BRAZILIAN POPULAR MUSIC

*For my parents with love and gratitude for their many sacrifices
and for my grandmother, "Miss Mam'zelle",
who lives on in our happiest memories*

Brazilian Popular Music

Caetano Veloso and the Regeneration of Tradition

LORRAINE LEU
University of Bristol, UK

LONDON AND NEW YORK

First published 2006 by Ashgate Publishing

Published 2016 by Routledge
2 Park Square, Milton Park, Abingdon, Oxfordshire OX14 4RN
711 Third Avenue, New York, NY 10017, USA

First issued in paperback 2016

Routledge is an imprint of the Taylor & Francis Group, an informa business

Copyright © Lorraine Leu 2006

All translations are the author's own, unless otherwise stated.

Lorraine Leu has asserted her moral right under the Copyright, Designs and Patents Act, 1988, to be identified as the author of this work.

All rights reserved. No part of this book may be reprinted or reproduced or utilised in any form or by any electronic, mechanical, or other means, now known or hereafter invented, including photocopying and recording, or in any information storage or retrieval system, without permission in writing from the publishers.

Notice:
Product or corporate names may be trademarks or registered trademarks, and are used only for identification and explanation without intent to infringe.

British Library Cataloguing in Publication Data
Leu, Lorraine
  Brazilian popular music : Caetano Veloso and the regeneration of tradition. –
(Ashgate popular and folk music series)
  1 . Veloso, Caetano – Criticism and interpretation 2. Popular music – Brazil –
History and criticism 3. Tropicalia (Music) – Brazil – History
  I. Title
  781.6'4'0981

Library of Congress Cataloging-in-Publication Data
Leu, Lorraine.
   Brazilian popular music : Caetano Veloso and the regeneration of tradition /
Lorraine Leu.
       p. cm—(Ashgate popular and folk music series)
   Includes bibliographical references and index.
   ISBN 0-7546-3655-0 (alk. paper)
    1. Popular music—Brazil—History and criticism. 2. Tropicalia (Music)—History and criticism. 3. Veloso, Caetano—Criticism and interpretation. I. Title. II. Series.

   ML3487.B7L48 2005
   781.64'0981—dc22

2005014111

ISBN 13: 978-1-138-27507-2 (pbk)
ISBN 13: 978-0-7546-3655-7 (hbk)

Typeset in Times Roman by N^2productions.

Veloso cutting an androgynous figure on stage. © Abril Imagens.

Contents

List of Illustrations   viii
List of Music Examples   ix
General Editor's Preface   x
Acknowledgements   xi

1 Culture, Politics and the Weight of Tradition in 1960's Brazil   1

2 Style and Sexual Politics in the Tropicália Period   24

3 "You Don't Know Me At All" – Challenging Vocal Traditions   59

4 Language, Meaning and Memory: The Songwriting Tradition   84

5 The Tradition of the Love Song in Brazil   103

6 Unidentifiable Objects of Desire: Caetano Veloso's Love Songs   124

Conclusion   146

Appendix: Interview with Caetano Veloso   149
Bibliography   157
Index   175

List of Illustrations

1 Facing the music – Caetano Veloso, Gilberto Gil and Os Mutantes confront the hostile crowd at the September 1968 International Song Festival — 48

2 Cover of the 1968 *Tropicália* album — 49

3 Publicity shot for *Manchete* magazine, 1968 — 50

4 Cover of the 1968 album *Caetano Veloso* — 51

5 Caetano Veloso, Gilberto Gil and other Tropicalists perform during the *Divino, Maravilhoso* television programme — 52

6 Veloso indulges in typically provocative antics on *Divino, Maravilhoso* — 53

List of Music Examples

1	*Tropicália*	64
2	*Alegria, Alegria*	66
3	*Enquanto seu lobo não vem*	68
4	*Gilberto Misterioso*	79

General Editor's Preface

The upheaval that occurred in musicology during the last two decades of the twentieth century has created a new urgency for the study of popular music alongside the development of new critical and theoretical models. A relativistic outlook has replaced the universal perspective of modernism (the international ambitions of the 12-note style); the grand narrative of the evolution and dissolution of tonality has been challenged, and emphasis has shifted to cultural context, reception and subject position. Together, these have conspired to eat away at the status of canonical composers and categories of high and low in music. A need has arisen, also, to recognize and address the emergence of crossovers, mixed and new genres, to engage in debates concerning the vexed problem of what constitutes authenticity in music and to offer a critique of musical practice as the product of free, individual expression.

Popular musicology is now a vital and exciting area of scholarship, and the *Ashgate Popular and Folk Music Series* aims to present the best research in the field. Authors will be concerned with locating musical practices, values and meanings in cultural context, and may draw upon methodologies and theories developed in cultural studies, semiotics, poststructuralism, psychology and sociology. The series will focus on popular musics of the twentieth and twenty-first centuries. It is designed to embrace the world's popular musics from Acid Jazz to Zydeco, whether high tech or low tech, commercial or non-commercial, contemporary or traditional.

Professor Derek B. Scott
Chair of Music
University of Salford

Acknowledgements

Of all the people who have contributed in one way or another during the process of writing this book, I owe the greatest debt to my former PhD supervisor, David Treece. I have benefited from Dave's teaching and intellectual generosity since I arrived at King's College, London as an undergraduate, and he was responsible for stimulating my interest in Brazilian popular music in the first place. I have been very fortunate to have his guidance and friendship over the years.

I would also like to express my gratitude to Sean Stroud for his interest in my work, for many illuminating conversations on Brazilian popular music and for all of the articles and books he has tracked down for me in archives and second-hand shops in Brazil and elsewhere.

I wish to thank a number of other individuals and organisations whose assistance has been invaluable. I met David Hesmondhalgh at a crucial moment when I first embarked on my PhD research and he set me firmly on the path of popular music scholarship. Philip Tagg offered welcome advice and extremely useful suggestions for essential reading. The insightful comments made on an earlier draft of the manuscript by Derek Scott, Series Editor, and Ashgate's Commissioning Editor, Rachel Lynch, greatly facilitated the process of bringing this work to fruition. Thanks are also due to those who responded to sections of this work when presented as papers, in particular at the annual conference of the *Journal of Latin American Cultural Studies* in July 2000 and the Latin American Popular Music conference at the Institute of Romance Studies, University of London in December 2003. Funds were made available for the formatting of the manuscript by the Department of Hispanic, Portuguese & Latin American Studies at the University of Bristol, and the University's Faculty of Arts Research Fund met the costs of reproducing the photographs contained herein. I would also like to thank the British Academy for funding my doctoral studies and the Anglo-Brazilian Society for financing an important, final research trip to Brazil before completing the PhD. I wish to acknowledge permission to include a version of Chapter 4 that appeared previously in abridged form in the *Journal of Romance Studies* 3.1, Spring 2003, under the title "Language and Memory in Popular Song: Brazil's Caetano Veloso".

In Brazil, Peter and Maria Helena Schambil provided a home away from home during my research trips and took a keen interest in my work. I am indebted to them for their many kindnesses, their hospitality and friendship. Silviano Santiago offered help and advice during my first research trip, for which I was extremely grateful. From Salvador, Vonaldo Lopes Mota collected and sent me the latest news and reviews of Caetano Veloso's work. José Eriberto da Silva, at TV Globo's Centro de Documentação in Rio de Janeiro patiently and tirelessly found me all of the footage I requested. Equally helpful were archivists at the Museu da Imagem e do Som in Rio and in São Paulo, especially Andrêa Palmer at the latter. I also wish to thank Alex Pereira at Polygram Brasil for providing me with music videos, and Gilda Mattoso for arranging the interview which is transcribed in the appendix. I am deeply grateful to Caetano Veloso for generously giving his time so that we could discuss aspects of his work that were of particular relevance to the issues addressed in this study.

I reserve final, loving thanks for Ian Morris, whose easy going approach to life and tremendous sense of fun saw me through the completion of this book.

Chapter 1
Culture, Politics and the Weight of Tradition in 1960's Brazil

Imaginary identities, sentimental adventures, a taste of what reality represses: pop songs open the doors to dream, lend a voice to what is left unmentioned by ordinary discourse. But pop is not only a dream machine ... it is the unofficial chronicle of its times, a history of desires existing in the margins of official history .... In setting out a history of today, popular culture etches the contours of a history of tomorrow in that it 'feels' a social atmosphere in its earliest, unformulated stages; pop music senses the current and projects a first image of it, long before the politicians have grasped its real nature or had the time to quell it, before words have been found to express it or betray it.[1]

In the course of visits to Brazil in recent years, my choice of Caetano Veloso as the subject of research on a national musical tradition has frequently provoked the question: "Why Caetano and not Chico?"[2] Chico Buarque's importance to Brazilian cultural history as a poet and samba composer was once famously described by a journalist as the only consensus shared by the whole nation. There is a public perception that his life's work of polishing and refining samba is more valid as a form of expressing the national than Veloso's hybrid work, with its polemical and inconclusive notions of Brazilianness. It is undoubtedly Veloso's treatment of tradition that "disqualifies" him as a spokesperson on national tradition for many Brazilians. Rejecting the idea of tradition as a static and hallowed national patrimony, Veloso's work emphasises the importance not only of the continuity of tradition, but also of rupture, which allows tradition to be reworked and made relevant to a contemporary context. Speaking to me about the relationship between tradition and rupture in his work, he observed: "That's the story of my life! I always find myself trying to examine that relationship and interpret it as best I can."[3]

Veloso's contribution to the tradition of Brazilian popular music and his importance within the history of Música Popular Brasileira (MPB) are significant. MPB developed in the mid 1960s out of a split within the bossa nova phenomenon that had made a huge impact in Brazil and beyond. Bossa nova emerged in the late 1950s at a moment of great optimism that a new age of progress was dawning in Brazil. This confidence was inspired by a policy of frenetic development pursued by the government of Juscelino Kubitschek, responsible for the construction of the futuristic city of Brasília on an arid plateau in the interior of the country. Kubitschek's other enduring legacies, rampant inflation, massive foreign debt and the human cost of his promise of "fifty years progress in five", would be felt later. However, at the time that bossa nova appeared, the most pressing concerns for its mainly middle-class songwriters and public were loves won and lost and the sun, sand and sea of the good life in the affluent beach districts of Rio de Janeiro.

By the time that the radical populist João Goulart came to power in 1961, Brazil was a country mired in a severe financial crisis. Convinced that attempts to solve the crisis he had inherited could only bring political unpopularity, Goulart concentrated on what he called "basic reforms" as a means of creating a political following. The prospect of educational, tax and particularly, agrarian reform which had the potential to significantly alter the political balance and divert wealth away from the privileged sectors of society, soon created fierce opposition to Goulart's government. The conservative middle classes took to the streets to persuade the military to move against Goulart. With the support of the US government, the military conspiracy began on 31st March 1964, bringing to an end a period of nearly two decades of populist politics in Brazil.

MPB emerged as a musical response to the rethinking and re-articulating of Brazilian identity after the coup. The term does not connote a coherent movement or style, and came to encompass most of the popular music produced in Brazil until the 1990s.[4] The crisis of populism that was produced by the overthrow of Goulart was articulated within the new current of music as a crisis in representing the popular. Brazilian sociologist Renato Ortiz identifies two main currents of thinking on a national-popular culture in the 20th century, which prevailed up until 1968 and the military's draconian Fifth Institutional Act, known as the AI–5.[5] The first emerged in the 1920s and 1930s, and conceptualised "popular" as "folkloric". This perspective advocated fashioning a national identity by reviving and preserving the folkloric traditions of the Brazilian people. The second school of thought developed around the mid 1950s and was characterised by a concern to politicise popular traditions. This period saw the activities of ISEB, the Instituto Superior de Estudos Brasileiros (Higher Institute for Brazilian Studies), Paulo Freire's literacy campaign and the Centros Populares de Cultura (Popular Culture Centres or CPCs).[6] Before 1964, left-wing cultural activity was dominated by the CPCs, whose production of "popular revolutionary art" was fuelled by debates on modernisation, democratisation, nationalism and "faith in the people". The CPCs had responded to the ascendancy of the left in politics under the Goulart administration by declaring that "in our country and at this stage of our history, outside of political art, there is no popular art."[7] The middle-class CPC poet sought to educate the people and raise consciousness in the intellectual, by relying on the power of the word to bring about social transformation: "With almost evangelical zeal, he mythifies the power of the word to effect change and his goal becomes to play on the emotions and to create guilt: to play on the emotions with his moving denunciations of poverty, and create guilt in the presumed critical and revolutionary conscience of the intellectual"[8]

Under the Goulart government left-populist cultural production was predicated on the politicisation of traditional cultural forms and on the viability of a link between the middle-class producers of this culture and the working classes. After 1964 these fundamental assumptions were undermined. In the first place, the "Economic Miracle" initiated by the new regime relied on a huge influx of foreign capital and led to an increasing internationalisation of Brazilian society and culture. Secondly, the growth of the mass media as a result of heavy investment by the military government began to result in a conceptualising of "popular" as that which drew a large audience.[9] Additionally, the classification "popular" was always a complicated one, given the fact that a consistent characteristic of Brazilian popular music has been its ability to combine the erudite and the popular within the creative space of song. Significantly, the military also succeeded in breaking organised contacts that had been created by intellectuals and cultural producers with workers and students during the Goulart government. Having deprived the cultural left of its public, the state felt able to allow a considerable degree of artistic freedom during the first four years following the coup. As a result, left-wing cultural activity continued to flourish until 1968 and the Fifth Institutional Act (AI–5). Two strong currents of nationalism emerged from this early period of the dictatorship. The military's programme for economic development was accompanied by an intense nationalist propaganda drive, communicated via a mass media system with close links to the State. All over Brazil bumper stickers and TV and radio advertisements proclaimed the army's ominous message to dissenters: "Brazil – love it, or leave it." The left responded to this authoritarian nationalism by embracing its own nationalist ideology, with cultural production inspired by traditional regional popular culture, the conditions of the urban worker and a rejection of the government's modernising project.

Before 1964 cultural expression under the CPCs had been dominated by literature. After the coup, having failed in their revolutionary aims and cut off from the popular classes, committed cultural production turned away from literature, which did not appear to answer the needs of the current political circumstances, towards the spectacle – theatre, cinema, music and the plastic arts.[10] In December 1964, Teatro Arena presented *Opinião* (*Opinion*), one of the first cultural responses to the coup, whose title samba proclaimed: "They can arrest me/ They can beat me up/ They can leave me to starve/ But I won't change my opinion" (Podem me prender/ Podem me bater/ Podem até deixar-me sem comer/ Que eu não mudo de opinião). *Opinião* staged the meeting of the popular classes with the middle classes which was made impossible by political circumstances. Although it expressed some uncertainty about this contact, the musical retained the nationalist, populist ideals of pre-1964 Brazil.[11] By 1967, however, reactions to the social and political scene took on a very different character, with the release of Glauber Rocha's film *Terra em Transe* (*Land in Anguish*), the story of an intellectual who wrestles with the question of his role in society and eventually commits suicide when confronted with his futility. The film constituted an incisive critique of populism, class alliances and even artists of the left and had a profound influence on the cultural scene, stimulating a wave of cultural production which came to be described as "Tropicalist".

The name "Tropicália" derives from an installation by plastic artist Hélio Oiticica. It was borrowed by Veloso for the song that was to be a significant statement of intent with regard to his relationship with the tradition of Brazilian popular music. The song was included on the 1968 album *Caetano Veloso* and in the same year, the name "Tropicália" was given to the album that resulted from the collaboration of a group of like-minded musicians and performers. After the release of the *Tropicália* album, the term began to be applied to other areas of the arts that shared similar aesthetics and concerns. For Celso Favaretto, the main point of contact between them was a radical social critique, based on a contemporary rearticulation of Modernist poet Oswald de Andrade's theory of *antropofagia*, or cultural cannibalism, a selective devouring of foreign culture by national culture.[12] However, although the circulation of ideas between artists from different spheres was one of the most prominent characteristics of the period immediately following the coup, it is important not to generalise, or homogenise Tropicália into a single cultural movement. Despite their points of contact, the application of the term "Tropicalist" to these distinct forms of cultural production can be misleading, particularly as it was only in the field of popular music that artists defined their movement and agenda as "Tropicalist". My references in this work to the "Tropicalists" and "Tropicália" therefore, are to the group of composers and performers who collaborated under that name.

The influence of Brazil's Cinema Novo (New Cinema) on the Tropicalist musical aesthetic is evident in the cinematographic quality of much of the imagery of the movement's songs during this period. Cinema Novo techniques, such as fragmentation, juxataposition and the characteristic dreamlike quality of its narratives, can be seen in the lyricism and structures of Tropicalist song.[13] For Glauber Rocha, the movement's most prominent theoretician, Cinema Novo combined *auteur* cinema with a social conscience and the creation of a language of underdevelopment, capable of turning limited resources into artistic invention. This "estética da fome", or "aesthetic of hunger", was at the heart of Cinema Novo's vision of Brazil. According to Rocha, hunger was the distinctive characteristic of life in underdeveloped countries, whose societies were perceived by developed countries as existing in a "strange tropical surrealism". The originality of Cinema Novo on the international film scene would lie in its representation of this hunger, and of violence, its "most noble cultural manifestation".[14] Violence would not only be the way for Brazilian cinema to assert its individuality, it would also offer a way of negotiating cinema's problematic position within the film industry. After years of attempting to produce "anti-industrial" cinema, Cinema Nova finally acknowledged that the market and industrial distribution were necessary evils and instead turned its attention to confronting the challenge of working within these parameters.[15] An additional complication was that the international distribution agency for Brazilian films, EMBRAFILME, was a state organisation, supported by a repressive regime. Cinema Novo film-makers explored the concept of cannibalism which had also begun to re-emerge in the theatre and on the music scene, exemplified by Joaquim Pedro de Andrade's *Macunaíma* (1969), and later by Nelson Pereira dos Santos's *Como era gostoso o meu francês* (*How Tasty was my Little Frenchman*, 1971). The development of a radical and aggressive poetic language within the existing conditions of production was of great significance to Veloso and the Tropicalists, who would develop forms of critical expression within the country's growing, elite-controlled mass media.

Film-maker Arnaldo Jabor has observed that although Tropicalist music was inspired by Cinema Novo, after the arrival of the Tropicalist performers on the cultural scene, Brazilian cinema began to be influenced in turn by the aesthetics of Tropicalist music and the movement's determination to confront the complexity of Brazilian society.[16] The *Udigrudi*, or underground cinema, which developed in the late 1960s, constituted a reaction to what it saw as early Cinema Novo's optimistic notion of the "aesthetic of hunger", capable of transforming the relationship between centre and periphery. It sought instead to convey a sense of hopelessness about the peripheral condition, through Tropicalist techniques such as bricolage, kitsch and the interest in the most devalued products of the culture industry. Julio Bressane's *Matou a família e foi ao cinema* (*Killed his Family then went to the Cinema*), for example, mixes pornography with pop songs, the horrific with the erotic, and Tropicalist muse Carmen Miranda with scenes of urban squalor. Underground films relied on the recycling of styles through parody, which aimed at attacking and shocking the spectator. Unlike Cinema Novo's stylised violence, however, there was nothing redemptive about the violence portrayed in these films, or in the provocation of the spectator.[17]

It was in the theatre that violence towards the public would be explored most fully, in the work of José Celso Martinez Corrêa's Teatro Oficina. Zé Celso's version of Oswald de Andrade's 1933 play, *O Rei da Vela* (*The Candle King*), which he dedicated to Glauber Rocha, sought to break definitively with the practices of traditional theatre, developing instead an attitude of "cruel, total provocation" (provocação cruel e total), whose aim was to mobilise the public through aggression. Oswald's play constituted a wide-ranging attack on the landed aristocracy, the industrial bourgeoisie, imperialism, fascism and socialism. Zé Celso's production combined conventional theatre with review theatre, farce, the circus and the *chanchada*,[18] to create a tone of irony and mockery that would later become a prominent characteristic of the Tropicália movement. Reception to the play was usually divided between those who applauded it enthusiastically and those who walked out of the theatre, scandalised by its shocking scenes.

This "theatre of aggression" also drew on Oswald's and the Modernists' valorisation of forms of artistic practice considered inferior by erudite culture.

Attacking the norms of good taste and good behaviour, Zé Celso sought an "arte suja", or "dirty art" which relied on an anarchic, provocative language of mockery. This language was to resonate in subtler and highly sophisticated ways in Tropicalist musical expression, and the dialogue with Modernism was to form an important part of the Tropicalist ethos. Oswald's corrosive satire included a critique of socialism, and Zé Celso intended that his production should not only attack the public, but also the attitudes and forms of expression of the cultural left.[19] This approach, which involved provoking both the left and the right, was one that the Tropicalists would also adopt.

Zé Celso's next production would take the idea of violence in performance to unprecedented levels in Brazilian art and culture. He chose Chico Buarque's play *Roda Viva* (*Rat Race*), in which a pop star succumbs to the pressures of his stardom and commits suicide, after which he is literally devoured by his public. In Zé Celso's version, this devouring was represented by a raw liver being torn apart by the actors, spraying blood onto spectators. Actors also singled out and poked fun at well-known individuals among the audience, or turned on members of the public in the front row, challenging them with questions such as, "Have you done your duty and killed a communist today?" The commercial success of *Roda Viva* in spite of its attacks on the public surprised even Zé Celso and led him to envisage new approaches to cultural consumption:

> One has to provoke the spectator, call him an idiot, repressed, reactionary. The aim is to create a series of Vietnams in the field of culture, a war against official culture, made for easy consumption. Today effective theatre means guerrilla theatre, with the weapons of anarchic, cruel theatre, as ugly as the ugliness and apathy in which we live today.[20]

The opinions of the critics were divided over the theatre of violence, applauding its daring, but also commenting that it allowed the public some short-term relief from the frustrations of the period without compelling them to take any action. Yet for José Celso, the new theatre was the sign of a revolution to come in society and politics, which had to begin by awakening and shocking the "dead and slumbering audience" (a platéia morta e adormecida).

In the visual arts attention was refocused on questions of formal innovation and the creation of "happenings", which sought to involve the public, extending their role as mere spectators. The climate of experimentalism was dominated by the development of this new, more provocative relationship with the public, as avant-garde artist Rubens Gershman remembers: "We began to create a series of installations which would involve and even insult the spectator. It was one more way to raise consciousness in the spectator about what we were trying to do." Gershman gives the following example:

> So, at that time, for example, [Carlos] Vergara made a hole in a wall and placed a notice near it asking the public to take a look and see what was inside. The hole was

quite low down, the spectator had to assume a ridiculous position, half-kneeling, to be able to look inside. Then when the person looked into the hole, the artist had written something like: Instead of looking like an idiot, crouched in this ridiculous position, peering into this hole, why don't you take up a position with regard to what is going on around you today ...[21]

In the area of the plastic arts, Hélio Oiticica was the artist most closely associated with the Tropicalist musical group. In April 1967, his installation "Tropicália" was exhibited at the Museu de Arte Moderna (MAM) in Rio. The work consisted of two tents which Oiticica called "penetráveis", or "penetrables" and which represented a humble domestic interior with plants and parrots, and with sand and pebbles underfoot. After making their way through a kind of labyrinth in the main tent, the public would come across a television set, which was left switched on. The installation suggested Rio's precarious *favela* dwellings, constructed with resourcefulness out of available discarded materials. It also articulated two of Oiticica's key practices and concerns, his collection and reuse of material which the city had rejected and discarded and the importance which he placed on public participation in art: "The corporeal, tactile, visual, semantic, etc, participation of the spectator."[22] This last concern was of fundamental importance to Oiticica's *parangolés*, a kind of costume, or wearable sculpture. Fashioned frequently out of discarded material and displayed on the body of the wearer, *parangolés* blurred the boundaries between plastic art and performance art. They borrowed from performance art both a resistance to the idea of transcendence in art and the view of art as property. Many of the wearers of Oiticica's *parangolés* were friends of his from the Mangueira *favela* where he spent much of his time, and their *parangolés* frequently commented on social deprivation and marginalisation. Oiticica's creations represented a politicisation of the body, as well as of the socio-cultural space, since they facilitated an "invasion" of the space of erudite art and culture by the most excluded individuals in society. The political implications of dressing the body would not have been lost on Veloso, who maintained a friendship with Oiticica and for whom the artist made two *parangolés*.

Celso Favaretto has identified several structural affinities between Oiticica's work and Tropicalist song, based on a shared concern to problematise the artistic forms with which they communicated:

> they effect a cultural de-centring with critical processes that combine construction with de-consecration; they dislocate the discussion of the relationship between art and political intervention, transcending the opposition between "committed art" and "alienated art"; they define relationships between aesthetic production and social critique, in which the latter focuses more on process and form than content. They are, therefore, forms of production that have the simultaneous effect of defining aspects of culture, while they deconstruct the languages that presume that culture to be totalising.[23]

By dialoguing with different artistic and cultural forms and experimenting with the diverse aspects of popular song, including lyrics, melody, vocalisation, dance and gesture, the Tropicalists explored to its limits song as an art form and as a form of critical and/or commercial communication. Oiticica's work also juxtaposed different artistic and cultural practices, and like Tropicalist song, was open to ideas from the international avant-garde in elaborating a radical critique of Brazilian society and culture.

By the late 1960s, poetry also began to be expressed in terms of performance. The *poema processo* emerged, which considered populist poetry artificial and unsatisfactory and most contemporary poets distant from the conditions of the moment. The movement sought to valorise the act of reading and concentrated on the visual construction of its poems. Following on from the Concretist view of the poem as an object for immediate consumption and use, *poema processo* even created edible poems, in various flavours. In a society which the military was attempting to reduce to silence, they frequently bypassed the word altogether in favour of signs and codes and made use of drawings and cartoons in their poems. In January 1968, in order to emphasise their claim that conventional poetry had lost its validity, they created an aggressive "happening" on the steps of the Teatro Municipal in Rio, tearing up the work of celebrated poets such as Carlos Drummond and João Cabral.

In popular music, there occurred a split within the bossa nova genre, as composers and performers like Carlos Lyra and Nara Leão, prompted by the social and political conditions that followed the coup, rejected the highly personal lyrical formula of "love, smiles and flowers". The protest song which emerged from this split, denounced urban and regional poverty, called for land reform and rejected imported cultural forms and with them cultural and economic imperialism. As the movement gathered momentum, its traditionalist ideology became increasingly belligerent in its rejection of foreign influences in Brazilian music.

The emergence of popular music criticism in Brazil was closely tied to the heated debate on the national-popular that developed at this time. This debate was played out at the music festivals organised by the main television stations and also in the pages of newspapers and magazines across the country. The limited size and reach of the book publishing industry in Brazil meant the widespread involvement of Brazilian academics in journalism. For many academics commenting on popular music it seemed more logical to write about a popular cultural form in a medium that would be accessible to a greater number of people. The pages of the press also offered the immediacy appropriate to the intensity of the debate, allowing scholars to intervene in and keep up with the momentum of the discussions of the day. Early music criticism in Brazil was dominated by the ideological agendas and the feverish social and political climate of the period following the coup. Critics frequently mirrored the priority given to political concerns over aesthetic values that was evident in protest song. As Marcos Napolitano has observed, two main lines of thinking dominated popular musical scholarship at the time. The first maintained that popular music had an obligation to engage fully with the ideological debates of the moment, and even that song had a role to play as the rallying cry for the creation of a revolutionary consciousness in Brazil. The second predominant concern was with the notion of cultural appropriation to explain the ruptures occurring in Brazilian popular music at the time.[24] This line of thinking was epitomised by the work of music journalist José Ramos Tinhorão, who severely criticised the appropriation of the music of "the people" and of black Brazilians, to cater to the tastes of the recording industry and its white, middle-class public.[25]

In 1966 Caetano Veloso made a polemical intervention into the debate on the function of Brazil's popular music, by emphasising the importance of adopting what he called the "linha evolutiva". Through this evolutionary path popular music post-bossa nova would articulate the transformations to Brazilian society brought about as a result of modernisation and internationalisation. The evolutionary path of musical creativity advocated a definitive break with the previous ideologically-laden perspective from which popular music had been judged. The concept re-focused attention on the importance of aesthetic considerations in musical production and criticism, and the need to rework and rearticulate traditions to produce contemporary forms of musical expression. As he commented in an interview:

> Lately, the question of Brazilian popular music has been posed in terms of a duty to and a need to communicate with the Brazilian people. That is, there is constant discussion of whether the key thing is to have an ideological stance on the problems of the country and whether the music can be considered good, given that it conveys this stance clearly. Or alternatively, there is the question of whether we should just return to or accept primitive Brazilian music …. Well, Brazilian music is becoming modernised but it continues to be Brazilian when all of the material is utilised (and understood) in the context of an experience and a vision of Brazilian reality … If we have a tradition and we want to create something new within it, we have to have more than just a sensibility for it, we need to have a knowledge of it. And it is this knowledge that will offer us the possibility of creating something new and coherent with it. Only a return to [music's] evolutionary path will make us aware of the whole picture and able to make informed creative choices and judgements.[26]

In the same interview, and at a time when bossa nova had been discredited by nationalist criticism as a degraded form of samba which had sold out to an international market, Veloso credits bossa nova master João Gilberto with taking the first important step towards the regeneration of the Brazilian popular music tradition: "As a matter of fact, for me João Gilberto represents the exact moment that this happened: the material of musical modernity utilised to re-create, to renovate, to take a step forward in Brazilian popular music."[27]

The dialogue between the modern and the traditional initiated by bossa nova would be maintained and developed by Veloso throughout his career. Reflecting recently on the impact of bossa nova on Brazilian popular music, he contrasts his work with that of Chico Buarque within the context of bossa nova's engagement with the old and the new:

> So Chico took precisely this element of continuity in bossa nova and explored it to its limits. And what I wanted from bossa nova was to take the element of rupture. Bossa nova ... was a scandal when it emerged – a huge rupture, but it was a huge rupture that would have precisely the effect of maintaining continuity. Or in other words, regenerating the creative material of Brazilian popular music. And this was what Tropicalism sought to do as well, ... in a way, what has characterised my performance over the years, has been an interest in always reviving the value of rupture, whenever rupture is actually necessary and appropriate, because of its capacity to regenerate what is vital within a tradition.[28]

This statement sums up Veloso's life's work of negotiating between these two poles of Brazilian popular music expression. It also points to what I believe is his most significant contribution to the art form, an approach which simultaneously draws on and disrupts tradition, in order to reinvent it.

The idea of the evolutionary path is taken up enthusiastically by poet and literary theorist Augusto de Campos in *Balanço da bossa e outras bossas*, a seminal work of Brazilian popular music criticism, originally published in 1968. The collection of essays occupied an intermediate position between academia and journalism, consisting of articles previously published in newspapers, which were written by academics, a maestro and an avant-garde composer. As well as the role played by the press in disseminating debate on popular music, the collection is evidence of the interest in developments in popular music from diverse individuals and groups. The work discusses the radical possibilities that the evolutionary path presents to Brazilian popular music in the context of the ideological debates of the time. It was not until the 1970s, however, when the heat of these debates on the national-popular had been cooled somewhat by repression and exile, that it was possible to undertake a systematic analysis of MPB inspired by the evolutionary approach.[29]

Celso Favaretto's *Tropicália: Alegoria, Alegria*, published in 1977, maintains that Tropicália compelled a re-think of the whole notion of political art in Brazil. Favaretto's work represents an important contribution to the debate on popular music and the national, because of his discussion of the radical character of the Tropicalist aesthetic. He examines the use of allegory and the "allegorical process" as key to understanding artistic expression of the modern and the national. This form of expression is characterised by fragmentation and plurality, which are the sources of its critical energy. Favaretto also highlights the importance not just of melodies and lyrics in an analysis of Tropicália, but also of the different codes that constituted Tropicalist performance. Favaretto widened the discussion of "nation" in contemporary Brazilian popular music to consider how processes of modernisation, and the ambivalences and contradictions they brought to ideas of national identity, were negotiated in Tropicália.

Veloso's challenging contribution to the national question and the function of popular music came at a crucial time for music criticism in Brazil. His insistence on confronting the problematic issue of a national tradition at this moment of crisis in its expression represented a significant intervention in the history of Brazilian popular music, which would decisively affect its future development. His approach to music-making would be fiercely attacked and rejected by the dominant current of cultural production at the time. However, his concern to create a dialogue between the national and the international and between the traditional and the modern would eventually legitimise this kind of crossover as a means of imagining and constructing the national, given the new social realities of Brazil.

By distancing itself from predominant cultural and political thinking, Tropicália sought to call attention to the crisis of revolutionary ideologies and existing forms of expression and affiliation. It rejected what it saw as the populist didacticism of the protest song movement and its attempts to speak on behalf of the masses. The movement sought to relate more closely to what an individual experience of, and response to social and political conditions might be, as opposed to the organised and collective experience represented by the left. This meant counterposing critical exchanges and discussion to ready-made ideologies, and advocating pluralism against the cultural hegemonies of both right and left. The Tropicalists' participation in popular song festivals turned the music festival stage into a space in which national tradition was hotly disputed, a dispute which was then transmitted live into Brazilian living rooms via the television sets rapidly proliferating throughout the country at this time.[30]

As will be explored further in the following chapter, Veloso and the Tropicalists sought critique and debate by changing the nature of the relationship with the audience. They also turned their attention to a still largely overlooked dimension of the ongoing dispute over the "popular" in Brazilian music – popular in the sense of being liked by the people – which represented a validation of public tastes. Tropicália was attempting to restore taste to the realm of personal choice rather than political affiliation. One of the Tropicalists' chief concerns was to bring about a revolution of aesthetics and taste in Brazil, in which style played a prominent role.[31]

As a movement Tropicália had a brief life, in keeping with its creators' wishes. However, its impact on the ways in which music is produced and performed in Brazil is still being felt today, and it remains a highly significant moment in Brazilian cultural history. The Tropicalists did not attempt to bring about a social revolution, instead, they believed that a musical revolution, a radical reworking of musical, lyrical and performing conventions would compel an examination and a questioning of the ideologies which upheld consecrated cultural practices. As David Treece has pointed out, it is difficult to imagine how Brazilian popular music would have developed after 1968, were it not for the contribution of the Tropicalists in reshaping and revitalising its traditions. Treece has observed that by 1968 political music had pared down the aesthetic resources of popular song to the extent that it was in danger of being reduced to nothing but "partisan, propagandist pronouncements on behalf of this or that pre-determined position, rather than critical and creative activities of reinvention."[32] Veloso and the Tropicalists reappraised the tradition of mixture and absorption of diverse materials which had, in fact, always been a characteristic of Brazilian popular music.

The 1970s, therefore, saw the proliferation of various "scenes" which Brazilianised foreign genres and trends. Jazz fusion, for example, exemplified by artists such as Hermeto Pascoal, Wagner Tiso and Egberto Gismonti, added Brazilian percussion and Brazilian musical and lyrical themes to the genre. Extraordinarily, only two years after a violent confrontation at the televised song festivals, when supporters of nationalist protest song rejected Veloso's contribution and foreign influences on Brazilian popular music in general, the winning song of the national section of the 1970 Festival Internacional da Canção (International Song Festival) would be "BR–3" (Antônio Adolfo and Tibério Gaspar), an offering from the new Brazilian soul music scene. Festival vocalist Toni Tornado also added a rousing rock delivery to the chorus in his performance of the song.[33] Leading exponents of Brazilian soul and funk included Tim Maia and Banda Black Rio, while artists like Luiz Melodia mixed these two genres with blues and *samba-canção*, and Jorge Ben and the Trio Mocotó experimented with a mixture of samba and soul. Meanwhile, the Northeastern rock/pop phenomenon, fuelled by the appetite created by the Tropicalists for the mixture of the regional with the international, produced artists such as Alceu Valença, Elba Ramalho and Geraldo Azevedo. The Tropicalist reclaiming of the dialogue with foreign genres was therefore immediately evident in popular music production during the following decade, and has been an established dimension of Brazil's popular music expression since.

In the chapters that follow, I have sought to create interpretive frameworks that allow for analysis of the dynamic processes which contribute to the creation of artistic meaning in popular song. Veloso's trajectory within the history of Brazilian popular music has often served to illuminate the relationships between music and society, between cultural expression and social values. However, in this work I have resisted an approach that takes a set of social and political relationships as the starting point of an attempt to explain how music conveys a particular message. Instead, I have sought to foreground the music itself and its performance, in order to reveal how musical expression can articulate, critique and influence these relationships. My approach has therefore been led by a sensitivity to the material – to the fact that in popular music, we are presented with multiple texts in the act of enunciation of the song. This work will therefore consider the visual text of performance, including the attendant iconography of popular music, for example, album covers, promotional material and television appearances; the musical text, or the musical structures of the songs; and the lyrical text, or the words of the songs.

Mindful of the historical role played by popular music in the long-running debate on the national in Brazil, this work also seeks to explore how popular song comments on and contributes to ideas of Brazilian cultural traditions and identity. Veloso's most significant role in the history of MPB has been as an innovator of Brazil's musical traditions. His approach to Brazil's musical heritage has been to valorise and cannibalise, and so create new song forms and modes of expression that add to Brazil's already extraordinarily heterogeneous traditions. Before continuing, in the following chapters, to consider the ways in which he draws on and disrupts social conventions and the conventions of popular music expression in Brazil, it is useful to make mention of three significant traditions in Brazilian society and culture with which Veloso has engaged, or which he has sought to challenge.

The Baroque, Carnival and Patriarchal Traditions

The traditions of the baroque and of carnival resonate throughout Veloso's work and are particularly evident in Tropicalist language, style and theatrics. Below I outline some of the key features of these traditions, which, as will become evident, contribute to Tropicália's aesthetic and forms of expression. Baroque literature began to be produced in Brazil from the mid 16th century in the writings of the Jesuits, continued to flourish into the 17th century, and even penetrated writing in the 18th century, blending with other movements, such as Neoclassicism and Arcadianism, and confounding traditional classifications of the genre.[34] Indeed, according to Nicolau Sevcenko, rather than speaking of a baroque era, it is more useful to understand how the baroque marks the whole of Brazil's cultural history. He maintains that if there is one fundamental feature of Brazil's diverse forms of cultural expression, it is their "latent baroque quality" (barroquismo latente), whose typical characteristics include a "contradictory impulse, the exaltation of the senses, the rapture of the celebration, the co-existence of difference, an attraction to the irrational".[35]

This idea of the persistence of a baroque tradition in Brazilian culture has been consistently argued by Haroldo de Campos, who considers the baroque "a form which is a constant of Brazilian sensibility, traversing our cultural space in various guises or at various moments of our history."[36] Campos provoked a long-running debate on the importance of the baroque in Brazil with his critique of Antônio Candido's 1959 study, *Formação da literatura brasileira*. Campos took issue with the exclusion of the baroque from Candido's history of Brazilian literature, which the latter saw as outside of, or prior to the systematic organisation of Brazilian letters. Accusing Candido of attempting to homologise literature and the nation, Campos saw Candido's idea of an "integrated" Brazilian literature as a romantic, idealistic view, which could only be sustained by excluding or minimising the contrasts of the baroque.[37] The debate led to a great deal of thinking and rethinking about the legacies of the baroque tradition, introducing a different view of the history of cultural expression in Brazil. Campos's re-evaluation of the baroque in literature highlighted its subversive approach to classical genre divisions and literary conventions. For him, baroque expression in Brazil represents a kind of revenge of the tropics on the metropolis. Borrowing a phrase from the Cuban neo-baroque writer, Lezama Lima, he describes it as the "art of the counter-Conquest" (arte da contraconquista), which takes great liberties with language, with a non-linear view of history that allowed it to make surprising connections.[38]

This freedom with language and style, as well as the surprising contrasts, are two of the most prominent elements of the Brazilian baroque. As Sevcenko observes, as a form of expression conceived to articulate contradictions, the logic of the baroque is unstable, interactive and interpellative.[39] These contradictions were due to the baroque's initial role as the culture of transition between old and new in the Western world. Baroque style offered a means of creatively and dynamically synthesising some of the tensions of the initial phase of the "modern age". Over the years, baroque style would continue to play the role of negotiating the experience of the modern in Brazilian cultural life. The language of the Brazilian baroque was marked above all by hybridity, a mixture of languages initially necessitated by the Jesuits' evangelising mission, which was to acquire a much more radical nature in the language of the most significant of the baroque poets, Gregório de Matos. The latter's "lexical miscegenation" (miscegenação lexical)[40] produced a Portuguese laced with Hispanicisms, colloquialisms, neologisms and words taken from indigenous and African languages. It was developed to express baroque dualisms of religiousness and sensuality, mysticism and eroticism, the spiritual and the carnal, making for a poetry of the serious and the satirical, the sublime and the ridiculous. As Afrânio Coutinho has pointed out, the importance of the baroque in Brazil is that it produced a local expression of a universal style.[41] It represents, therefore, an initial cannibalisation of foreign culture and its adaptation to a Brazilian milieu. Outside of the field of literature, the nature of the European baroque was modified in the popular imagination, so that in religious art and sculpture, differences specific to a tropical environment were incorporated into the official iconography, transforming it and producing uniquely Brazilian sensibilities.[42] The sumptuousness of the religious feasts and processions of the baroque were adapted by a society hungry for public entertainment and there occurred a confusion of the sacred and the profane in many of the feasts and pilgrimages.[43] Several of these religious celebrations represented some of the most memorable events of Brazilian colonial life, such as the processions to mark the inauguration of a new church in Vila Rica, Minas Gerais, in 1733, a "monumental happening", according to Affonso Ávila, who likens the colour, choreography and grandeur of the event, to Rio's contemporary carnival processions.[44]

This exuberant tropicalisation of European baroque style resulted in a temporal, lexical and visual hybridity that has a consistent presence in Brazilian artistic and cultural expression. It is a sensibility that the Tropicalist movement adapted and shaped to their own socio-cultural space, dominated by the antitheses of their particular experience of modernity. The result was an artistic style with baroque's appeal to the senses and sensuality, and characterised by baroque invention and radical innovation of established forms and genres.

The heterogeneity of the baroque would also find an echo in Brazilian carnival, which Roberto Da Matta calls a polysemic parade, because it brings together "a little of everything", and so "refers to various symbolic subuniverses of Brazilian society".[45] Da Matta maintains that carnival's most fundamental aspect as a national ritual is the combination of symbolic and real elements from contradictory, usually separate domains, to create an open social field, characterised by encounter, mediation and polysemy. This causes the organised reality of daily life to unravel into many levels, producing the heterogeneity characteristic of carnival: "... Carnival has multiple levels, innumerable events, focuses, focuses within focuses, ... all permitting a fantastic relativisation of social reality ..."[46] These processes, which emphasise the dynamic nature of carnival, could also be used with reference to Tropicália, with its open-ended forms of expression and representations of Brazilian society and culture, which create confrontations and dialogues between antagonistic fields, and so generate multiple meanings and images. Tropicalist expression feeds on what Richard Parker sees as carnival's most prominent feature: "its ability to encode and articulate so many different, often contradictory, meanings, and to thus open itself up to so many divergent interpretations."[47]

A considerable body of work exists on carnival and on Brazilian carnival, which I do not intend to summarise here. Instead, I would like to point to some of the key concepts associated with carnival which are relevant to the Tropicalist movement. One of carnival's most discussed characteristics is its ability to temporarily suspend, reverse, or invert social hierarchies.[48] These are all disruptive actions, which subvert the concept of rank and status around which society is organised. Roberto Da Matta is perhaps the commentator who provides the most detailed and penetrating examination of the hierarchical constitution of Brazilian society and how carnival simultaneously reflects and undermines these structures. Da Matta views carnival as one of three fundamental forms through which Brazilian society is ritualised, the others being the military parade and the religious festival. Each of these forms of expressing social structure is entrusted to a group with a specific place in national life (the people, the military, the Church), so that even the cycle of festivals reflects the hierarchical system of "everyone knowing their place". However, unlike military parades and church festivals, carnival sets out to oppose the political and religious order of the nation. The result of this temporary suspension of the rules of hierarchy, is the license of carnival – stripped of conventional social roles, its participants enjoy the freedom to choose and change identities, to momentarily redefine their social world.[49]

Bakhtin's influential work on carnival and the social world of Rabelais, emphasises the original, popular character of carnival, as a festival celebrated through the initiative of ordinary people. He argues that the reversals and transformations of what the authorities pretend are immovable hierarchies, emphasise relativity and processes of becoming, instead of stability and eternity. This ever changing, renewable, "gay time", "affirms the people's immortal, indestructible character. In the world of carnival the awareness of the people's immortality is combined with the realisation that established authority and truth are relative."[50] This concept of time is an important key to carnival's transgressive power. By opposing itself to linear and "official" historical time, it calls into question the absoluteness of the order and structure of the social world. This anti-linear and anti-absolutist attitude represented a fundamental Tropicalist strategy for understanding and expressing the complexities of their society. Cultural critics such as Umberto Eco tend to agree with Bakhtin's formulation of carnival as manifesting a desire for subversion, but take issue with its actual revolutionary potential. Instead Eco describes carnival as a transitory social disturbance, which is only revolutionary when it is unexpected and unauthorised.[51] Nevertheless, while carnival may ultimately be an illusion that ends up reiterating the prevailing order, it can often articulate alternatives, by revealing the desire and the possibilities for social transformation.

In an examination of how processes of carnivalisation have pervaded Brazilian society, Da Matta elaborates Gilberto Freyre's influential concept of the importance of the domains of the house and the street to an understanding of the Brazilian social system. Referring to the protagonist of Jorge Amado's *O Pais do carnaval*, who feels his Brazilian identity most keenly when performing two activities – dancing the samba at carnival time with a *mulata* and beating his disloyal mistress – Da Matta observes a dichotomy between the street (a place of carnivalesque behaviour) and the house (the site of violent, patriarchal behaviour) in the protagonist's perception of his Brazilianness. In the novel national identity is related to carnival and an authoritarian attitude to female sexuality. However, the divide is far from entrenched, as the novel actually performs an inversion by situating the mistress in the house instead of the street, and with the upper-class character celebrating carnival in the street, with a *mulata*, instead of in the house or social club.[52] This inversion, or mixing of domains suggests a more complicated relationship between house and street, and is typically carnivalesque. It also reflects the inversion of social and sexual roles that is characteristic of carnival.

Indeed, the changing of gender roles is a key manifestation of what Bakhtin viewed as the two most important elements of popular festivals such as carnival. The first is travesty, or mocking disguise, which suggests a renewal not just of clothing, but also of the social image, and the second is the subversion of hierarchic levels. For Da Matta, carnival's feminisation of the world served to reveal the "other side" of Brazilian society, of a group usually restricted to the home.[53] Richard Parker sees carnival in Brazil as a time for reflecting the diversity of the sexual universe, for celebrating confusion and ambiguity over polarised gender classifications, and echoing Da Matta's emphasis on the polysemic nature of carnival, points out that the transvestism of carnival is not a unified symbolic inversion, but a set of transformations: "Celebrating confusion and ambiguity, but building up subjective meanings as varied as their subjects, these multiple transvestisms push and pull at the seams of any system of meanings that would seek to separate the world into two distinct, opposed, and hierarchically related categories ...".[54] During his Tropicalist period, Veloso would make strategic use of the pervasive ambiguity of the carnivalesque, in an attempt to create a proliferation of meanings in his songs and performances.

Parker points to carnival transvestism as offering an opportunity for a marginal sector of society to briefly occupy a position of centrality. Indeed, despite the existence of cross-dressing in carnival since its origin, transvestism did not begin to be discreetly acknowledged in press coverage of the festivities until 1958.[55] Da Matta has observed that the blurring of the divisions between the sexes presents a threat to the reinforcement of positions of patriarchal power and prestige in society.[56] Veloso's feminisation of his body and of his social world, within the particularly macho and hierarchical culture of a military regime, was perceived as a threat to the organisation of social power and to the rhetoric of civic responsibility and family values disseminated by the regime.

The power of the patriarchal figure has a long history in Brazilian society. When the Portuguese colonial governing apparatus proved to be wholly inadequate for controlling the extent of the territory of Brazil and its enormous slave labour force, it fell to the patriarch to assume the role of imposing social control and organisation. As a result, the patriarchal family, organised around the *casa-grande*, or mansion, became the most important social model during the colonial period. This model was dualistic in nature, with the patriarch, his wife and legitimate children at its core, and a set of individuals dependent on the *casa-grande* on the periphery. The patriarch himself functioned as a link between the two, thus enjoying one of the most prominent roles in society and the immense power that accompanied it.[57]

The order of this society was intensely hierarchical and male/female relations were based on extreme opposition, underlined by sexual freedom for men and the virtual domestic imprisonment of women. This resulted in the sharply delineated male and female spaces that Freyre conceptualised as the divide between house and street, with the man's place in the public domain, while women were confined to the domestic sphere. As Parker observes, the patriarchal order in Brazilian history also represents more than a model for social organisation, it became an important ideological construct and a system of representation, through which Brazilians still structure their social interactions and relations.[58]

In Parker's opinion, the legacy of patriarchal ideology is perhaps felt most in the construction of gender in Brazil. He sets out in detail how the hierarchy of the patriarchal system still influences the language of the body and sexual meanings and classifications, centred around the *machão*, who embodies the power, violence and virility traditionally associated with masculinity. However, although he argues that everyone understands the fundamental principles of this gender hierarchy, Parker demonstrates the ways in which it has been questioned in modern Brazilian life, by alternative sexual practices and approaches to the question of sexual meaning, which coexist and intertwine with traditional values. This alternative system of meanings and practices, although always developed with reference to traditional structures of gender and sexuality, focuses on the possibilities of subverting these structures, that is, on the diversity of sexual pleasure.

This "ideology of the erotic" plays with the dichotomy in Brazilian culture and society between the house and the street, undermining the division between private and public, by privately transgressing accepted social norms. In contrast to these conventions, which are based on distinctness, dualism and hierarchy, erotic ideology emphasises the diffuse, multiple and polymorphous. In fact, Parker describes the erotic as a transient carnivalisation of daily life, since by "Breaking down the separations of daily life in the fleeting moments of desire, pleasure and passion, the erotic offers an anarchic alternative to the established order of the sexual universe: an alternative in which the only absolute rule is the transgression of prohibitions."[59] Additionally, he makes the point that while the social dislocation which resulted from the processes of modernisation, urbanisation and industrialisation has contributed to undermining the legitimacy of the family, Church, and the State, the ideology of the erotic is more than simply a result of modernity, but has a complex and intimate relationship with key traditions of Brazilian culture, evident for example, as a subversive undercurrent within the plantation economy and the patriarchal order.

The political system that replaced the colonial slave-owning order was still based largely on *coronelismo*. The *coronel*, or "colonel" was not necessarily an individual invested with military rank; the term was used as a mark of respect for large landowners. Power had passed from the hands of the former slave-owners of Bahia, Pernambuco and Rio de Janeiro to Republican landowners in São Paulo, and by the turn of the century, Minas Gerais, who played the role of patrons at a local level. This clientelism was important in accommodating the shift in the political economy to export-led development, and meant that the political system of the First Republic was heavily reliant on local oligarchic control. By the 1930s the Depression had led to a repudiation of the assumptions on which this development was based, revealing the limitations of the First Republic's elitist political system. Subsequent political events – leading to the creation of Getúlio Vargas's authoritarian Estado Novo (New State) in 1937 and the return to democracy in 1945 – were aimed at establishing a measure of state autonomy over the elites, but the transition to democracy ended up replicating and perpetuating the contradictory social and political alliances of the Old Republic. The 1945 transition and the period of democracy which followed preserved the apparatus of the interventionist state created under Vargas from 1937, and when the military regime was installed in 1964, state-supported clientelism became the basis of its political strategy. This was to endure throughout the 1970s and peaked in the 1982 municipal, congressional and gubernatorial elections, when the military intensified its manipulation of state patronage at local level in a desperate attempt to gain advantage.[60]

The tradition of clientelism, therefore, has a long history in Brazilian life, which can be traced back to the organisation of colonial society. Fernando Henrique Cardoso has explained the coexistence of authoritarianism with processes of modernisation in society under the military regime installed in 1964, by referring not only to the colonial legacy, but also to the tradition of elitist political control and of a strong state.[61] Brazil's "bureaucratic-authoritarian" regime of 1964–85 represented the culmination of a process by which power became less personal (in the hands of the "colonels") and more institutional (in the hands of the military). The transfer of power from colonial patriarch, to Republican *coronel*, to the military, meant that Brazilian society came to be marked profoundly not only by relationships of patronage, but also by the values and attitudes of machismo, even as it was undergoing processes of internationalisation and modernisation initiated by the military after 1964. Tropicália played heavily on the coexistence of traditional values with the effects of modernisation, and pre-modern representations of the body were combined with the physical experience of living in a capitalist society. In the 1960s, a worldwide discussion had re-emerged on the role of civilisation and capitalism in the decline of the pre-eminence of the body. This discussion led to a number of works that sought to rescue the erotic body, one of which, Herbert Marcuse's *Eros and Civilisation* (1969), was read by Veloso and was also widely read on the Brazilian artistic scene at the time. The following chapter examines how the Tropicalist threat to the persistent tradition of patriarchialism, combined with a desire to reclaim the desiring body from the capitalist order, would be perceived in many quarters as undermining the very fabric of Brazilian social life and organisation as envisaged by the State.

Notes

1. Hennion, "The Production of Success", 205.
2. The two songwriters are often referred to by the public and by critics by their first names.
3. Interview with the author, see Appendix.
4. For a discussion of the different variants of MPB during its early period see Treece, "Guns and Roses", 1–29.
5. The AI–5 suspended Congress and removed the right of habeas corpus. After its introduction censorship, repression and violence against civilians intensified.

6. Ortiz, *A Moderna Tradição Brasileira*, 149–66. ISEB was founded in 1955 and was responsible for the influential idea that contemporary Brazilian society was based on a dichotomy between the "authentically national" and that which was "anti-national". On Paulo Freire's literacy campaign see his *Pedagogy of the Oppressed* and *Cultural Action for Freedom*.
7. (em nosso país e em nossa época, fora da arte política não há arte popular). From the "Anteprojeto do Manifesto do Centro Popular de Cultura, redigido em março de 1962", in Buarque de Hollanda, *Impressões de Viagem*, 131.
8. (Evangelicamente, ele mitifica o poder de conversão da palavra e seu movimento intencional passa a ser o de comover e culpar: comover pela denúncia da miséria, culpar pelo investimento na suposta consciência crítica e revolucionária do intelectual.) From Buarque de Hollanda, *Impressões de Viagem*, 26.
9. Ortiz, *A Moderna Tradição Brasileira*, 149–66.
10. Buarque de Hollanda, *Impressões de Viagem*, 29–32.
11. Buarque de Hollanda, *Impressões de Viagem*, 33–4.
12. Favaretto, "A canção tropicalista", paper presented at BRASA III, King's College, Cambridge, 7–10 Sep., 1996. The concept of cultural cannibalism is discussed more fully in Chapter 4.
13. Buarque de Hollanda, *Impressões de Viagem*, 52.
14. Quoted in Buarque de Hollanda and Gonçalves, *Cultura e participação nos anos 60*, 43–4.
15. Ramos, "Uma forma histórica de cinema alternativa", in Mello (org.), *20 Anos de resistência*, 83.
16. In Buarque de Hollanda and Gonçalves, *Cultura e participação nos anos 60*, 88–9.
17. King, *Magical Reels*, 114–15.
18. *Chanchadas* were popular comedies which began to be made in the 1940s and which drew audiences mainly from working-class sectors of society.
19. Ventura, *1968: O Ano que não terminou*, 90.
20. É preciso provocar o espectador, chamá-lo de burro, recalcado e reacionário. O objetivo é abrir uma série de Vietnans no campo da cultura, uma guerra contra a cultura oficial, de consumo fácil. O sentido da eficácia do teatro hoje é o sentido da guerrilha teatral ser travada com as armas do teatro anárquico, cruel, grosso como a grossura e apatia em que vivemos.

    Ventura, *1968: O Ano que não terminou*, 93.
21. Buarque de Hollanda and Gonçalves, *Cultura e participação nos anos 60*, 28.

    Então, na época, por exemplo, o Vergara fez um furo na parede e botou um cartaz pedindo aos expectadores que olhassem o que tinha nele. E era um buraco bem baixinho, a pessoa tinha de ficar de forma ridícula, meio ajoelhada, pra poder olhar no buraco. E lá, quando o sujeito olhava, estava escrito qualquer coisa como: ao invés do Sr. ficar nessa atitude ridícula, olhando neste buraco, por que não toma uma atitude em relação às coisas que estão acontecendo em sua volta ...

22. (Participaçãó corporal, tátil, visual, semântica etc., do espectador.), Hélio Oiticica in MAM catalogue, *Nova Objetividade Brasileira*, 1967, cited in Buarque de Hollanda and Gonçalves, *Cultura e participação nos anos 60*, 29.
23. operam descentramento cultural com procedimentos críticos que combinam construtividade e dessacralização; deslocam a discussão sobre as relações de arte e participação superando a oposição entre "arte participante" e "arte alienada"; definem relações entre fruição estética e crítica social, em que esta se desloca do

tema para os processos e procedimentos. São, assim, produções que afirmam dois sentidos simultâneos: designam aspectos da cultura enquanto desconstróem as linguagens que a pressupõe totalizada.

Favaretto, "A canção tropicalista", 2.
24. Napolitano explores the prevailing approaches to writing on popular music at this time in "A música popular brasileira nos anos 60", 123–49.
25. Tinhorão has published many rigorously researched histories of Brazilian popular music that are widely read by scholars in the field. He differed from most commentators on popular music in the 1960s in that he rejected the possibilities for realising a national-popular ethos through a form of cultural expression which he considered to be dominated by market demands. See Bibliography for a list of Tinhorão's work.
26. A questão da música popular brasileira vem sendo posta ultimamente em termos de fidelidade e comunicação com o povo brasileiro. Quer dizer, sempre se discute se o importante é ter uma visão ideológica dos problemas brasileiros, e se a música é boa, desde que exponha bem essa visão; ou se devemos retomar ou apenas aceitar a música primitiva brasileira .... Ora, a música brasileira se moderniza e continua brasileira à medida que toda informação é aproveitada (e entendida) na vivência e na compreensão da realidade brasileira ... Se temos uma tradição e queremos fazer algo de novo dentro dela, não só temos que senti-la, mas conhecê-la. E é este conhecimento que vai nos dar a possibilidade de criar algo novo e coerente com ela. Só a retomada da linha evolutiva, pode nos dar uma organicidade para selecionar e ter julgamento de criação.

Cited in Napolitano, "A música popular brasileira nos anos 60", 137–8. Interview originally published in *Revista Civilização Brasileira*, 7, May 1966, pp. 375–85.
27. (Aliás João Gilberto para mim é exatamente o momento em que isto aconteceu: a informação da modernidade musical utilizada na recriação, na renovação, no dar um passo à frente da música popular brasileira.) Cited in Napolitano, "A música popular brasileira nos anos 60", 138.
28. Interview with the author, see Appendix.
29. One of the first key contributions to this line of thinking, came in the form of Vasconcellos's *Música Popular* which explored three distinct phases of MPB. The first encompasses the period 1962–67, which saw the shift from protest song to the political and cultural impasse which resulted from the coup. The second, between 1967–68, he calls the period of "disillusioned song", characterised by Tropicália and its new critical perspective on Brazil's history. Vasconcellos sees the movement as the most daring and productive incorporation of political material into MPB. The third period (1969–74) is described as that of the "culture of depression", characterised by the irrational and the escapist, which does not fulfil the creative possibilities raised by Tropicália.
30. In 1960 only 9.5% of urban homes possessed a television set; by 1970, the figure was 40%. This level of growth was stimulated by government incentives and massive investment after 1964, when the military sought to develop a modern communications network which would support their programme of centralised authoritarianism. Skidmore, *The Politics of Military Rule in Brazil*, 111.
31. The ideological implications of style and the association of style with values will be discussed in Chapter 2.
32. Treece, "Rhythm and Poetry", in Brooksbank Jones and Munck (eds), *Cultural Politics in Latin America*, 37.

33. *Festivais, Volume 1*, GloboDisk, 0028–2, 1997.
34. Coutinho, *An Introduction to Literature in Brazil*, 69 and 71.
35. (impulso da contradição, exaltação dos sentidos, êxtase da festa, convivência das disparidades, atração das vertigens.) Sevcenko, "Entre a ordem e o caos", 61.
36. (uma constante formal da sensibilidade brasileira, percorrendo, através de mutações o variações epocais, o nosso espaço cultural.) Campos, "A Poesia do Barroco", 146.
37. Campos summarises the argument in "A Poesia do Barroco", 146–7.
38. Campos, "A Poesia do Barroco", 148. See also Campos, *Ruptura dos Gêneros na Literatura Latino-Americana*, 35.
39. Sevcenko, "Entre a ordem e o caos", 66.
40. Campos, "A Poesia do Barroco", 146.
41. Coutinho, *An Introduction to Literature in Brazil*, 98.
42. As part of his work for the state heritage council SPAHN (Serviço do Patrimônio Histórico e Artístico Nacional), the Modernist writer Mário de Andrade describes a colonial engraving in a church in the interior of São Paulo in which tropical fruits are included in the Last Supper:

> The detailed engraving of a watermelon opposite Christ, in the Last Supper, is a raw touch of delicious ingenuousness. One cannot help smiling, when faced with this cornucopian national table. The copier must have been Brazilian, or perhaps Portuguese with an intimate acquaintance with our national exuberance ... He could not restrain himself, he failed to understand the mystical frugality of Da Vinci's table, he filled empty plates with engravings of watermelons ... It is perhaps more on account of the abundance of the laden table, rather than because of the engravings of a possible native watermelon, that these paintings reveal Brazil.

Quoted in Resende, "Brazilian Modernism", 213.

43. Ávila, "Barroco, Estilo de vida, Estilo das Minas Gerais", 99. Gilberto Freyre gives a colourful account of this fluid attitude to religion held by the Portuguese colonisers:

> theirs was a liturgy social rather than religious, a softened, lyric Christianity with many phallic and animistic reminiscences of the pagan cults. The only thing that was lacking was for the saints and angels to take on fleshly form and step down from the altars on feast-days to disport themselves with the populace. As it was, one might have seen oxen entering the churches to be blessed by the priests; mothers lulling their little ones with the same hymns of praise that were addressed to the Infant Jesus; sterile women with upraised petticoats rubbing themselves against the legs of São Gonçalo do Amarante; married men, fearful of infidelity on the part of their wives, going to interrogate the "cuckold rocks", while marriageable young girls addressed themselves to the "marriage rocks"; and finally our Lady of Expectancy being worshipped in the guise of a pregnant woman.

The Masters and the Slaves, 30.

44. The festivities unwound over several days, the highlight was the procession which transferred the Host from the Chapel of the Rosary to the church being inaugurated. The long, choreographed procession wove its way along colourfully, perhaps comparable only to the modern carnival parades of Rio. There were innumerable local brotherhoods in costume with their standards and patron saints, preceded by musical groups, dance troupes, festive floats and mythological figures on horseback.

As festividades, desenroladas durante vários dias, tiveram seu ponto máximo na procissão de trasladação do Santíssimo da Capela do Rosário para a igreja que então se inaugurava. O longo cortejo constituiu uma colorida trama coreográfica, só comparável talvez aos desfiles do moderno carnaval carioca. Viam-se em trajes de gala as inúmeras irmandades locais com seus estandartes e santos padroeiros, precedidas de conjuntos musicais, grupos de dançarinos, carros alegóricos e figuras mitológicas a cavalo.

Ávila, "Barroco, Estilo de vida, Estilo das Minas Gerais", 99.
45. Da Matta, *Carnivals, Rogues and Heroes*, 39.
46. Da Matta, *Universo do Carnaval*, 28, 41, 42 and 114.
47. Parker, *Bodies, Pleasures and Passions*, 163.
48. Bakhtin, *Rabelais and His World*.
49. Da Matta, *Carnivals, Rogues and Heroes*, 26, 33, 30 & 84–5.
50. Bakhtin, *Rabelais and His World*, 245, 82, 213 and 256.
51. Eco, "The Frames of Comic Freedom", in Sebeok (ed.) *Carnival*, 1–9.
52. Da Matta, *Carnivals, Rogues and Heroes*, 63–8.
53. Da Matta, *Universo do Carnaval: Imagens e Reflexões*, 48.
54. Parker, *Bodies, Pleasures and Passions*, 146.
55. See Pereira, *Carnaval Brasileiro*, 141–7, for an account of transvestism in carnival balls.
56. Da Matta, *Universo do Carnaval: Imagens e Reflexões*, 55.
57. See Candido, "The Brazilian Family", in Smith and Marchant (eds), *Brazil: Portrait of a Half Continent* and Freyre, *The Masters and the Slaves*, on patriarchy and the *casa-grande*.
58. Parker, *Bodies, Pleasures and Passions*, 30–31.
59. Parker, *Bodies, Pleasures and Passions*, 134.
60. I summarise here some of the key points of Cammack's analysis of these political processes in, "Brazil: The Long March to the New Republic", 21–58.
61. Cardoso, "On the Characterization of Authoritarian Regimes in Latin America", in Collier (ed.), *The New Authoritarianism in Latin America*, 33–57.

Chapter 2

Style and Sexual Politics in the Tropicália Period

"The left booed me, they pelted me with bananas. Until the day I was arrested by the military and then, exiled from the country. But not even the army took me for a left-wing sympathiser. My expulsion from the country ... was based on *aesthetic considerations and on a possible violation of certain customs and traditions of the Brazilian people*." Caetano Veloso[1]

"Oh, this business of music meddling with politics, big beards, long hair ... The only music I'll waste my time on is classical music or a nice samba-canção."
Erasmo Dias, Public Security Secretary for São Paulo during the military dictatorship[2]

In 1967 television audiences all over Brazil succumbed to the charms of a wide-eyed, angelic-looking young Bahian with an astounding memory for the classic sambas sung by the radio stars of the 1940s and 50s. The producer of TV Record's hit programme Esta Noite Se Improvisa (Improvise Tonight) had stumbled upon Veloso in a bar near the television studio. He had been helping his sister, Maria Bethânia, herself a rising star, to practise for the musical game show, in which contestants had to beat each other to the buzzer if they were able to sing a recognisable song containing a key word given by the presenter. Veloso won the contest so many times he began to make his living by selling off the cars that were awarded as first prize. He had accompanied his sister's growing popularity very closely, composing for her and acting as a chaperone at their father's request, but until his success on Esta Noite he had not viewed himself as a potential performer. His accidental popularity surprised not just Veloso, but his sister's formidable promoter Guilherme Araújo, who had not previously considered the timid young man as stage material. With characteristic perspicacity, however, Araújo quickly identified Veloso's beguiling innocence and vulnerablitity as the source of his appeal. But while the public were being seduced by the ingénue, already they had also begun to react to an aspect of his appearance that unsettled them. While other singers were showered with flowers from the studio audience, Veloso was greeted with a hail of combs, so he could tame his unruly locks, which did not match the slick dinner-suited image characteristic of television showmanship[3].

By the end of the following year, on 23rd December 1968, Veloso and his Tropicalist co-collaborator, Gilberto Gil, would be taken from their homes in São

Paulo in the early hours of the morning by plain-clothes military officers, and would spend the next two months imprisoned in Rio as threats to national security. This chapter examines Veloso's transformation from a *bom moço*, or "nice young man", into an *enfant terrible* and how the sexual politics which he developed and advocated during the Tropicália period differed from the cultural politics of the day. I will discuss the political significance of his ambiguous style and divergent sexual identity in the context of late 1960s Brazil, illustrating how Veloso turned to the representation of desire and pleasure to recover a dialectical and critical relationship between individual and social identities. Style and sexuality have always been closely linked to the process of image-making throughout Veloso's career, but the two were fundamental during the Tropicália years in 1967 and 1968, playing a vital role in the communicative process, with all of the resulting complexities and controversies that characterised his relationship with the public during this time.

Style and Popular Music

The comments in this chapter's epigraphs immediately reveal the political implications of style. When Veloso was imprisoned in Rio, one of his first experiences of bodily deprivation was the shaving off of his hair, a prominent personal trademark. Long hair and a beard, hippie clothes and macumba beads were elements of a language of signs inscribed on the body that spoke of pleasure, *preguiça* (indolence) and underdevelopment and constituted an anti-discourse to the law-and-order ethic of the military regime. Veloso has even stated that he and Gilberto Gil were prevented from working after their release, because their shaved heads would have represented a potent testimony to the violation of their personal freedom: "... they shaved our heads, they had no proof we'd done anything, but they didn't have the courage to let us go, because they couldn't decide ... Do we release them and let them appear on television with their heads shaved?"[4]

The question of the vital importance of style to considerations of pop culture was emphatically raised in Britain with the publication of the newspaper critic and jazz singer George Melly's *Revolt Into Style* in 1970. Melly highlighted the ways in which pop was able to translate the spirit of its time into "objects ... or fashion or behaviour",[5] emphasising heavily the visual dimension of pop. In the area of academic publishing, the importance of iconography in subcultural analysis was firmly established with the publication of Dick Hebdige's *Subculture: The Meaning of Style* in 1979. Hebdige was based at the Centre for Contemporary Cultural Studies at Birmingham University, which had published a seminal collection examining the relationship between subcultural groups and class.[6] Hebdige widened the scope of the Birmingham Cultural Studies group, by attempting a non-class-specific reading of subcultural styles. He drew on the post-structuralist semiotic theory of polysemy, in which each text is seen to be capable of generating an infinite range of meanings. The concept was closely associated at that time with the French group, Tel Quel, which borrowed from modernist and avant-garde aesthetics and modelled themselves on Brechtian epic theatre, in order to transcend conventional theories of art. The Tel Quel group concerned itself with the productivity of language – the process by which meaning is constructed – rather than with the final product. This process was epitomised by the term "signifying practice", in which art became "the triumph of process over fixity, disruption over unity", and (using Eisenstein's terms for the principles on which he based his montage) "collision" over "linkage".[7] These concerns resonate in the Tropicalist aesthetic developed a decade earlier, which also drew in part on Dadaist and Surrealist collages, "ready-mades" and dreamscapes, Brecht's theatre of alienation, and modernism as it was articulated in Brazil.

Hebdige's attempts to reveal "the ideological dimension of signs" in his study of the meaning of style have been widely discussed and its limitations widely critiqued. He does not, for example, engage with the fundamental issue of gender and sexual politics in relation to style.[8] In fact, he has been accused of implying that style and politics cannot really be reconciled, and that the politics of style is restricted to a temporary, symbolic power to shock.[9] However, his work helped to establish the concept of polysemy within cultural studies, which would subsequently inspire the more complex vision of cultural process as "hybridisation". Tropicalist cultural expression is profoundly and consciously hybrid in nature. It was oriented around a dialogue between different historical epochs, different art forms and between erudite and popular culture.

From *bom moço* to *enfant terrible*

Veloso's passage from game-show popularity to superstar was meteoric, and came about as a result of the third TV Record Festival of Brazilian Popular Music in 1967. His success with the song "Alegria, Alegria" (Joy, Joy) made him an overnight sensation and THE hot topic of the press. This festival in effect served as the first public platform for the split between exponents of protest song and the nascent Tropicália movement. The arena chosen to launch Veloso's strategic use of style as the politics of change and of choice was the festival stage, the main focus of Brazilian popular music at the time and a prominent feature of the landscape of its cultural politics. The essential contradiction of the festivals is that although they were viewed by the left-wing members of the audience as an oppositional space, they were organised by the television stations, part of the mass media system supported and promoted by the State.[10] For the fan of protest music, however, attendance at a festival at least offered an opportunity to gather in public and to express solidarity and support for ideologies of zealous nationalism and anti-modernisation aimed at opposing those promoted by the military regime. The festivals offered the space for the development of a counter-culture, evident in other spheres of the arts, such as the theatre, cinema and the plastic arts, in which cultural expression became increasingly politicised. The desire to participate in this movement and express a need for action was underlined with a style favoured in particular by college and university students in São Paulo, described retrospectively in a BASF company leaflet: "The students wore long-sleeved khaki shirts, faded Lee jeans (with back pockets for keeping the marbles they used to fling at the mounted military police to throw them off balance) and rough tennis shoes, suitable for street battles."[11] Of course, not all of the students who adopted this style would have participated in demonstrations and street disturbances. It was a question, rather, of appearing ready to do so. The Tropicalists were aware that style had become a key vehicle for the enactment of social concerns in view of the difficulty of direct activity, but showed themselves to be in favour of plurality instead of authority, of individual self-renewal, instead of the adoption of a uniform. They therefore set out to invade and explore the ambiguities of the festival space and in so doing, ended up defying the authority of both the left and the right.

Protest song found majority support at the time among young people and students in particular. This points to a particular characteristic of Brazilian youth culture at the time, its willingness to embrace a traditional attitude in its concern to protect the ideal of national purity in the fight against imperialism. Commenting on what he saw as the conservative stamp of the music of Brazilian youth at this time, Gilberto Gil reflected: "If we always thought like that, we would be playing our music with indigenous instruments. We have to think in universal terms. These days the world is very small, there is no place for regionalisms."[12] Despite setting themselves up as an oppositional force to the right wing and to authoritarianism, the militant nationalism of some students meant that in their approach to culture, especially music, they ended up reproducing the bullying tactics of the extreme right. The Tropicalists, attacked by both the left and the right, relied heavily on style as a way of visually reinforcing their position as neither.[13] Brazilian youth culture's attempts to standardise musical tastes compromised the right to choice contained in the politics of style. Tropicália aimed to elevate the question of individual choice to central importance, as a way of reacting to social and political events of the time.

The desire for participation that created feelings of community and solidarity had therefore given way to a highly organised and even aggressive form of participation. As we will see, Veloso compared the bullying of the cultural left to that of the paramilitaries of the CCC (Comanda de Caça aos Comunistas [Combat Communism Command]), who had invaded the Ruth Escobar Theatre in São Paulo and attacked the actors appearing in Zé Celso's radical production of Chico Buarque's play, *Roda Viva*. This aggressive participation at music festivals initially took the form of booing, which turned increasingly to violence in the form of verbal attacks and the hurling of objects at performers. The debate over the issue of booing had been raging for some time, and some performers believed that it was all going too far when a singer's right to perform was not respected. The bossa nova composer Sérgio Ricardo had been among those who viewed both applause and booing as important forms of participating in the polemic surrounding Brazilian popular music, and as a sign of the maturity and lucidity of the public. However, at the third Festival of Brazilian Popular Music in 1967, Ricardo was unable to perform his song about a popular footballing hero, "Beto Bom de Bola" (Beto Brilliant with the Ball), because of the audience's vociferous disapproval that a song generally considered weak in melody and arrangement had qualified for the finals. The audience's unrelenting provocation caused Ricardo to lose control and shouting from the edge of the stage, "You win! This is Brazil! This is an under-developed country! You're all animals!", the singer smashed his guitar and threw it at the crowd before storming off the stage.[14]

In addition to the Sérgio Ricardo incident, several festival performers were humiliated and some reduced almost to tears by the violent reaction of the crowd. The festivals had become an oppressive space, in which musical tastes and attendant political views were imposed through the rule of the mob. This is brought out very clearly in a review of the festival written by the poet and critic Augusto de Campos, in which he also describes the role of the mass media and its and the public's fascination with the Festival:

> Throughout all of this, a passionate public, some knowledgeable about popular music, but in the main composed of hipno-tv-ised supporters, accompanied, telexpectantly, the progress to the next round of 12 of the 36 songs presented. They did so with a fanaticism previously evident only at football matches or political rallies. Outside of the theatre, there were daily reports in the press, gossip on the radio, opinions and general commotion. Inside the theatre a crowd of supporters – a live plebescite – judging the songs, the performers and the jury, with the "yeas" or "nays" of applause or abuse. Booing had its own place in the festival and almost transformed it – as the papers have said – into a "hecklefest".[15]

The confusion between culture and politics that occurred at this time is exemplified in the festivals, where hard reflection on the country's situation was in danger of being substituted with aesthetic and ideological battles.[16] A prime example of this was the incident surrounding Geraldo Vandré's performance of "Caminhando: pra não dizer que não falei das flores" (Marching: so you'll not say I didn't speak of flowers), during the third International Song Festival in 1968, organised by TV Globo. Ferocious support for Vandré's moving protest song compelled him to appeal for calm. Amidst the shouting and fighting, Vandré called for respect for his rivals to first place, Tom Jobim and Chico Buarque, and reminded the audience of the role of artists and of the limitations of the festivals:

> Antônio Carlos Jobim and Chico Buarque de Hollanda deserve our respect, our role is to write songs, on this occasion the role of judge belongs to the jury over there ... (booing) Please, please, there's just one more thing, to those of you, those of you who still think that you support me by booing others ... (chanting, shouting and

booing) ... People! People! Please, look, just one more thing, there's more to life than festivals![17]

Prior to the 1967 festivals, Gilberto Gil had been organising meetings of Brazilian artists from across the spectrum to discuss the development of new directions in Brazilian popular music. The disagreements in evidence at these meetings between future Tropicalists and more traditional performers prefaced the hostility and the definitive split in the popular music scene that were to crystallise after the 1967 TV Record Festival in São Paulo. Gil was the first performer to introduce electric guitars into the festivals, followed by Veloso in the presentation of "Alegria, Alegria", a song which opened with images of contemporary life disseminated by the mass media:

> Caminhando contra o vento
> Sem lenço sem documento
> No sol do quase dezembro
> Eu vou!
> O sol se reparte em crimes
> Espaçonaves, guerrilhas, em Cardinales bonitas
> Eu vou!
> Em caras de presidentes
> Em grandes beijos de amor
> Em dentes pernas bandeiras
> Bomba e Brigitte Bardot
> O sol nas bancas de revista
> Me enche de alegria e preguiça
> Quem lê tanta notícia? ...
> Eu vou! Por que não? Por que não?

(Walking against the wind/ Nothing to identify me/ In the almost December sun/ I go!/ The sun serves up crime [O Sol was the name of a countercultural publication]/ Spaceships, guerillas, pretty Claudia Cardinales/ I go!/ Into presidents' faces/ Passionate kisses/ Smiles, legs, flags/ Bombs and Brigitte Bardot/ The sun on the newspaper stands/ Fills me with joy and laziness/ Who reads all that news anyway? .../ I go! And why not? Why not?)

The subject in the song is bombarded with these images as he wanders through Copacabana, "consoled" by some of the products of a consumer society mentioned in the second part of the song – Coca-Cola, TV and pop music. He deals with the flood of modern, international culture with subversive pre-modern and national characteristics – *alegria* and *preguiça* – carnivalesque exuberance and stereotypical Brazilian indolence. The first part of the song seems to suggest that the individual can hold his own and be selective when confronted with the international cultural onslaught, "who reads all that news anyway?", he asks. The refrain "I go! And why not?" and the repeated line "Nothing to identify me" appear to constitute a defiant declaration of individual freedom with regard to the subject's construction of identity, both in the context of international mass culture and of military rule. However, the critical force of the song lies in the gap it exposes between the dream of modernity and the reality of modernisation. In the second half of the song the lyrics emphasise that reality: the limited, partial reach of the modernising project, which never gets to "the heart of Brazil". The song as a whole oscillates between the ideal of a truly modern, democratic Brazil "with no guns" and "with no hunger", and a Brazil which is still without books and educational opportunities.[18]

In the preliminary qualifier, the mere presence of Veloso's backing band, the Beat Boys, dressed in pink suits with Beatles haircuts and playing electric guitars, provoked booing even before he appeared on stage. Determined to perform the song, Veloso then burst onto the stage with such an irate expression that he literally bullied the audience into hearing the song out, emphasising the defiant "Porque não?" (Why not?) of the lyrics. To his surprise he ended up being warmly applauded by the majority of the audience. By the final of the competition, "Alegria, Alegria", with its snapshots of modern, urban Brazil and modernised marchinha beat, had won over the crowd and was placed fourth by the jury.

The press could not get enough of the new star and frequently made direct links between his physical appearance, his sex appeal and his musical style, such as Eli Halfoun's article, headlined "Caetano: já é alegria demais" (Caetano: enough Joy now):

> But what was most influential in Caetano's success was his appearance: thin, uncombed, and untidy, which earned him the nickname "Hunger Strike", the Bahian began to gain the sympathy of young girls, who saw him as a "vulnerable little thing". That was enough for the "vulnerable" Caetano to discover the secret of his success, and he threw himself into the make-believe. He started inventing a so-called universal sound, and even he himself doesn't really know what it is.[19]

Here Halfoun goes as far as suggesting that the new sound has come about as a result, a product of the image projected. Affronted by the commodification of the performer, and his awareness of the consumability of style and willingness to engage with the market, the journalist concluded: "He has commercialised his every attitude and gesture, the unruly hair, the untidiness and the appearance of the 'shy, vulnerable young boy' ..."[20]

The role of the impresario Guilherme Araújo in the packaging and the exposure of the early Veloso cannot be underestimated. Brazil's first manager in the modern sense facilitated by the mass media, Araújo fed the interest of the public by leaking bits of information to the media, ranging from details of forthcoming releases, to the fact that he had sent for a special hair stylist from Rio, capable of dealing with Veloso's unruly coiffure. With Araújo's encouragement Veloso became a performer in many spaces, satisfying the desire of the Brazilian public for both the public and private personae of the star. In the minds of the public the gap between the "real" Caetano Veloso of everyday life and the singing star became increasingly smaller. The most memorable example of this is Veloso's wedding in November 1967. Although the interest in and attention accorded to pop star weddings is today an accepted part of the showcase of their lives, this occasion was without precedent at the time. Thanks to the television cameras, the press and the PR skills of Guilherme Araújo, who was reputed to have leaked details of the secret ceremony to the media, the whole nation was able to share in this "intimate" moment of the singer's personal life. If the couple were not expecting the pop of flash bulbs, they were, however, aptly attired for a show – Veloso in the distinctive roll-neck with sports jacket of the kind he had worn to perform "Alegria, Alegria", this time with a large crêpe flower in the buttonhole and his bride in a miniskirt and Red Riding Hood-style cape in shocking pink satin. There was a veritable stampede in the small church in Salvador, Bahia, with fans crammed in to witness the touted "hippy wedding", singing "Alegria, Alegria" and trying to rip a bit of the bride's dress, or a strand of Veloso's hair as trophies. Not to be outdone by the modern media, the whole affair was later recounted in verse form by the oral poet Expedito Ferreira da Silva.[21] The couple needed a police escort to reach the altar, and the groom's mother fainted in the scrum; Araújo, however, was heard to remark: "This is wonderful! Just wonderful!"[22]

If his manager was already convinced of the headline-grabbing potential of style, Veloso himself also needed no further proof that the star was desired as much as his music. He obliged and offered himself up to the public, while constantly re-elaborating the self he presented. Using his body as a site of dialogue and conflict between the individual and his society, Veloso defined and redefined a self facing all of the contradictions and complexities of a distorted modernisation and the increasing influence of international culture. His bodily code depended on a dynamic of instability, which emphasised the importance of prompting questions rather than attempting to provide answers. Drawing on an international pop aesthetic and re-articulating it within a local context or framework, he aimed to provoke discussion on the position of Brazil within the global cultural system, and the position of the individual faced by the contrasts and shifts of modern society.

For example, much was made of the fact that so many members of the Tropicália group came from or had close connections to the state of Bahia. The ingenuousness that the public had identified, and to which it had been initially attracted in Veloso, appeared to be linked to preconceptions with regard to the naiveté of the recently arrived migrant. However, as Veloso began to rework the relationship between the migrant and the city, emphasising the energy and creativity with which the overwhelming urban scene of São Paulo could be confronted, the public's opinion of him began to change. Referring repeatedly to his origins, the press soon began to make mention of his "savage" appearance, and view his performances as a kind of barbarian invasion of a civilised space. Confounding easy classification, however, and refusing to reinforce the entrenched geo-social divide in Brazil, Veloso set about engaging head-on with all that was modern and international in the city of São Paulo, without compromising his regional identity. Style offered a vital and instantaneously communicable means of defining the self, and Veloso made use of its dynamic of transience and mutability, celebrating the opportunity it offered to emphasise difference.

The Tropicalist attack on conventional aesthetics – on "good taste" – formed a part of this promotion of difference and led them to embrace lowbrow cultural forms and objects and elevate them to a status on a par with those of official, national culture. This attitude was highly ambiguous – both celebratory and self-mocking – and reflected the Tropicalists' aim not to replace one set of value judgements with another, but to create a space in which they could productively comment on each other. For example, Veloso explains the adoption of Carmen Miranda as an emblem of Tropicália in the following way: "… Carmen Miranda was, first of all, a source of both pride and shame, and then, a symbol of the intellectual violence with which we wished to confront our reality, the implacable gaze which we wished to turn on ourselves."[23] The use of kitsch and camp culture facilitated a process of constant questioning that threatened to destabilise conventionally held views on national symbols. In January 1972, in his first show after his return from exile in London, Veloso appeared on stage dressed and dancing like Carmen Miranda. Veloso's feminisation of his body provoked the desired scandal and polemic and in invoking Miranda he also made reference to her status as an icon for gay men in Brazil and internationally, and the use and fetishisation of elements of her style in gay culture.

Veloso's attention to style and the visual aspect of performance was inspired in part by Miranda, whose use of dance, physical and vocal gestures and costume was primarily responsible for her rise to international fame. By the early 1940s "South American fever", the fashion craze inspired by Miranda, had captivated New York. Department stores displayed the now famous turbans and baianas, derived from the traditional dress of black Bahian women and first used by Miranda in a performance of Dorival Caymmi's "O Que é Que a Baiana Tem?" (What Does the Baiana Have?) (1939). The ambivalence of the conquest of New York and later Hollywood through the use of caricatured and exoticised images of Brazil was embraced by the Tropicalists, who acknowledged that the stereotypes disseminated by mass culture could offer new possibilities for critically confronting and revealing the realities of Brazilian society.

Although Carmen Miranda's extensive cultivation and use of style was extraordinary, the prominence of style in the tradition of Brazilian popular music was not without precedent. Without the benefit of film to disseminate images, the figure of the *malandro*, or wily rogue, inspired a whole sub-genre of samba from the late 1920s to the beginning of the 1940s, when the Estado Novo's promotion of an ethic of discipline and hard work did away with him.[24] The key values upheld by *malandragem* were courage, elegance and the *jeitinho* (or ability to find a way around laws, rules and regulations), which were important in the alternative order that the *malandro* created from his position at the margins of society. His style reflected his pride, sense of honour and the ambivalence of this position of marginality which was often coupled with aspirations to social acceptance.²⁵ The Panama hat conformed to the rules of good breeding concerning the wearing of hats in public, however, as immortalised in Wilson Batista's samba, "Lenço no pescoço" (Handkerchief Round My Neck) (1933), it was worn at a jaunty and somewhat defiant angle and served as a foil in the event of a fight. The *malandro*'s tie or neckerchief also represented a nod to gentility, but was invariably the brightly coloured tie of a dandy. His silk shirt, worn as a sign of quality and means, was also adopted because silk could not be easily cut by a knife, while his *tamanco*, or distinctive style of slip-on footwear was easy to shed when fighting broke out.²⁶

It is impossible to ignore the elements of camp in all of this dandyism and flair. Indeed the most notorious *malandro* of all, Madame Satã, was Brazil's first transvestite stage artist. Satã, who controlled the Lapa area of Rio de Janeiro in the 1930s, was equally famous for his valentia (courage) as for his homosexuality, and it was in defence of the latter that he was originally drawn into a life of malandragem.²⁷ The dandification of conventional elements of clothing represented a parody of the image of respectable and upstanding citizens, at the same time as highlighting the malandro's exclusion from that social group. The white linen suit which became closely associated with the *malandro* is perhaps most emblematic of this and was taken up by the Tropicalists as one of their prominent stylistic trademarks. In a 1979 article Richard Dyer describes camp culture as belonging to a marginal group in society which takes up commodities which the anarchy of capitalism has produced and puts them to a "contrary" use from that intended by the dominant culture. This has the potential to subvert, but also has reactionary implications.²⁸ The Tropicalists were initially labelled reactionary by the left, who failed to appreciate the irony with which these commodities were used.

The questioning of the value of Carmen Miranda as both a national symbol and a prominent figure on the world stage had particular relevance for the Tropicalists' international outlook. Precedents set in popular music were the *sambas-canção* and *sambas-exaltação* of Ari Barroso which conquered Hollywood through homogeneous stock imagery of an exoticised Brazil; and bossa nova, whose revolutionary style took the world by storm, but whose innovations were appropriated outside Brazil, emptied of their context and reduced to lift and shopping mall music. In spite of this, to the Tropicalists it was simply delusional not to acknowledge international influences on Brazilian cultural expression – for example, the popularity of the tango and bolero in the 1940s and 1950s. The Tropicalist bolero, "Soy loco por ti América" (Crazy About You America), recognised the influence of Latin American culture on Brazil, and provoked a wave of criticism from conservative elements of society and cultural purists, both for its references to guerrillas and freedom fighters, and for its use of "Portunhol", a mixture of Portuguese and Spanish. The Tropicalists' mix of national and international was therefore reflected in their musical style – electric guitars in a samba or bolero – in their forms of dress – hippie clothes and *malandro* suits – and their language – heady collages of traditional rural life and fast-changing urban scenes. Veloso's succinct summary of one of the concerns of the Tropicalist movement was that it sought a "saudosismo do futuro" (nostalgia for the future), a phrase which can be applied to its musical aesthetic as well as its sense of style. Rejecting the vulnerability that the protest movement assumed in the relationship between countries of the periphery and of the centre, they aggressively and selectively devoured aspects of international culture and made them into a uniquely Brazilian cultural product.

Veloso's notorious performance of the song "É Proibido Proibir" (Prohibiting Prohibited) at TV Globo's third International Song Festival in 1968 epitomised the radical impact of his style on an audience composed to a large degree of left-wing student supporters of protest song. At that festival he sought to reclaim this crucially important performing space as an arena in which difference and conflict could be expressed and played out, not just shouted down. Instigated by his manager, Veloso had written "É Proibido Proibir" using the slogan of the student protest movement in Paris, a phrase also entirely appropriate for the current political conditions in Brazil. The spare lyrics of the song deliberately confuse the spheres of private and public, linking a revolution taking place within the eroticised space of the home with the burning cars of the revolution out in the streets:

> Me dê um beijo meu amor
> Eles estão nos esperando
> Os automóveis ardem em chamas
> Derrubar as prateleiras
> As estantes
> As estátuas
> As vidraças
> Louças, livros, sim
> E eu digo sim
> E eu digo não ao não
> E eu digo é proibido proibir

(Give me a kiss my love/ They're waiting for us out there/ The cars are going up in flames/ Knock down the shelves/ The bookcases/ Statues/ Window panes/ Dishes, books, yes/ And I say yes/ And I say no to no/ and I say prohibiting prohibited)

Veloso decided to turn his performance of the song with its inflammatory chorus into a "happening". The booing started before he appeared on stage. The crowd, already predisposed to rejecting the song for its "American" sound, were further incensed by the presence of the rock trio Os Mutantes (The Mutants) and their electric guitars, and by the appearance of Veloso in an outfit carefully chosen for this appearance. Juxtaposed on Veloso's lean, androgynous body was a futuristic suit of black and lime green plastic, with a necklace of animal teeth, Afro-Brazilian macumba beads and electrical wires, a style statement that communicated visually the triumph of individual choice and the "nostalgia for the future". It was a juxtaposition that had disturbed and angered the crowd during the preliminaries, not only because it departed from the formal attire expected at such events, but because of its irreverence and de-essentialising of symbols associated with Brazil (see Figure 1).

That 1968 TV Globo Festival was riddled with controversy from the preliminaries to the finals, providing the scene for the ultimate clash between supporters of traditional popular music vs. Tropicalists, or anyone seen to be departing from protest forms. The chief co-ordinator of the Festival, Renato Corrêa de Castro, had expressed the hope that booing would have no place in that year's festival, because "The public is more enlightened now, more musically knowledgeable. And their anger is clearly focused on other things."[29] The latter part of the comment referred to the almost daily student protests taking place on the streets of São Paulo and made a direct link between political protest and the public's behaviour at festivals, assuming that the expression of anger and protest in the streets would absorb the hostility previously evident in the performing space. It seemed rather to inflame it further. During the preliminaries, Guilherme Araújo had had boards distributed among Tropicalist supporters (always the minority), which read "Tropicalism is freedom" and "Tropicalism is critique", and during the semi-finals, when Geraldo Vandré began his stirring "Caminhando" (Marching), a board went up with the comment: "Folklore is reactionary". This provoked a punch-up in the crowd between the two groups of fans, which required police intervention to bring under control. In the semi-finals the atonal, "modern-sounding" introduction of "É Proibido Proibir" as played by Os Mutantes immediately elicited a hail of missiles and Veloso further incensed the crowd by repeating a highly erotic and provocative dance he had performed during the preliminaries and which had led to cries of "Queer! Queer!". The journalist Carlos Calado describes the gestures and movements that led to the vociferous rejection of Veloso's body politics:

> Caetano appeared swaying his hips. He invented an aggressively erotic dance, with thrusting pelvic movements, which recalled the sexual act. The crowd, unimpressed, replied with some choreography of their own: in one co-ordinated movement, the majority of the crowd turned their backs to the stage, while they continued to boo and shout.[30]

It was not only Veloso's irreverence in simulating the sexual act in dance, but the way in which he insisted on "camping it up", his slight, androgynous body wiggling with an almost feminine allure, which infuriated the crowd. Relativising and destabilising sexuality and the erotic, the most private aspect of an individual's life, Veloso placed the issue of free choice as regards sexual identity firmly on the cultural political agenda.

By the semi-finals, the crowd had decided that they would not even allow the song to be performed. Veloso persisted in the face of their hostility, but eventually erupted in a blistering attack on the public, denouncing the narrow-mindedness and reactionary attitudes "on the loose" in Brazil. This speech represents one of the most extraordinary moments of contemporary music history in Brazil:

> So these are the young people who say they want to be in power? I see you have the courage to applaud this year a song, a kind of song, which you didn't dare applaud last year, these are the same young people who are always flogging a dead horse. You don't get it, you don't get any of it! There's no Fernando Pessoa today![31] I came here today to say that it was Gilberto Gil and I who dared to enter the structure of the festival, not with fear, although I know that's what Chico de Assis would like,[32] but with courage, with courage to enter this structure and explode it! It was Gilberto Gil and I! You're all out of it! You'll never understand! Is this the flower of our youth, is this the flower of our youth?!
>
> You'll never control anybody! Do you know who you're like? Do you know who you're like? ... You're like those people who went to *Roda Viva* and beat up the actors. You're just like them, just like them! ... The problem is that you all want to police Brazilian music! This year Maranhão [a fellow festival performer] presented a song with a Charleston arrangement, do you know what it was? It was the same song, "Gabriela" from last year that he didn't dare sing, because it was too "American". But Gil and I have opened the way, what is it that you want? I came here to put an end to all of this! I want to say to the jury – you can disqualify me! I don't want to have anything to do with this! ...
>
> Gilberto Gil is here with me to put an end to the festivals and all the imbecility that reigns in Brazil! Put an end to it, once and for all! That's the only reason we entered the festival! ... We don't pretend that we don't know what this is all about! We had the courage to enter all of the structures and withdraw from all of them, and as for all of you?! ...
>
> If you have the same attitude to politics that you have to aesthetics, then we're done for! ... God's on the loose!![33]

The speech denounced the policing of taste at the festivals, seen as akin to the violence meted out to the actors of the play *Roda Viva*. In addition to upbraiding the public for a lack of courage to experiment, Veloso publicly recognised the ambivalent nature of the Festivals, a compromised performing space, but one which the Tropicalists were willing to enter in order to subvert it from within. The incident provoked an unprecedented level of violence from the public. Gil, who had joined Veloso on stage to lend support, left the stage bleeding after he was struck by something flung from the crowd. Following the incident, one of the festival organisers offered Veloso the opportunity to appear in the final, provided he compromise by not wearing the plastic suit (!), which he refused. In his absence the festival still provided moments of conflict and aggression, particularly when Geraldo Vandré took second place to Tom Jobim and Chico Buarque. This incident represented a defining moment of crisis in the relationship between performer and public.[34] By the following year, the impact of the AI–5 (Fifth Institutional Act) was being felt at the festivals, with many composers and performers in exile or severely censored. The festivals ceased to be a space of confrontation or debate of any kind, with the next TV Record festival banning protest song and electric guitars and restricting entries to "authentic" Brazilian compositions only.[35]

Caught in the crisis faced by cultural production, which had been organised around the idea of Revolution before 1964, and which then found itself involved in a growing culture industry, Tropicália responded by playing on the tension between these two poles of production. It shifted political considerations in popular music from social revolution to individual intervention. Tropicalist politics was the politics of the everyday, of the body and the desiring individual in society. Veloso in particular drew on this alternative politics in the new relationship that he sought to establish with the mass media, and the result was the opening up of spaces of provocation and tension within popular music. In the climate in which Tropicália was formed responses to repression also included the desperate guerrilla action of the urban centres, as well as the creation of a *linguagem da fresta*,[36] a new poetic language that operated surreptitiously in between the gaps of the allowed discourse. Tropicália's response was to draw on cultural guerrilla tactics and on elements of this new language to wage a kind of "semiotic guerrilla warfare",[37] conducted through a style that relied on a continuous reorganisation of signs and codes. Buarque de Hollanda and Gonçalves identify elements of guerrilla tactics in the character of student protest at the time, in the "fragmented language of the protest marches with their lightning-strike rallies, their rhetoric and their rhythms of centralisation/ decentralisation."[38] The idea of "guerrilhismo cultural" (cultural guerrilla warfare) was made explicit by José Celso Martinez in a statement on the role of contemporary theatre in Brazil: "These days effective theatre means guerrilla theatre".[39] In the case of Tropicália, as David Treece has observed, the group recognised the impasse which confronted the cultural left, which had been cut off from the popular base they sought to lead, and opted instead for a strategy of guerrilla action in the area of popular music.[40]

To return to the concept of polysemy that Hebdige applies to subcultural style, polysemy denies the existence of texts as a whole and of closed structures. Instead, it favours fissure and contradiction, or the "productivity of language" – its capacity to "generate a potentially infinite range of meanings".[41] For Hebdige, therefore, style does not simply reside in an object, in an item of clothing for example, but in the "signifying practices which represent those objects and render them meaningful".[42] Richard Middleton has two main questions about this concept: firstly, how do we identify expressive value faced with an infinity of meanings and secondly, does this approach not run the risk of reducing style to mere formalism?[43] In Tropicália an answer to these concerns lies in the body, which acts as the focal point of the process and gives it materiality. This is evident in Silviano Santiago's conceptualisation of the way in which different elements of Veloso's stylistic technique intrude upon, interact with and contradict each other, and how the performer allows each member of the audience to construct his or her own meanings out of the disordering of conventional meaning:

> The body serves the voice, as the clothing serves the lyrics and dance serves the music. Allowing these six elements of the equation not to work in harmony ..., but to contradict each other completely, a curious, permutational sense of playfulness is created, as if the singer on stage were a jigsaw puzzle which could only be assembled in the minds of the audience ... He wanted his body, as a piece of sculpture, in daily life and on the stage, to take on the contradiction ... He wanted his body, through its plasticity, to captivate the public and be the living image of his artistic message.[44]

This "curious, permutational sense of playfulness" is immediately apparent on the cover of the *Tropicália* album (see Figure 2). The electric guitars and Os Mutantes' ultra-modern Beatles hairstyles contrast with the Afro-Brazilian tradition represented in the dashikis worn by Gilberto Gil and Gal Costa, and the suggestion of underdevelopment in Tom Zé's portrayal of the newly-arrived migrant from the North-east, with his leather valise. The mock-serious expressions of the group lend an air of self-caricature to this portrait of Brazil. Arranger Rogério Duprat's straight-faced portrayal of the bourgeois intellectual taking tea, but from a potty, is a surrealist touch of the absurd, which disturbs our sense of reality by attributing an uncommon function to a common object. For the Modernist movement in the 1920s, the notion of the absurd was a fundamental characteristic and ethos of Brazilian society, and it was one that Veloso would explore to its limits. He sought to embody Brazil's absurdity, endowing it with a contradictory and unstable physical presence in his live performances and his iconography.

Hebdige likens the semiotic guerilla warfare practised in subcultural style to a process of bricolage. He describes subcultural bricoleurs as those who appropriate commodities and transform them, by placing them in a symbolic ensemble which erases or subverts their original, "straight" meanings. This is evident in Tropicália's iconography, for example in the publicity photograph taken for Manchete magazine before a festival performance of Veloso's "É Proibido Proibir", which demonstrates clearly the subersive power of bricolage (see Figure 3). The image parodies the Brazilian flag by juxtaposing its Positivist motto "Order and Progress" with a portrait of Veloso. The portrait has a cartoon, or comic-book quality that immediately suggests non-erudite, or non-"serious" mass culture. Veloso's "hippy" hairstyle and the shape of a heart also evoke a "Make love not war" counter-cultural ethos, directly contradicting the Positivist watchwords with the culture of *desbunde*, the laid-back attitude associated with drug-taking. The conflict between the ideals of order and progress and the reality of Brazil's underdevelopment are further emphasised in the hybrid figure of Veloso, reclining barefoot in an attitude of perennial *preguiça*, or indolence, and garlanded with symbols of the pre-modern in the animal tooth necklace and macumba beads, but dressed also in the plastic suit which suggests a modern cartoon superhero.

Veloso's 1967 composition "Tropicália" also relies heavily on imagery of the body in its surreal presentation of contemporary Brazil. The lyrics refer to the construction of the new capital city of Brasília during the Kubitschek presidency. The hugely ambitious project was completed in record time and intended as a gigantic monument to modern Brazil. The song challenges the triumphalism and immutability usually associated with the building of a monument. It pays tribute to a more representative Brazilian reality, symbolised in the idea of a hybrid body, characterised by unpredictability and imperfection, but also by resilience:

> O monumento é de papel crepom e prata
> Os olhos verdes da mulata
> A cabeleira esconde atrás da verde mata
> O luar do sertão
> O monumento não tem porta
> A entrada é uma rua antiga estreita e torta
> E no joelho uma criança sorridente feia e morta
> Estende a mão
> Viva a mata -ta -ta
> Viva a mulata -ta -ta -ta -ta ...
>
> No pulso esquerdo o bang-bang
> Em suas veias corre muito pouco sangue
> Mas seu coração balança ao samba de um tamborim
> Emite acordes dissonantes
> Pelos cinco mil alto-falantes
> Senhoras e senhores ele põe os olhos grandes sobre mim
> Viva Iracema -ma -ma
> Viva Ipanema -ma -ma -ma -ma
>
> Domingo é o Fino da Bossa
> Segunda-feira está na fossa
> Terça-feira vai à roça porém
> O monumento é bem moderno
> Não disse nada do modelo do meu terno
> Que tudo mais vá pro inferno, meu bem
> Que tudo mais vá pro inferno, meu bem
> Viva a banda da da
> Carmen Miranda da da da

(The monument is silver crepe paper/ The green eyes of the mulata/ In the green forest her hair veils/ The backlands moonlight[45]/ The monument has no door/ The entrance is an old, narrow, winding road/ And on its knee a smiling ugly dead child/ Holds out its hand/ Long live the mata -ta -ta[46]/ Long live the mulata -ta -ta -ta -ta/ Cheap Western flicks pulse in its left wrist/ Very little blood coursing through its veins/ But its heart dances to the beat of a tambourine/ It emits dissonant chords[47]/ Through five thousand loudspeakers/ Ladies and gentlemen it casts its large eyes over me/ Long live Iracema -ma -ma[48]/ Long live Ipanema -ma -ma -ma -ma[49]/ Sunday's the "Best of Bossa"[50]/ Monday's just the pits/ Tuesday maybe a day's work on the farm/ The monument is very modern/ But knows nothing about the latest fashions/ Everything else can go to hell, my dear/

Everything else can go to hell, my dear[51]/ Long live "A Banda -da -da"[52]/ Carmen Miranda -da -da -da -da)

The song makes the point that what constitutes Brazil is not static, but is unstable and renewable like carnival (silver crepe paper); hybrid, like the green-eyed mulata; unfinished and flawed (The monument has no door/ The entrance is an old, narrow, winding road); and sometimes ugly and grotesque (a smiling ugly dead child). Throughout the song references are also made to the traditional and the contemporary in Brazilian popular music, including the *toada*, bossa nova, samba and *iê-iê-iê* (Brazilian rock). The song portrays Brazil, therefore, as its people and its popular culture, not a monument of stone which aspires to the modern, but says nothing about the experience of the individual in society (The monument is very modern/ But knows nothing about the latest fashions).

One of the legacies of Kubitschek's developmentalist project was a marked increase in foreign influences on Brazilian society and culture. The cover of the album which includes the song "Tropicália" is one that evokes international mass culture with its kitsch comic-book graphics, but with a strategically placed Tropicalist symbol – a bunch of bananas – in one corner (see Figure 4). The idea of the comic-book superhero suggested in the publicity shot for Manchete is taken up again in the album in the song "Superbacana" (Supercool). In the song Veloso presents himself as a kind of Brazilian superhero pitted against the cowboys of Uncle Sam. He uses his sensual, desiring body to confront the overwhelming power of industrialisation and consumerism and exercise the freedom to embrace or reject its products. The affirmation of individual choice and identity construction in "Alegria, Alegria", reiterated in the phrase "Sem lenço sem documento" (Nothing to identify me), is echoed here in the line "Nada no bolso ou nas mãos" (Nothing in my pockets and my hands):[53]

> O espinafre biotônico
> No comando do avião supersônico
> Do parque electrônico
> Do poder atômico
> Do avanço econômico
> A moeda n° 1 do Tio Patinhas não é minha
> Um batalhão de cowboys
> Barra a entrada da legião dos super-heróis
> E eu superbacana
> Vou sonhando até explodir colorido
> No sol dos cinco sentidos
> Nada no bolso ou nas mãos
> Superhomem superflit supervinc superhist supershell superquentão ...

(Biotonic spinach/ Supersonic jet command/ Electronic industrial estate/ Atomic power/ Economic progress/ Uncle Scrooge's pennies aren't mine/ A gang of cowboys/ Bars the entrance of the legion of superheroes/ And I, Supercool/ Keep dreaming until I explode colourfully/ In the sun of the five senses/ Nothing in my pockets and my hands/ Superman SuperFlit Supervink Superhist SuperShell Superhot ...)

The song is under a minute and a half long, with the unrelentingly optimistic tone of a radio jingle. The use of inflated imagery and the top speed at which it is sung lend a comic air, which questions the value of supersonic travel and atomic energy to the average individual. The heroic stance that fed into Tropicalist style was often subject to self-parody, creating confusion over whether the performer was playing the role of comic hero or tragic clown. For the Tropicalists exceptionality was perhaps the most heroic of values and it was a quality that Veloso and Gil sought to praise on the stage of a 1968 show at the Sucata nightclub, with the erection of a banner made by Hélio Oiticica bearing the provocative tenet "Seja marginal, seja herói" (Be a criminal, be a hero). The banner showed an image taken from the newspapers, which Oiticica had used in his installation, "Homenagem a Cara de Cavalo" (Homage to Cara de Cavalo). The piece was made up of a black box with a plastic bag of simulated blood next to it and was surrounded by four photographs of the body of Oiticica's friend, the notorious young criminal known as Cara de Cavalo, who had been gunned down by police in Rio. The text that accompanied the box read: "Aqui está e aqui ficará. Contemplai o seu silêncio heróico." (Here he lies and here he will stay. Contemplate his heroic silence). It was a statement in praise of the anti-hero and in favour of anarchic freedom that incensed the authorities and was partly responsible for the closure of Veloso and Gil's show.

The mixing of politics with aesthetics through the manipulation of imagery is also prominent in the work of one of the Tropicalist collaborators, the lyricist Torquato Neto and his conceptualisation of Tropicalism. Writing in 1968 on the emergence of the movement, he focuses heavily on dress: "for the men, white linen suits [like those traditionally worn by malandros], with large collars and red rayon ties; women should adopt the old-fashioned look of Luiza Barreto Leite [a Brazilian actress] or Alencar's Iracema."[54] The style-led attack on conventional tastes was therefore an integral part of the Tropicalist ethos, present from the moment of the movement's inception. This is what made Tropicália's message so seductive, it offered not just discourse in the wind, but a whole way of life, a sensibility which would speak volumes about individual choice. The clothing, hairstyles, jewellery were all invested with meanings which created a new language of resistance difficult to police, and which offered the opportunity to participate in this resistance by adopting these stylistic codes of opposition.

In a particularly evocative article, the writer Caio Fernando Abreu reminisces about the impact of a Tropicalist performance on him as a young man of twenty. All the excitement, the novelty of the moment, is experienced by Abreu through the body, a body which appears to have been altered that night to experience the new reality of the sensual and the sensorial. What dominates in Abreu's memories is the visual style:

> Luminous flashes: Gil's patterned robes, Nara Leão's brightly coloured satin clothes, Gal's hair styled to look like Angela Davis's. And that little blonde with the fringe, is her name really Lee, like the jeans? Prince Caetano with his eagle's profile, so tiny, so strong, inaugurating the monument at the top of Rêgo Freitas Street, one night in August. Overwhelmed, dazzled, we tried to understand.[55]

In addition to an attack on tastes, the performance also constituted an attack on the senses that dazzles and puzzles. Converted to the cause of Tropicalism, Caio Fernando Abreu gave his body over to the symbols of the new way of life: "there was a new word on our lips. Tropicalism, that was its name. That same week, I bought some Amazon-green satin trousers, some umbanda necklaces in Cathedral Square. I let my hair grow, smoked my first joint. And I went in search of Brazil."[56]

The creation of effects by exciting the senses suggests the persistence of the culture of the baroque. The playfulness and wit of the baroque are present in Tropicalist lyricism and stylistic techniques, such as assonance, paradox and oxymoron, and the baroque fondness for illusion in the Tropicalist instability of meaning. Tropicália also shares the baroque's concern for the erosion of the divide between high and low culture, and between the sacred and the secular. José Celso Martínez's comments on the "death" of Tropicália, which was shown on TV Globo and which he was involved in staging, reflect this confluence of sacred and secular: "We wanted to enact a profane mass, which began by exalting Tropicália and ended by destroying the whole set, just like on the last day of carnival in years gone by."[57] The mixture of sacred and profane to create a new Tropicalist spirituality of the sensual relied on the body to give it materiality. In the staging, the contamination by the profane was further conveyed in Veloso's clothing, dressed in a white suit at the start of the programme, he ended the dramatisation with the suit stained with red dye.

Veloso's contemporary, Chico Buarque, had also been engaged in focusing on the body as a means of apprehending social meaning, an approach in which issues of gender and sexuality were central. These questions were posed within the lyrics and imagined subjects of his songs, whose searching, problematising and frequently radical messages had no visual manifestations in either Buarque's personal or public life. Veloso, however, sought to materialise the relationship between social issues and gender through style, which functioned not just to reflect and reinforce the song texts, but itself constituted a visual text, consisting of performances at highly theatrical shows, appearances on television and in the newspapers, and on album covers. He elaborated and made explicit use of style to encourage the public to use these visualisations as a means of making sense of the music and the society from which it emerged.

In that society, dominated at the time by a military dictatorship, the body could be described, in Bryan Turner's words, as "the target of the colonisation of the everyday world by the public arena of (male) reason."[58] Veloso sought to resist this patriarchal rationale by feminising his body through the use of make-up, clothing and dance, effecting whimsical transformations that exposed male identity as role-playing, as poses that cannot be held indefinitely. He sought to code sexuality in terms of plurality and divergence, in an attempt to open up cultural spaces in which the audience could consider different representations of desire and masculinity. It was a measure of the audience's confusion that Veloso's shows at the time were invariably sold out, but that he continued to suffer abuse from the audience for his ambiguous presentation of his sexuality.

The military discipline and machismo that dominated Brazil at governmental level was propagated socially through militaristic symbols of nationhood and the promotion of heterosexuality based on marriage and the family. This formed part of an overall effort to control the population, recalling Foucault's theory of the micro-politics of the regulation of the body and the macro-politics of panopticism, with the body and populations being "two places around which the organisation of power over life was deployed."[59] By deregulating the body, Veloso sought to destabilise that system of overall control, raiding the storehouse of conventional gender signs and codes and re-articulating them, sometimes aggressively, frequently ironically, and re-inserting them into an alternative context that transformed them according to individual desire. Style injected that all-important element of ambiguity into this oppositional discourse. Traditionally seen as a female concern, Veloso's deployment of style undermined official masculinity and constituted a rejection of the promotion of heterosexuality in the social order.

On the question of his clothing, Veloso has commented: "I feel comfortable in this ambiguous clothing; it's a way of using a style whose language is simultaneously compromised and liberated. *It's a position from which to contemplate the moment.*"[60] This statement recognises the ideological constitution of the body and the idea that although individuals have a certain freedom to construct their bodies, the conditions under which they do so are not normally of their own choosing. However, as Arthur Frank has observed, "these ideologies are not fixed; as they are reproduced in body techniques and practices, so they are modified. The government of the body is never fixed, but always contains oppositional spaces."[61] The Tropicalists' Miss Banana competitions, for example, parodied the showcasing of women's bodies, exposing and sabotaging the event from within. With regard to the music industry, Veloso has stated that style offered him a way of critiquing and challenging the control that the industry sought to exercise on performers:

> what we had to do ... was not passively accept formal wear for television and live performances, but effect a critique of clothing as well. A critique of appearance so we could feel free in that world of mass entertainment. It's a world that is often very conformist because of the concern to maintain an audience or sell a product, so the tendency would be to do everything not to displease the public, to increase sales ... Sometimes the individual ends up as this conformist figure in order to be accepted by the majority, a kind of Hollywoodian repression of the personalities of the artists. Our generation wanted to do away with all that.[62]

The tactic of simultaneously drawing on and subverting official codes and discourses is, of course, very much a feature of carnival, and Veloso made extensive use of the style of carnival to demonstrate sexuality and gender as shifting and contestable terrains of personal and social power. What he sought, however, was a continuous carnivalisation, not a temporary transgressive inversion. Veloso and the Tropicalists enacted multifarious voices, positions and identities by changing their appearance frequently during shows. The body became a kind of visual polyphony of the codes and conventions of Brazilian society subjected to individual whim and choice. In his representations of gender through style Veloso was not concerned to set out the "right" concepts of sexual politics against the "wrong". Rather, he sought to highlight the elusive nature of sexuality against the grain of absolutism, by suggesting a kind of open-ended eroticism, whose meanings disappear just as they begin to emerge.

Veloso's Tropicalist style could not have had the impact that it did, despite its shock value, were it not for the deliberate and careful cultivation of the mass media. The movement stated its intention to explore the ambivalence of consumerism in producer/arranger Rogério Duprat's wry comments to his fellow Tropicalists on the sleeve notes of the collaborative album: "How are you going to cope with the revelation that records are made to be sold …? Are you aware of the risks you are running? Do you know that you can make a lot of money with this? Do you have the courage to make a lot of money?"[63] The movement examined the risk of control by large commercial enterprises versus the opportunity to reach greater numbers of people. The refusal to distinguish between aesthetics and the market formed part of the movement's de-sacralising project with regard to protest song. It made use of the issue of consumerism to confront the polarisations with which popular music was being defined, between politically committed and alienated, national and international, popular and commercial.[64] "Conquistar a massa" (conquering the masses) formed an important part of the aim of the movement from the very beginning and necessitated a style which, as previously mentioned, performed the crucial function of visualising Tropicalist ideas for its public, especially considering the meteoric passage planned for the movement through the Brazilian socio-cultural scene. The mass media – television, in particular – was intended as a means by which the movement could communicate its ideas rapidly to a wider public.

Veloso consciously sought to construct an image that would also work within the new kind of intimacy afforded by television and a home audience. As Silviano Santiago has pointed out:

> He had realised that musical talent wasn't everything, that it wasn't enough, because now he was confronted with more than just the public before him at live performances. There was now another audience to deal with, a much larger and more demanding one, seated in their armchairs at home, who filled the commercial breaks with running commentary and family jokes.[65]

When I interviewed him, Veloso remarked on the creation of his image as a response to television:

> I wanted to emphasise the fact that we were involved in the mass media. And I wanted to make explicit the idea of an image specially designed for television. So it was both a kind of re-affirmation of what I was doing, it was mass media entertainment and a critique of the mass media and its attitudes. So we were parodying those images at the same time that we created them – I mean, we had no illusions that simply by singing a few songs we could influence the political position of the listener, or make the best aesthetic choices to save the purity of Brazilian national identity. At the end of the day, that just seemed ingenuous to us. First of all we wanted to say that we were there as television personalities singing for millions of people and that in this world of mass entertainment interesting things were happening, including experimentation with form and political daring.[66]

Veloso went on to give examples of such experimentation as his choice of costume for the performance of "É Proibido Proibir" and his continuous change of image, which he then linked to his intention to always make explicit his place within a televisual culture:

> And this daring was evident for example, when I sang "É Proibido Proibir" with green and black plastic clothes, with beads around my neck and necklaces of electric wires and plugs and my hair the way it was, and Os Mutantes with science fiction-style clothes. And at another time I wore African garments, or suddenly I appeared in a suit, or Bahian robes over jeans ... Throughout my career, my appearance has taken the most varied forms, because from the beginning we wanted to make clear our awareness of ourselves as stage and screen personalities ...[67]

He also sought to encourage a response to the "presence" of the performing body on the screen and in the living room, a presence often reinforced by spectacular behaviour, gestures, antics, theatre, or simply by the natural plasticity of his lean body and long hair. His body itself as a creation, a work of art and as artifice became the focus of public contemplation in which everyone could participate by turning on the TV and consuming him. One effect of this consumption was the copying of his style, facilitated by the increasing reach of the mass media, which offered something vital of the star himself. Santiago notes that on Veloso's return to Brazil after the period of exile in London:

> The superstar plays the role ... of model: the dungarees that Caetano was wearing when he arrived in Galeão airport suddenly proliferates throughout the city, as if by magic. Young people, consuming the superstar, in a carnivalesque and anthropophagic fashion, end up imbibing, in the ritual and the feast, his charm and the intoxicating life he represents.[68]

Veloso's guest appearances on television included participation in the Discoteca do Chacrinha (Chacrinha's Disco), the zany game show of Brazil's king of kitsch.

Chacrinha was a Tropicalist *avant la lettre* whose relationship with his public was based on aggression and mockery, such as his trademark throwing of bananas, pineapples and salted cod into the audience. The programme celebrated a sensibility based on the unrefined and the irreverent, which the Tropicalists saw as a raw expression of aspects of Brazilian identity. Veloso's antics on the programme, however, irritated sections of the public and the media and he was accused by the journalist Nelson Motta, a Tropicalist sympathiser, of confusing the public: "adopting contradictory and dangerous attitudes, a world away from the serious and deeply thought-provoking idea of Tropicália. A bit of seriousness would not do him any harm."[69] It was, in fact, the high seriousness of dominant culture with which Veloso's self-caricature wished to engage. Following in the footsteps of the Modernists, the Tropicalists advocated a different approach to the attempt to approximate high and low cultures. Where protest song maintained a reverential attitude to popular culture, Tropicália adopted an ironic, iconoclastic and demystifying stance and accompanying sense of style.

Television became the main channel for expression of the Tropicalist aesthetic after the closure of the Sucata nightclub show. The programme *Divino, Maravilhoso* (Just Divine) on TV Tupi was conceptualised by Veloso as a weekly "happening", with very little planned in advance of the live transmission. TV Tupi's director, Fernando Faro, understood the value and importance of the Tropicalists' experimental modes of communication: "I believe in the programme Divino Maravilhoso, because if the Tropicalist performers are discussed, that is a sign of their popularity. If they are attacked, it's because they communicate more forcefully. If they irritate, cause confusion, it's because they communicate outside of the accepted codes."[70] His comments pointed to a new Tropicalist definition of popularity, associating it with discussion and controversy. The visual impact and directness of television were exploited to the full and the programme's imagery was crucial to the performance of the songs. Setting and costuming played important roles in the theatricality of the performances, which were based on freedom and improvisation. Attired in a style quite unprecedented for Brazilian television, Veloso wore a military jacket, but the authority of this garment traditionally associated with a highly disciplined and combative male body was undermined by Veloso's androgynous figure. This effect was intensified by the allusion to the "barbaric" and "primitive" contained in the animal tooth necklace he wore as an accessory, the sandals associated with a hippy lifestyle, and jeans, the symbol of universal youth and leisure (see Figures 5 and 6). He would no more allow the style of his body to be controlled than that of his music: "Este é o som livre! É mutante, não pode parar!" (This is free sound! It's mutant, unstoppable!), he affirmed during the first programme. The vocal and bodily gestures used in the Sucata show were re-employed and combined with scenifications devised specially for television, such as that created around a large cage that Veloso had requested to be built on stage, from behind which the performers conducted a banquet of the marginalised – beggars and hippies. At the programme's end Veloso broke out of the cage singing Roberto Carlos' *iê-iê-iê* hit, "Um leão está solto nas ruas" (A Lion's Roaming the Streets).

Given the new intimacy of television, Veloso had guessed rightly that the shock of the Tropicalist style would hit home even more strongly than it had done at the music festivals, or in nightclubs. Television reached a wider audience and crucially, entered the home, provoking immediate criticisms from the guardians of morality. After the very first show the station began to receive letters of complaint, protesting at the programme's corrupting influence on the young. Given the emphasis on anarchy and individual freedom of the programme, it is surprising that the censors allowed it to be aired at all. The last straw came when Veloso enacted a scene whose discourse relied on ideas of divergent sexuality and violent death, couched in the traditional family celebration of Christmas. In the pre-Christmas Eve show Veloso included in the repertoire "Anoiteceu" (Night Fell), by Assis Valente, a samba composer at his peak during the 1930s and 1940s, who had been persecuted because of his homosexuality and was thought to have committed suicide as a result. In his most open and blunt denunciation yet of attempts to control and police sexuality, Veloso performed the song with a gun pointed to his head. On the following day, he and Gilberto Gil were arrested in São Paulo and transported to a military prison in Rio.

The "arte participante" or committed art of Tropicália's left-wing contemporaries had set the scene for a critical examination and denunciation of the inequities of Brazilian society. They had been less successful, however, in capturing the ambiguities and complexities of that society. Tropicália ambitiously sought to reflect aspects of Brazil in all its contradictions and paradoxes. Recognising the limitations imposed by political and social conditions, Tropicália sought to destabilise and critique existing ideas and attitudes with regard to the national and the popular in Brazilian music and society. The Tropicalists recognised that a carefully elaborated style would be one of the key means by which they would create an impact, draw attention to their ideas and encourage a reaction to the movement. Veloso's elaboration of style during the brief and intense heyday of Tropicália constituted a radical cultural response to the social realities of Brazil at the time. Using his body as a site of dialogue and conflict between the individual and his society, Veloso defined and re-defined a self asserting the right to be all things, held in a tense and fragile balance that offered shifting positions from which to view his world.

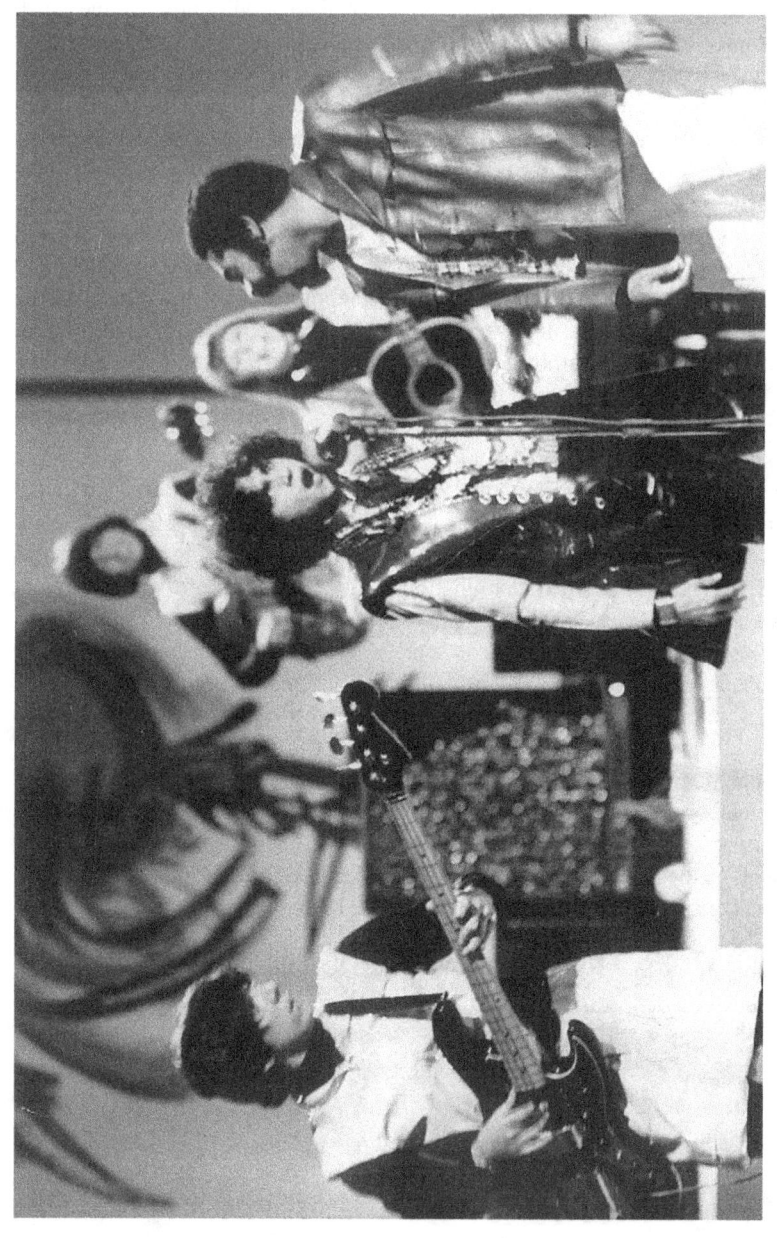

Figure 1   Facing the music – Caetano Veloso, Gilberto Gil and Os Mutantes confront the hostile crowd at the September 1968 International Song Festival. (Agência Estado)

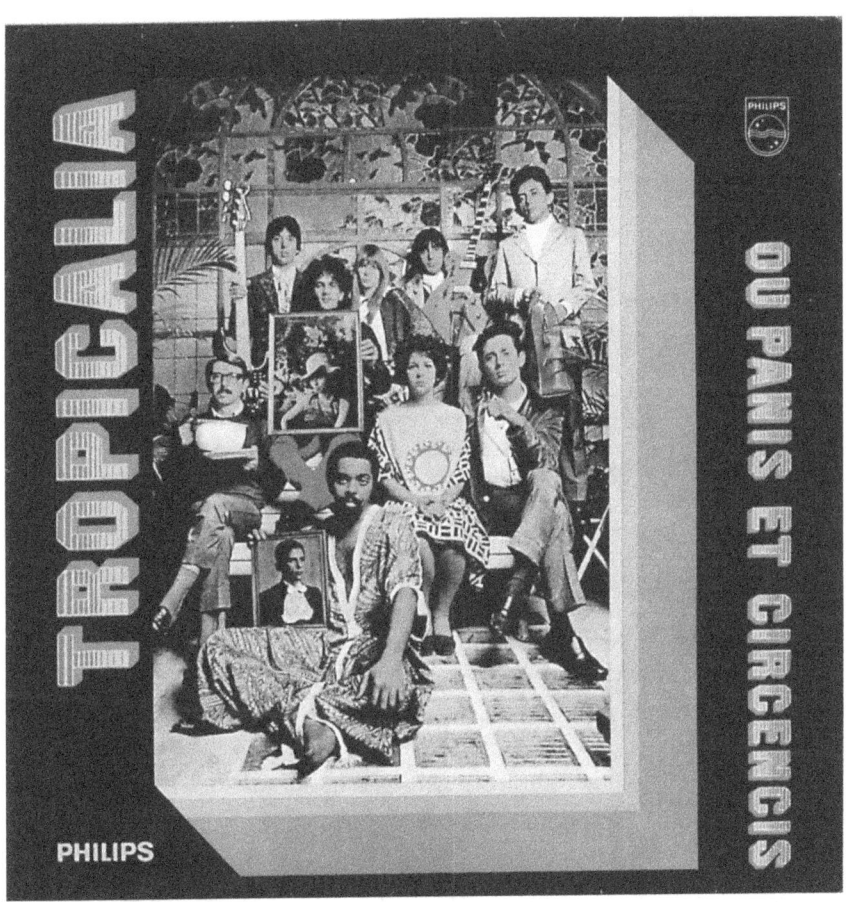

Figure 2 Cover of the 1968 *Tropicália* album. (Universal Records)

Figure 3   Publicity shot for *Manchete* magazine, 1968. (Manchete Press)

Figure 4 Cover of the 1968 album *Caetano Veloso*. (Universal Records)

Figure 5 Caetano Veloso, Gilberto Gil and other Tropicalists perform during the *Divino, Maravilhoso* television programme. (Paulo Salomão/Abril Imagens)

Figure 6 Veloso indulges in typically provocative antics on *Divino, Maravilhoso*. (Paulo Salomão/Abril Imagens)

Notes

1. (A esquerda me vaiava, me jogava banana. Até o dia em que fui preso pelo Exército e depois, expulso do país. Mas nem o exército me confundiu com a esquerda. Minha expulsão ... estava ligada a *razões estéticas e a uma possível violação de certos costumes e tradições do povo brasileiro*.) Cited in Fonseca, *Esse Cara*, 51, emphasis mine.
2. (Ih, essa coisa de música metido a político, de barbicha, cabeludo ... A única música que perco tempo em ouvir é a clássica ou um belo samba-canção.) Cited in Fonseca, *Esse Cara*, 143.
3. See Calado, *Tropicália*, 115.
4. (... rasparam a nossa cabeça, não tinham prova de nada, mas não tinham coragem de soltar, porque não conseguem decidir ... Solta, deixa voltar para a televisão com a cabeça raspada?) Cited in Pereira and Buarque de Hollanda, *Patrulhas ideológicas*, 112.
5. Melly, *Revolt Into Style*, 7.
6. Hall and Jefferson (eds), *Resistance Through Rituals*, first published as *Working Papers in Cultural Studies* no. 7/8, 1975.
7. Hebdige, *Subculture*, original publication (London: Methuen: 1979); edition consulted (London: Routledge:1997), 119.
8. See McRobbie, "Settling Accounts With Subcultures", 66–80.
9. McRobbie, "Settling Accounts With Subcultures", 78; Clarke, "Defending Ski-Jumpers", 84.
10. Treece, "Guns and Roses", 4. For a detailed analysis of the cultural politics of the festivals and the role played by television see Stroud, "'Música é para o povo cantar'", 87–117.
11. (Os estudantes usaram camisa cáqui de manga comprida, calça Lee desbotada [do bolso de trás para atirar bolas de gude que desequilibram os cavalos dos PMs] e tênis grosseiros, especiais para batalhas de rua.) "Rock In Brasil: o balanço das gerações", leaflet published by the Projecto Cultural das Empresas do Grupo BASF no Brasil.
12. (Se pensássemos sempre assim, estaríamos tocando nossas músicas com instrumentos indígenas. É preciso pensarmos em termos universais. O mundo hoje é muito pequeno, não há razão para regionalismos.) Calado, *Tropicália*, 131.
13. While Veloso sought to position himself outside of the traditional left, Marcelo Ridenti makes a convincing case for Tropicália's "poetic identification" with the extreme left, dedicated to armed guerrilla warfare against the military dictatorship. See *Em Busca do Povo Brasileiro*, 278–80.
14. (Vocês venceram. Isto é Brasil. Isto é país subdesenvolvido! Vocês são uns animais!) Extract from Campos, "Festival de viola e violência", *Correio da Manhã*, 26/10/67, in sleeve notes, *Sérgio Ricardo (História da Música Popular Brasileira)*. Abril Cultural, no. 37, 8; Video footage: "Festivais MPB – Anos 60, TV Record", Arquivo Projeto Alta Fidelidade, Universidade de Paraná, Curitiba.
15. Por isso tudo, um público apaixonado, em pequena parte de conhecedores de música popular e, na maioria, de torcedores hipno-TV-tizados, acompanhou, telespectante, a classificação das 12 dentre das 36 músicas que foram apresentadas. Com uma ferocidade que até aqui só ocorria nas competições de futebol e da política. Fora do teatro, as reportagens diárias dos jornais, as fofocas do rádio, os palpites e os 'bolos'. Dentro um público de torcedores – plebescito vivo – julgando as músicas, os intérpretes e o júri, através do 'sim' e 'não' do

aplauso ou do apupo. A vaia constituiu um capítulo à parte e quase transformou o festival – como se disse pelos jornais – em 'festivaia'.

Campos, *Balanço da bossa e outras bossas*, 128.
16. Treece, "Guns and Roses", 27.
17. Antônio Carlos Jobim e Chico Buarque de Hollanda merecem o nosso respeito, a nossa função é fazer canções, o função de julgar nesse instante e do júri que ele está ... Por favor, por favor, tem mais uma coisa só, pra vocês, pra vocês que continuam pensando que me apoiam vaiando ... Gente! Gente! Por favor, olha, tem uma coisa só, a vida não se resume em festivais!

Transcribed from live recording at the Maracanãzinho stadium in Rio de Janeiro, in *Geraldo Vandré: Prá não dizer que não falei das flores*. Som Maior. 303.2001–B. 1979.

18. Eu tomo uma Coca-Cola/ Ela pensa em casamento/ Uma canção me consola/ Eu vou/ Por entre fotos e nomes/ Sem livros e sem fuzil/ Sem fome sem telefone/ No coração do Brasil/ Ela nem sabe até pensei/ Em cantar na televisão/ ... Sem lenço sem documento/ Nada no bolso ou nas mãos/ Eu quero seguir vivendo amor/ Eu vou/ Por que não? Por que não?

I have a Coca-Cola/ She thinks about her wedding day/ A pop song consoles me/ I go/ Among photos and names/ With no books and no guns/ No hunger no phone/ In the heart of Brazil/ She has absolutely no idea/ I've dreamt about a TV singing career/ ... Nothing to identify me/ Nothing in my pockets or my hands/ I just want to go on living my love/ I go/ And why not? Why not?

19. Mas o que mais influiu no sucesso de Caetano foi a sua figura: magro, despenteado, e displicente, o que lhe valeu o apelido de "Marcha de Fome", o baiano começou a ganhar a simpatia das menininhas, que viam nêle uma 'coisinha desprotegida'. Foi o bastante para que o 'desprotegido' Caetano descobrisse ali a 'fonte do seu sucesso'. E resolveu aderir completamente à pilantragem. Começou inventando um tal de som universal, que na realidade nem êle mesmo sabe o que seja.

Eli Halfoun, *Ultima Hora*, 2/12/67.
20. (Comercializou todas as atitudes e os gestos, o cabelo despenteado, a displicência e a figura do 'rapaz tímido e desprotegido' ...) Halfoun, *Ultima Hora*, 2/12/67.
21. "Casamento de Caetano deu em versos de cordel", anon., *Ultima Hora*, 23/01/68.
22. See Calado, *Tropicália*, 152–7.
23. (Carmen Miranda foi, primeiro, motivo de orgulho e vergonha, e depois, símbolo da violência intelectual com que queríamos encarar nossa realidade, do olhar implacável que queríamos lançar sobre nós mesmos.) Fonseca, *Esse Cara*, 36. Veloso writes about the significance of Carmen Miranda to Brazilian cultural history in "Carmen Mirandadada", Perrone and Dunn (eds), *Brazilian Popular Music and Globalization*, 39–45.
24. The Estado Novo (New State) was declared by the populist president Getúlio Vargas in 1937. It conferred dictatorial powers on Vargas, whose regime concerned itself with the consolidation of Brazilian identity through the officialisation of cultural expression.
25. Matos, *Acertei no Millhar*, 70.

26. Durst, *Madame Satã*, 50.
27. Durst, *Madame Satã*, 16–18.
28. Dyer, "In Defence of Disco", 413.
29. (O público já está mais esclarecido, mais educado musicalmente. E o seu desabafo está bem definido em outras coisas.) Calado, *Tropicália*, 218.
30. (Caetano entrou rebolando. Inventou uma dança agressivamente erótica, com movimentos pélvicos para frente e para trás, que lembravam uma relação sexual. A resposta dos desafetos também veio quase em forma de coreografia: num movimento coordenado, grande parte da platéia virou as costas para o palco, sem parar de vaiar e gritar.) Calado, *Tropicália*, 221.
31. Veloso was planning to read a poem by Pessoa during the performance of the song.
32. Music critic and member of the jury.
33. Ventura, *1968, O Ano que não terminou*, 201–4.

> (Mas é isso a juventude que diz que quer tomar o poder? Vocês têm coragem de aplaudir este ano, uma música, um tipo de música, que vocês não teriam coragem de aplaudir no ano passado, são a mesma juventude que vai sempre, sempre matar amanhã o velhote inimigo que morreu ontem! Vocês não estão entendendo nada, nada, nada, absolutamente nada! Hoje não tem Fernando Pessoa! Eu hoje vim dizer aqui que quem teve coragem de assumir a estrutura de festival, não com o medo que o Sr. Chico de Assis pediu, mas com a coragem, quem teve essa coragem de assumir esta estrutura e fazê-la explodir foi Gilberto Gil e fui eu, não foi ninguém. Foi Gilberto Gil e fui eu! Vocês estão por fora! Vocês não dão pra entender! Mas que juventude é essa, que juventude é essa?
>
> Vocês jamais conterão ninguém! Vocês são iguais sabe a quem? São iguais sabe a quem? ... Àqueles que foram a *Roda Viva* e espancaram os atores. Vocês não diferem em nada deles, vocês não diferem em nada! ... O problema é o seguinte: vocês estão querendo policiar a música brasileira! O Maranhão apresentou esse ano uma música, com arranjo de charleston, sabem o que foi? Foi a "Gabriela" do ano passado que ele não teve coragem de, no ano passado, apresentar, por ser americana. Mas eu e o Gil já abrimos o caminho, o que é que vocês querem? Eu vim aqui pra acabar com isso! Eu quero dizer ao júri: me desclassifique! Eu não tenho nada a ver com isso! Nada a ver com isso!
>
> ... Gilberto Gil está comigo pra nós acabarmos com o festival e com toda a imbecilidade que reina no Brasil! Acabar com isso tudo de uma vez! Nós só entramos em festival pra isso! ... Não fingimos, não fingimos, aqui, que desconhecemos os que seja festival não! ... Nós, eu e ele, tivemos coragem de entrar em todas as estruturas e sair de todas, e vocês?
>
> E vocês? Se vocês em política forem como são em estética estamos feitos! ... Deus está solto!!

34. Treece, "Tropicália: A Canção Popular e a Cultura de Massas", 55.
35. Stroud, "'Música é para o povo cantar'", 89–90.
36. Vasconcellos, *Música Popular*, v.
37. The term is used by Hebdige, citing Umberto Eco, in *Subculture*, 105.
38. (... linguagem fragmentada das passeatas com seus comícios-relâmpago, sua retórica e seu ritmo de centralização/descentralização.) Buarque de Hollanda and Gonçalves, *Cultura e participação nos anos 60*, 67.
39. (O sentido da eficácia do teatro hoje é o sentido da guerrilha teatral.) Buarque de Hollanda and Gonçalves, *Cultura e participação nos anos 60*, 63.
40. Treece, "Tropicália: A Canção Popular e a Cultura de Massas", 54.

41. Hebdige, *Subculture*, 119 and 117.
42. Hebdige, *Subculture*, 127.
43. Middleton, *Studying Popular Music*, 165–6.
44. O corpo está para a voz, assim como a roupa está para a letra e a dança para a música. Deixar que os seis elementos desta equação não trabalhem em harmonia ..., mas que se contradigam em toda sua extensão, de tal modo que se cria um estranho clima lúdico, permutacional, como se o cantor no palco fosse um quebra-cabeça que só pudesse ser organizado na cabeça dos espectadores ... Quis que seu corpo, qual peça de escultura, no cotidiano e no palco, asumisse a contradição ... Quis que seu corpo, pelo seu aspecto plástico, cativasse o público e que fosse ele a imagem viva de sua mensagem artística.

    Santiago, *Uma Literatura nos Trópicos*, 151 and 150.
45. "Luar do Sertão" (Backlands Moonlight), title of a 1914 *toada* by Catulo da Paixão Cearense & João Pernambuco, and one of the most well-known songs in Brazilian music history.
46. "Mata" means forest or jungle. It is also a very fertile area of the North-east of Brazil between the coast and the drought-ridden hinterland, where sugar cane was traditionally grown.
47. A reference to bossa nova's dissonant chords.
48. Iracema is the title and main character of José de Alencar's 1865 novel, which portrays the founding of the Brazilian nation as the result of a coupling between a Portuguese colonist and an indigenous Indian princess. Their mixed-race offspring is presented in the novel as the bedrock of the Brazilian people.
49. Well-to-do beachfront district of the South Zone of Rio de Janeiro.
50. "O Fino da Bossa" ("The Best of Bossa") was a 1960s television programme showcasing the stars of bossa nova and MPB.
51. This is the title and refrain of a 1965 hit song by Brazil's erstwhile king of rock and now most popular crooner, Roberto Carlos.
52. Title of a 1966 hit song by Chico Buarque.
53. In 1998 a collection of artwork inspired by Veloso's songs was exhibited at the Paço Imperial in Rio, entitled "A Imagem do Som de Caetano Veloso". The exhibition included an installation by Jair de Souza inspired by "Superbacana", which consisted of a billowing cape in the green and yellow of the Brazilian flag, with a pair of two-toned shoes placed next to it, suggesting the *malandro* as the quintessential Brazilian superhero. *A Imagem do Som de Caetano Veloso*, 118–19.
54. (... para os homens, ternos de linho branco, com golas bem largas e gravatas de rayon vermelho; as mulheres devem copiar antigos figurinos de Luiza Barreto Leite ou Iracema de Alencar.) From "Texto de *Os Últimas Dias de Paupéria*", reproduced in *O Estado de São Paulo, Cultura*, 7/08/93.
55. Flashes luminosos: o camisolão estampado de Gil, o cetim coloridísimo de Nara Leão, o cabelo de Gal eriçado feito o de Angela Davis. E aquela lourinha de franja, o nome é mesmo Lee, como a calça? Príncipe Caetano com seu perfil de águia, tão pequenino, tão forte, inaugurando o monumento no alto da rua Rêgo Freitas, em certa noite de agosto. Intimidados, deslumbrados, tentávamos compreender.

    Abreu, "Comprei calças de cetim verde-amazônia", *O Estado de São Paulo, Cultura*, 7/08/93.
56. (... levávamos uma palavra nova nas cabeças. Tropicalismo, esse era o nome. Na mesma semana, comprei umas calças de cetim verde-amazônico, uns colares de umbanda na Praça da Sé. Deixei crescer o cabelo, fumei o primeiro baseado. E

comecei a procurar pelo Brasil.) Abreu, "Comprei calças de cetim verde-amazônia", *O Estado de São Paulo, Cultura*, 7/08/93.
57. (Queríamos realizar uma missa profana, que começava exaltando a Tropicália e, no fim, destruiríamos todo o cenário, da mesma forma que ocorria no último dia dos carnavais antigos.) Cited in Wady Cury, "Morte da Tropicália seria exibida na Globo", *O Estado de São Paulo, Cultura*, 07/08/93.
58. Turner, "Recent Developments in the Theory of the Body", 8.
59. Foucault, *The History of Sexuality*, 139.
60. (Me sinto bem com essa roupa tão ambigua; é uma maneira de usar um estilo que tem a linguagem ao mesmo tempo comprometida e ao mesmo tempo livre. *É uma posição de ver o tempo.*) *O Globo*, 21/07/84, cited in Fonseca, *Esse Cara*, 29. Emphasis mine.
61. Frank, "For a Sociology of the Body", 47.
62. Interview with the author, see Appendix.
63. (Como receberão a notícia de que um disco é feito para vender … Sabem vocês o risco que correm? Sabem que podem ganhar muito dinheiro com isso? Terão coragem de ganhar muito dinheiro?) *Tropicália Ou Panis et Circensis*. Philips, 6436.303, 1968.
64. Celso Favaretto, "A Canção Tropicalista", conference paper, BRASA III, King's College, Cambridge, 7–10 Sep., 1996, 2.
65. (Tinha se dado conta de que o talento musical não é tudo, não é suficiente, pois agora não só tinha um público ativo diante dele, na platéia, como também um outro, bem mais vasto e exigente, sentado nas poltronas das salas de estar e que preenchia os minutos de silêncio dos commerciais com comentários e piadas caseiras.) Santiago, *Uma Literatura nos Trópicos*, 149.
66. Interview with the author, see Appendix.
67. Interview with the author, see Appendix.
68. (O superastro funciona … como modelo: a jardineira que Caetano vestia ao chegar ao Galeão de repente se prolifera pelos quatro cantos da cidade, como que reproduzida por mãos de fada. Os jovens, consumindo o superastro, carnavalesca e antropofagicamente, passam a receber, no ritual e na festa, seus fluidos de encanto e de inebriante vida.) Santiago, *Uma Literatura nos Trópicos*, 154.
69. (… tomando atitudes contraditórias e perigosas, longe da idéia séria e profundamente inquietante da sua *Tropicália*. Um pouco de seriedade não faz mal a ninguém.) Cited in Calado, *Tropicália*, 235.
70. (Acredito no *Divino, Maravilhoso*, porque se os artistas tropicalistas foram discutidos, isto é um sinal de popularidade. Se foram agredidos, é porque se comunicaram com mais força. Se eles irritam, causam perplexidade, é porque essa comunicação foi feita fora dos códigos.) Calado, *Tropicália*, 192.

Chapter 3

"You Don't Know Me At All" – Challenging Vocal Traditions

You don't know me,
Bet you'll never get to know me,
You don't know me at all,
Feel so lonely ...

The song "You Don't Know Me" appears on the 1972 album *Transa* (Tryst) and the refrain quoted above can be taken as a clue to the relationship between Veloso and his listening public around this time. During the initial period of his career up to the *Araçá Azul* (Blue Araçá) album in 1972, Veloso's relationship with his listeners is by no means a straightforward one. He established himself as a demanding performer who delighted in testing, provoking and surprising his public. Yet by the time he had left for exile in London in 1969, Caetano Veloso was already a superstar in Brazil. This chapter will examine the role of Veloso's capricious voice in the construction of this contradictory singer/listener relationship. Although Veloso's work can furnish any number of songs whose vocalisations are worthy of comment, the analysis of the recorded voice in this chapter will focus on the period between 1968 and 1972. This is because during no other period of his career does he elaborate and sustain so concerted a project to probe the expressive potential of the voice. This period represents a significant moment in his career, in which he explores the dimensions and possibilities of communicating with the voice. It is also the period of most intense repression by the military dictatorship that took control of the country in 1964.

The importance of vocal style has been and continues to be explicitly addressed in British and American popular musicology since the publication in 1968 of a study by the ethnomusicologist Alan Lomax.[1] However, the centrality of vocal activity in creating meaning, in uniting form and content, has only recently begun to be fully acknowledged and systematically analysed in Brazilian popular music scholarship. The publication of Luis Tatit's *O Cancionista: Composição de canções no Brasil* (The Songwriter: Song Composition in Brazil), which examines the "dictions", or individual vocal styles of some of Brazil's most important performers, represents the most significant contribution yet to this area of study of popular song in Brazil. Likening the performer to a juggler, Tatit focuses on the relationship and interplay between words and melody in popular song. The singer's greatest resource in maintaining this juggling act is what Tatit calls the "intonational process" which extends speech into song. This process relies on the role played by the language of gesture in the junction of melodic sequences with linguistic elements. Tatit's approach focuses on the internal structure of the song, over an emphasis on its social context. While he may not engage overtly with social and political issues, the elements of song structure which Tatit demonstrates as feeding into the processes of song creation point to issues outside of the art form. In its examination of Veloso's early vocalisations this chapter seeks to combine a detailed analysis of elements of song structure and their role in the communicative process with a demonstration of how such elements, which are internal to a song, may comment on the social, political and cultural conditions which prevailed at the moment of its creation.

Even during initial, impressionistic listenings to Veloso's early material, I was immediately struck by the remarkable degree of its vocal diversity. These impressions crystallised on repeated listenings, to the point where it became clear that consciously or not, these vocalisations were expressing an intense need to create and provoke, if necessary, opportunities for dialogue with the public.[2] This chapter, therefore, sets out to explore the conditions out of which this need for dialogue arose and how the voice sought to create and maintain it. My decision to examine this particular period of Veloso's career from the point of view of the voice was the result of another consideration. This period, which is generally referred to as his Tropicalist period, has already been the subject of commentary in academic and journalistic works which have focused on various aspects of the movement, but not on the crucial role played by the voice at this time.[3] In this chapter, therefore, my concern is to add another perspective to the study of the Tropicalist period. I have used an examination of the voice as a window for observing the internal processes of communication at work in a song. I have then made links between these "inner workings" and the socio-political context that informs conscious performance choices, as well as the unconscious gestures of performance.

Tatit makes an interesting point in referring to Veloso's fascination with the singers of Brazilian radio's Golden Age in the 1940s and 50s, whose voices had so profoundly marked the sensibilities and affective memory of their listeners. He sees the early part of Veloso's career as concerned with finding an idiom for a contemporary *canção de rádio* (song for radio), the type of song that would exercise a hold on the listener's imagination as the songs of the 1940s and 50s had done. This concern to develop a new *canção de rádio* explains Veloso's attraction to the wide range of dictions evident in Brazilian popular music, not only those of the Golden Age performers like Orlando Silva, Vicente Celestino and Carmen Miranda, but also of contemporary performers such as Roberto Carlos and Jorge Ben. What these performers have in common is that they were all unabashedly commercial and extremely popular with the public, as well as being figures who had either been forgotten or were dismissed by protest song.[4] The attempt to reinvent a *canção de rádio*, therefore, reflected a desire to create a song form which offered an alternative to the explicit politics of protest song and which focused on the question of the listening experience and listening pleasure. In an important commentary on approaches to analysing popular music, Susan McClary and Robert Walser warn against ignoring emotional and physical responses to music when considering music's political power. They go on to discuss one of the pitfalls of popular music analysis from the perspective of the left:

> Part of the problem is one that chronically plagues the Left: a desire to find explicit political agendas ... in the art it wants to claim and a distrust of those dimensions of art that appeal to the senses, to physical pleasure. Yet pleasure frequently *is* the politics of music – pleasure as interference, the pleasure of marginalised people that has evaded channelisation. Rock is a discourse that has frequently been at its most effective politically when its producers and consumers are least aware of any political or intellectual dimensions ...[5]

As discussed in Chapter 2, in spite of its self-avowedly apolitical stance, the Tropicalist movement was characterised by the subversive potential of its alternative presentations of sexuality and Brazilian identity, conveyed in a performance and musical discourse that appealed emotionally and sensorially to listeners. This was apparent not only in the visual aspect of communication, but was also evident in Veloso's experimentation with another aspect of the communicative relationship during this period, based on the sound of the voice. Tatit says of the search for a new *canção de rádio* and Veloso's impulse to experiment at this time:

> This search was being undertaken throughout at least a six year period, some of this time greatly influenced by the conditions of exile. And from time to time the signs appeared, which are still clearly distinguishable, of two projects: the experimental vein left over from *Tropicália* and the new *canção de radio* that was increasingly taking shape.[6]

One of the key factors responsible for the so-called Golden Age of popular music between 1929 and 1945 was the arrival of radio in Brazil. The singer Mário Reis was a key figure of the Golden Age, who broke definitively with the *bel canto* style which had dominated until then, creating a more natural and colloquial singing style which made full use of the advantages offered by electromagnetic recording. According to Severiano and Homem de Mello, such was the importance of this new style that the history of popular song in Brazil can be divided into before and after Mário Reis. They see the second phase of the Golden Age (in particular between 1937 and 1942), as being dedicated to the cult of the voice, inspired perhaps by the extraordinary vocal abilities of radio's first idol, Orlando Silva.[7] Silva was greatly admired for his slow, quiet delivery, perfect tuning and the varied timbres and textures of his voice. Silva was the model to which many among the generation of young crooners and singing groups who would follow him in the 1940s aspired. These included Dick Farney and Lúcio Alves, crooners who inspired intense and unswerving loyalty from members of their respective fan clubs for their ability to create unprecedented climates of intimacy in their recorded performances. This period of popular music history was not only characterised by this new intimacy between the crooner and the public listening at home, but also by the remarkable degree of physical proximity between fans and performers and the social interaction enjoyed by fans with their idols. This was due to the public access to studio programmes and performances given by radio stations in Rio de Janeiro and the activities of the various, fanatical fan clubs. José Ramos Tinhorão has made an important and detailed examination of the radio station studio as a social space between the 1930s and 1950s. Tinhorão describes the studio programmes that emerged from the 1940s, live spectacles at which members of the public were welcome and which became a significant aspect of urban leisure for the popular sectors of society in Rio de Janeiro.[8] These programmes allowed for more intimate contact with the radio stars and led to a new kind of relationship between the artist and the public. Tinhorão also examines the extraordinarily active role of the members of the fan clubs in promoting their idols and points out that the beginning of the 1950s represents not only the peak of the studio programmes, but also of the promotional activity and influence of the fan clubs.[9]

One admirer of both Orlando Silva and Lúcio Alves was the then crooner João Gilberto, who would later reinvent the concept of intimacy with his radical and distinctive bossa nova style. As a reaction to bossa nova and to the current socio-political conditions, protest song would embrace collective consciousness-raising instead of seeking to create climates of intimacy in performance. Veloso sought to return to a more personal approach to communication in popular song by elaborating a new cult of the voice, which would not necessarily preclude social protest. Instead, he would manipulate intimacy to challenge prevailing attitudes to the relationship between performer and public. A rethinking of this relationship to focus on individual response reflected Veloso's and the Tropicalists' aim to present multiple voices and responses to contemporary realities.

Caetano Veloso's Voice: 1967–72

Because this chapter examines how vocalisations in recorded performance contribute to the total discourse of the songs, the lyrics and music of the songs will therefore be discussed as they relate to, or in the context of, vocal activity. During the period between 1967 and 1972 each of the albums produced contains its own vocal diversity and evolution. However, a clearly discernible movement is noticeable over the seven albums, starting with the relatively uncomplicated articulation of *Domingo* (Sunday) in 1967, to the more challenging vocal style of the Tropicália period, the intimacy and directness of the London albums, and the avant-garde experimentation of *Araçá Azul* in 1972.

In the sleeve notes to *Domingo* Veloso hints at the new and radical directions that his music would soon take: "My inspiration no longer wants to feed off nostalgia for old times and places, on the contrary, it wants to incorporate that nostalgia into a project for the future."[10] However, this first album is still suffused with bossa nova's predominant sentiment of longing and love, its thematic concerns of relationships and natural beauty, and its musical characteristics and intimate delivery. The songs lack the playful inventiveness and experimental vocalisations that had made early bossa nova so aesthetically revolutionary, and the uniformity of their style makes for a very untextured and subdued sound.

Overall, the vocal rhythmic scheme is simple and regular and the voices of Veloso and Gal Costa are mainly organised into independent parts. Unusually however, the two voices do not layer the sound, but are so similar as to be almost interchangeable. The seamlessness of the male and female voices is rather disconcerting for the listener, because it makes the process of identification of and with the individual voices difficult. If we cannot identify with the voice as either male or female, we experience a kind of disjunction of the voice from the (imagined) body, and the effect of the songs as a moment physically lived by the singer is somehow diminished. In *Domingo*, the lack of embellishment, the lack of variation in tone colour, volume and tempo, the minimal accentuation of notes and the evenness of the phrasing, mean that the presence of the singers in the song is not convincing. The romantic discourse also becomes confused: instead of the dialogue we might expect between the male and female voices, we get a homologous monologue, in which both voices are enunciating without differentiation or apparent ironic intent, the male courtship dialogue as scripted in songs such as "Avarandado" (Verandah-ed Dawn) and "Minha Senhora" (My Lady). *Domingo* underlines a moment in Brazilian popular music when bossa nova had all but been exhausted and making music offered a rather narrow choice between *iê-iê-iê* and variants of bossa nova, either the socially conscious protest song strain, or bossa jazz. Veloso's comments on the album sleeve indicate a realisation that it was time to develop a "future project" which would undermine the polarisation of musical styles in Brazil.

In his next album *Caetano Veloso* he follows through on this intention. In proposing his own radical aesthetic, the album's sleeve notes also acknowledge a huge debt to João Gilberto and the revolutionary aesthetic spirit that he brought to Brazilian popular music. Veloso draws on a number of musical forms including bossa nova, *iê-iê-iê*, *samba-canção*, *bolero*, *beguin* and *baião*, with nods to The Beatles and even Debussy and Stravinsky. In the sleeve notes he asserts his right to experiment with these fusions: "because I don't want to, in fact, I don't have to explain anything to anyone."[11] The song which opens this album would give its name to the Tropicália movement which followed, and sets the movement's agenda of multiplicity, contradiction and difference, both in terms of lyrical content and performance. The pace of the 12 songs on the 1968 album is quick-slow, quick-slow, and so on, so that the listener is never allowed to become complacent. The movement of the song "Tropicália", like that of the album, is that of speeding up and slowing down. The chorus's regular beat demands a foot-tapping response, but it soon becomes difficult for the listener to accompany the beat, as the music speeds up again and the singing voice becomes a torrent, bombarding the ear. The rapid fire of the voice with the pace of the music convey the unease, yet exultation of modern living.

The album begins (and ends) with the speaking rather than the singing voice. The proclamation that opens the album and the song "Tropicália" is believed to have resulted from an improvisation in the recording studio. On hearing the song's introduction, which was meant to evoke a tropical scene, the percussionist, Dirceu, recalled the letter sent by a royal scribe to the Portuguese king on the wonders of the newly "discovered" territory that would come to be known as Brazil. To test the sound, he gave his own humorous version of the historical document, in which he assigned a role to sound technician Rogério Gauss: "When Pêro Vaz Caminha discovered that the land of Brazil was green and fertile, he wrote a letter to the king: everything that is planted here grows and flourishes. And the Gauss of the time recorded it all."[12] The improvisation remained as a spoken introduction to the song, and sets the tone for the irreverence and freedom of the song and the album.

Veloso explains the different impulses out of which the song was composed as follows:

> I was thinking about an old samba by Noel Rosa called *Coisas Nossas* (Our Things), that listed scenes, typical figures and cultural characteristics of Brazilian life ... I imagined a song with similar themes and a similar structure ... With my mind racing, it occurred to me that Carmen Miranda rhymes with *A Banda* [the samba by Chico Buarque] (I'd been wanting to shout the name or brandish the image of Carmen Miranda for some time), and I imagined what it would be like to place side by side, images, ideas and elements which revealed the tragicomedy of Brazilian life, the simultaneously frustrating and amazing adventure of being Brazilian.[13]

Within the song itself there are differing modes of enunciation, including conversation, exclamation and narrative, and the movement of the song is from a more verbose and complex form of expression to the elemental musical and verbal language of the refrain. The voice performs verbal acrobatics in order to convey the multiple images of Brazil presented in the lyrics (Example 1). This will become a recurring hallmark of Veloso's vocal style, delivering extremely long phrases that create a tension within the song as the listener becomes increasingly aware of the physical demands of these phrases on the performer. This contrasts with the refrain, based on a series of "Vivas!" in which the last syllable of the last word of

Example 1 *Tropicália*

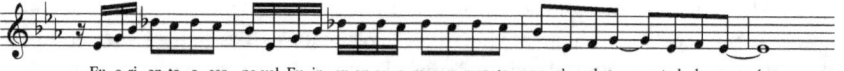

the phrase is repeated (Viva Maria -ia -ia/ Viva Bahia -ia -ia -ia -ia). The vocalisation therefore goes from being verbally and sonorously loaded to being stripped down to just one repeated syllable. This not only allows for fragments of words to be savoured as sound, but also conjures up a number of different references and meanings. For example, according to Veloso the exclamation "Viva Carmen Miranda-da-da-da-da!" referred not only to one of the muses of Tropicália, but was meant to evoke the Dadaist movement, as well as linking Carmen's name to that of Dadá, the notorious female companion of the backlands bandit Corisco.[14]

In addition to the polysemic nature of these words, highlighted by repetition, the web of cultural references in the song is rendered by a diversity of vocal activity. As well as marked accentuation, volume oscillates from mid to high range as the mode of enunciation changes from narration to exclamation and the tempo relies on the rhythms dictated by the voice. The vocalisation also quotes from two of Brazil's most popular composer/songwriters, one from the early part of the century, the other a more contemporary idol. Veloso's delivery of the phrase "luar do sertão" (the backlands moonlight) recalls the famous 1914 *toada* of the same name by Catulo da Paixão Cearense and João Pernambucano, one of the most famous songs of Brazilian popular music history. The second quote is musically substantially different from the original, but echoes a line from *iê-iê-iê* king Roberto Carlos's then recent hit, "Quero que vá tudo pro inferno" (Everything Can Go to Hell) (1965). It is delivered in a tone akin to that of everyday speech, which acknowledges the fact that the phrase from Carlos's song had passed into conversational use, as an expression of a feeling shared by many Brazilians at that time, faced with the existing social and political situation under the military dictatorship.

"Alegria, Alegria" (Joy, Joy) is another signature song on this album, which announced Veloso's intention to resist easy categorisation, with its challenging refrain: "Sem lenço sem documento/ Eu vou/ Porque não?" (Nothing to identify me/ I go/ And why not?). Veloso has explained that the song was composed especially to characterise the new approach to popular music which he and Gilberto Gil had been elaborating: "It had to be an upbeat march, contaminated in some way by international pop, and with a hint of affectionate criticism of the world from which this pop music emerged."[15] As mentioned in Chapter 2, the album cover, designed by Rogério Duarte,[16] reflected a pop art aesthetic with its lurid, cartoon-like graphics, including a bunch of bananas, a prominent Tropicalist symbol. The lyrics of "Alegria, Alegria", examined in Chapter 2, were inspired by a walk in Rio's Copacabana area, and describe the feeling of being both bombarded and stimulated by manifestations of mass culture.

Veloso has commented that "Alegria, Alegria" was intended as a song that would define the new Tropicalist approach to music-making that he had been discussing with Gilberto Gil. They preferred to "use a kind of sound which was associated with commercial music, and make the arrangement an independent element that both worked with and clashed with the song. In a way, what we wanted to do was sample bits of music and have a ready-made arrangement."[17] The dynamics of the song rely upon this effect of the independence of the arrangement and the vocalisation from the music. Although the melodies are quite simple, the harmonies are rapidly modulating, which has a somewhat unsettling effect on the listener and helps to create the critical distance that Veloso wished to introduce into the song (Example 2). By contrast, the vocals are alternately tenderly intimate and exultant, drawing the listener into the song and encouraging an emotional response. The vocals and arrangement create an impression both of disorientation and freedom in a big city. As Veloso explains: "As the song progressed, I saw that ... the necessary critical distance was there ... but, there was also the immediate pleasure of enjoying the song ... It was a way of leaving the listener both near and far from the world view of the character in the song who declares, 'I go'".[18] This tactic of approximating and involving the listener, while simultaneously creating conditions in which a critical distance is possible, combines the immediacy of a pleasurable response with a disruption of that pleasure, which allows for a consideration of the wider context of the song.

Veloso's range of vocal activity materialises the diverse and contradictory experience of living in a society undergoing a rapid, but partial process of modernisation, a modernisation addressed in negative terms by protest song. The double-edged, contradictory nature of his vocalisations encompasses both celebration and critique. The song reveals an individual who is both bombarded and empowered by the effects of modernity. In the songs of this period, however, the modern electronic instrumentation always remains subordinate to the voice, and although it may at times carry the melodic line while the voice is silent, it is usually the voice, that is, the individual, who ultimately retains control. The voice, therefore, serves as a link between the traditional and the modern, in effect negotiating the impact of internationalisation on Brazilian culture. However, the juxtaposition of modern and traditional musical practices in many of the songs had an unsettling effect on many listeners at the time.

In this album as a whole the listening experience is informed by vocalisations that consistently seek to disturb and unsettle. Veloso's insistence on the

Example 2 *Alegria, Alegria*

exploration and expression of difference makes repeated and unexpected demands on listeners. The consolation of the familiar is often denied by means of the twists and turns of the voice, whimsically and it seems at times, wilfully frustrating the ear. In other words, our experience of pleasure, which can be dependent on predicting understood musical and linguistic conventions, is momentarily ruptured when our expectations are not fulfilled. In his book *The Queen's Throat*, Wayne Koestenbaum comments: "Buying a record, you buy the singer's anatomy and the consolation that an imaginary body brings."[19] For consolation here, we may just as easily read pleasure. The quote from Koestenbaum suggests that when we listen to music, we feel a need for a bodily presence in the voice, what Barthes describes as "grain".[20] This process of materialisation of the singer in the listener's imagination is an important part of the listening experience. As Simon Frith observes, "the meaning of pop is the meaning of pop stars, performers with bodies and personalities, central to the pleasure of pop is pleasure in a voice, sound as body, sound as person."[21] The vocal alterations and transformations that occur from song to song during this period of Veloso's career therefore create a degree of uncertainty. Do we still "know" the singer, when part of the pleasure we derive from his performance lies in identifying the voice as that of Veloso's, as the body and the personality behind the song?

This uncertainty about the voice was to be carried over to the collaborative *Tropicália* album, in which a tone of *deboche* (mockery) often destabilises the suggested mood. The tone of *deboche* combines with feelings of exultation to capture a particular moment, which, as mentioned above, Veloso has described as "the simultaneously frustrating and exhilarating adventure of being Brazilian". For the Tropicalists the conditions of contemporary Brazilian society required commentary that confronted both the joys and sorrows of Brazilian life. Any celebration of Brazil was relativised by this ironic mocking, which exposed the realities of social inequity and repression and which also denied notions of homogeneity in Brazilian cultural identity.

These conflicting feelings and the concern to reveal the multi-dimensional nature of Brazilian identity are reflected in the album's vocalisations. *Tropicália's* material included *tango-canção*, *rumba*, *bolero*, *baião*, bossa nova, pop and rock. The diversity of song forms necessitated a variety of dictions. This, together with the ingenuity of Rogerio Duprat's instrumentation and use of background noises, make for a sonorous experience that is both stimulating and repeatedly surprising. This is evident in "Parque Industrial" (Industrial Estate), a typically mordant composition by Tom Zé, with himself, Veloso, Gilberto Gil, Gal Costa and Os Mutantes as vocalists. The song lyrics heavily satirise the industrialisation and developmentalist-nationalist projects adopted as the salvation of Brazil: "Pois temos o sorriso/ Engarrafado/ Já vem pronto e tabelado/ É somente requentar e usar" (Well we now have smiles/ In bottles/ They come ready-made and priced up/ Just re-heat and enjoy). The different timbres of the individual vocal parts suggest, however, a more complicated set of reactions and attitudes: Gil's is exultant,

Gal Costa's wistful, Veloso's vulnerable and Tom Zé's wry, while the repeated refrain "Porque é made, made, made/ Made in Brazil!" (Because it's made, made, made …) is proclaimed exuberantly in unison. The instrumental arrangement is by turns playful (reinforcing the wit of the lyrics) and mockingly triumphalist, in the military marching band style that pervades the song and is intensified in the refrain. Duprat also inserts phrases from the Brazilian national anthem, which he alternates with a quote from an advertising jingle for the painkiller Melhoral. The song reflects the rich texture of sound in the album as a whole: for example, there are also background noises of the happy cries of children in an amusement park, which seem to refer to and critique the official mantra of building a great future for Brazil's children. The track ends with the sound of wild applause, but in the context of the song's commentary, this applause sounds hollow and seems more of an ironic comment on blinkered national pride and the failure of the developmentalist thrust to change the lives of the majority of Brazilians.

Not all of the songs on the album, however, possess the ironic tone of *deboche*. "Enquanto seu lobo não vem" (Until Mr Wolf Comes), superficially a love song, is also an invitation to defy the control of public space exercised by the military. The song relies on the contrast between the intimacy and delicacy of the vocalisation and the defiance expressed in the lyrics. This disparity is evident for example in the first refrain, in which the name "President Vargas" is tenderly intoned in a manner appropriate to romantic music. The logic for this within the narrative of the song is a reference to President Vargas Avenue in Rio de Janeiro, since the song is a summons to the public to make themselves visible on the city's streets. The incongruity that we hear in the crooning of a name synonymous with dictatorship highlights the hidden agenda of the song's lyrical content. A similar aural incongruity lies in the accompanying chorus that warbles ethereally in the background the phrase, "Os clarins da banda militar" (The bugles of the military band). In spite of the fact that public space is controlled and regulated by the

Example 3 *Enquanto seu lobo não vem*

military, the song asserts the right to occupy that space, making reference to one of the city's most famous samba schools ("Vamos desfilar pelas ruas onde Mangueira passou" [Let's parade through the streets where Mangueira passed]). It also calls for transgressions in the private sphere and for the survival of solidarity underground: "Vamos por debaixo das ruas/ Debaixo das bombas, das bandeiras/ Debaixo das botas ... debaixo da cama" (Let's go underneath the streets/ Under the bombs, flags/ Under the boots ... under the bed). The mode of the love song is therefore very appropriate to the message of the song, allowing the voice to take on a tone of complicity and intimacy, while the layering of the song structure also gives the impression that the voice is operating undercover. The introduction dramatises this layering: we first hear a percussive sound, the *agogô*, to which a woodblock, then an acoustic guitar is added, followed by the bass (Example 3). After this textured pattern of sound has been built up, the vocals are introduced. As the song progresses strings and flutes are added. However, the progressively more strident addition of the military brass at the end of each line of the lyrics and the sound of the snare drums which punctuate the song act as a counterpoint to the quiet insistence of the voice, creating another incongruity which imbues the song with a feeling of tension and reflects the delicate balance of emotions expressed – love, solidarity, hope, challenge, resistance and sorrow.

The last song on the album, a version of "Hino ao Senhor do Bonfim" (Hymn to Our Lord of Bomfim) (J.A. Wanderley and P. Vilar), is a kind of religious anthem that celebrates the achievements of the citizens of Bahia, and also points to the regional origins of the Tropicalists. Throughout the song, however, Veloso's quite subdued delivery contrasts with the full-throated and exuberant rendition of the chorus. The tension between the two styles appears to give way at the end to the exalted sound of the chorus, only to have any feelings of triumphalism disintegrate, as the voices themselves degenerate into non-verbal utterances of wailing, moaning and screaming. This is finally silenced by the sound of cannons firing, with which the album's opening song also ends. The breakdown of the singing voice, the loss of the pleasure of singing and of listening to the voice, which ends up able to express only pain, represent a denunciation of censorship and the repressive socio-political conditions under which the Tropicalist movement was formed.

The cover of Veloso's next album, released in 1969, is blank except for the artist's name, which makes a comment on the widespread and intense censorship implemented after the declaration of the Fifth Institutional Act, or AI–5. Perhaps in response to the threat of silence, in this album manipulations of the voice are highly self-referential and self-contemplative. The voice becomes a form of meta-communication, either commenting on itself explicitly, or as a subtext, drawing attention to what it is doing, or is capable of doing. This album represents a crucial moment in this first phase of Veloso's work. It is a kind of watershed in which many of the vocal styles and forms of expression that he has already used converge, styles that he will use and elaborate upon in the next three albums.

The first song on the album, "Irene", begins with the voice of Gilberto Gil counting in the recording, "Um, dois, tres!", highlighting the process of song production right from the start. The lyrics consist of four lines repeated again and again, as though the two singers were improvising around the lines. This effect is reinforced by the way in which they play with the homologous sound of the words "Quero ver Irene rir" (I want to see Irene laugh), and the disruption of the song shortly after it begins, by the two voices engaged in laughing conversation. After this interlude by the speaking voices, they dissolve into a deflating sound that makes way for the musical introduction to start up again. The effect of this is to create an illusion that we as listeners are being involved in the process of constructing the song. Meanwhile, the repeated phrase "Irene ri Irene ri Irene", sung so that the words are confused, point to the role of the voice in uniting lyrics and music, as the voice dissolves the words into the melody.

The songs that follow are a showcase for the hybridity of Veloso's vocal style. In "Marinheiro só" (Lone Sailor), a folk song accompanied by electric guitars, the voice expertly negotiates this mixture of traditional and modern sounds. "Lost in the paradise" is a rock ballad in the Bob Dylan style. The vocals support the surreal lyrics, written in English, with a delivery which suggests sixties rock psychedelia. In "Atrás do trio eléctrico" (Following the Sound System) the voice shows off its virtuosity, with considerable skill displayed in enunciating the verbose lyrics, given the whirlwind pace of the melody. The song is a *frevo*, a carnival song form from North-eastern Brazil. Tricks and playfulness in the vocalisation, as well as the pace, the tone of fun and the vocal and verbal acrobatics evoke the atmosphere of carnival. "Os argonautas" (The Argonauts), which appears next on the album, presents a sharp contrast, with the musical flavour of Portuguese *fado* and the philosophical flavour of existentialism. This is followed by a samba, a tango, a rock ballad and a *samba-canção*. In Veloso's rendition of "Carolina", Chico Buarque's samba about the oppressive atmosphere created by the dictatorship, the voice makes such exaggerated gestures that this version was widely perceived as a parody of the original. Veloso had commented frequently on the difference in approach between himself and Chico and on one occasion had contrasted the songs of the Tropicalists with those of Chico in the following way: "We ... wanted something that was, in some way, ugly, while Chico continued to concern himself only with what was beautiful."[22] In his vocalisation of the song, Veloso makes the voice ugly – heavy and world-weary. The physical and the emotional, a body and heart filled with pain and longing, are communicated here through the straining voice, the pitch occasionally raised almost to the point of breaking down, the tempo slowed to a crawl.

Much is made of Veloso's ability to marry words and music perfectly as though it were a natural gift, but this is also one of the conscious concerns of his early music-making, to continually examine and re-examine the ways in which the voice works with language, sound and melody in the creation of song. As evident in the chorus of the song "Tropicália", the voice lingers over the words, prolonging and stressing the last syllables, as if drawing attention to the construction and deconstruction of the word. In the repeated syllables, such as "-ta -ta -ta -ta" and "-da -da -da -da", the voice itself becomes a percussive instrument, dissolving the divide between words and music. A similar function is performed by the voice in "Acrilírico" (Acrylyrical), the penultimate track of this 1969 album. Here there is virtually no instrumental music, with the voices and background noises instead providing the rhythms. The song is delivered entirely in the speaking voice, foregrounded against a variety of noises (including a door slamming, ice clinking in a glass, the sound of traffic) with which the voices interact. On the whole the piece sounds like the opening sequence to a film, and evokes a scene just after the opening credits have rolled, with characters going about their daily business in a big city. The voices have a measured, artificial quality, not the inconsistent rhythms of normal speech or conversation, and this stylisation seems designed to convert them into instruments, into music. Despite their restrained tones, however, the voices' control over the spoken word seems to have become usurped by the organism of the word itself, metamorphosing and multiplying into other words, other meanings, as the subject contemplates the past and future of his music-making:

> Ainda canto o ido o tido o dito
> O dado o consumido o consumado
> Do amor morto motor da saudade
> Quero canto de vinda
> Divindade do duro totem
> E futuro to-tal, -tal, qual quero canto

(I still sing of what's fled, had, said/ The fact the consumed the consummated/ Of love mourned motor of longing/ I want songs of divination/ Divinity of the defiant totem/ And a future so radi-cal, -call it singing what I want to sing)

The last song of the album, "Alfômega" (Alphomega), consists of the voices of Veloso and Gilberto Gil intoning "made-up" words, created by joining different words and syllables together. The vocal qualifiers here criss-cross a diffuse line between speaking and singing. The enunciation is syllabic, with the syllables markedly broken up by the voice and the music. The voice focuses on itself here, flagging its singing and speaking roles for the listener. The vocal gestures of the song, such as grating, noticeable breathing and whooping with excitement, relish the nebulous area between singing and speaking as a newly found freedom to make meaning. The lyrics support this focus on the voice as the breathing, feeling body, summarised in the Greek-derived invented word "somatopsicopneumático", which is repeated throughout the song. With "somato" suggesting things bodily, "psico" the mind or emotions, and "pneuma" breathing, this word succinctly summarises the act of song performance. These last two songs on this album make explicit Edward Cone's idea that song is a dual form of utterance, a combination of the explicit language of words and a continuum of symbolic gestures, or non-verbal sounds.[23] Veloso's work suggests a keen awareness of these two ways of producing meaning and the importance of the interaction of different musical parts to create the multiplicity of texts so vital to the message of his work.

Over the course of these seven albums, Veloso's voice takes on many different positions and personae. On Side A alone of the 1968 album, for example, the voice is by turns exultant and defiant, then tender, nostalgic, carefree, imbued with loss, and finally, mystical. This kind of vocal diversity defies the listener to draw any conclusions as to where the "real" Veloso might lie. During this period of his career, the heyday of Tropicália, despite his active courting of the mass media, the whirlwind of interviews and television appearances, and the divulgence of the most intimate details of his personal life, Veloso resisted singularity in characterisation because of the many roles played both in his visual presentation of himself, as discussed in Chapter 2, and in his vocalisations. There were so many manifestations of him that it made it difficult for the public to identify him exclusively with any one of them.

After being forced into exile in July 1969, and deprived of the many spaces in which he had been accustomed to performing, Veloso turned away from spectacle to introspection to express the pain of exile. In the 1971 album, *Caetano Veloso*, the first of two recorded in London, the relatively unfamiliar sound of Veloso's voice singing in English conveys keenly the sense of estrangement he experiences, singing for a Brazilian public (these albums were not actually heard on radio stations in London at the time), but in a foreign language. The sound of the voice in English is crucial to the album's key concepts of exile and alienation. The dynamics of the album rely, however, on the interaction within the songs between English and Portuguese. As the album progresses, there is an increasing presence, or intrusion of the Portuguese language into the songs. This recovery of the performer's native language parallels a process of the recovery of memory that will develop fully in the second London album. Indeed, as I seek to demonstrate below, these London albums function as spaces for the performance of memory.

The first track "A Little More Blue" represents the lowest emotional point of the album. The lyrics recount events in the artist's life that have affected his state of mind most profoundly. The first experiences he recalls place him in the context of the Brazilian past he has been compelled to leave behind (the moment of exile, the national outpouring of grief over the death of Carmen Miranda, his arrest), while the latter connect him to the present London reality (seeing a late film and missing the last tube home). The vocalisation of these verses is extremely subdued and the rhythm so slow that at times it sounds almost like spoken verse. Only the chorus (the repeated line "I feel a little more blue than then") is embellished and the song ends with this line becoming increasingly ornamental, until the last word, "then", acquires the nasal twang that a word ending in "-en" would have in Portuguese. What we hear in this song is a subtle process by which memories of Brazil are linked to more recent experiences in London, and in which the past intrudes upon the present, not only in the song lyrics, but also in the Brazilianising of the English word.

The third song, "Maria Bethânia", has a pulsating, distorted bass line and the first verse has a regular and insistent rock 'n' roll rhythm, to accompany the rock 'n' roll vocalisation in English. However, in the chorus, when the name of Veloso's sister is actually introduced, the timbre of the voice suddenly becomes very tender and the addition of strings creates an effective contrast to the first verse and an appropriate climate for the realm of affective memory. The presence of that memory is heard in the following verses, which maintain their rock 'n' roll sound, but into which the strings are inserted. In terms of the vocalisation, there is still a marked contrast between the verses and the chorus. In the verses, the phrases are quite long and the English sounds stifled, like an unnatural sound for the voice, one that requires effort. In the chorus however, the English (the language of exile) actually flows into and becomes the Portuguese (the language of home and belonging). Lyrics, music and vocalisation therefore demonstrate the beginning of a process of reconciling past and present:

> Maria Bethânia, please send me a letter
> I wish to know things are getting better
> Better, better, better, better, Bethânia

By the end of the song it is the sound of Portuguese that dominates, in an entire passage of nasalised sounds without words. This passage is accompanied by an instrumental flourish to highlight it further, before the song fades to the pulsating rhythm of the bass guitar.

Past and present are continually in dialogue in the album and produce the complexity of feelings of the exile. In "London, London" on Side A, the experience is one of "silent pain and happiness", including feelings of relief and peace, given the social and political conditions prevailing in Brazil at the time. "In the Hot Sun of a Christmas Day" on Side B, whose title – continually repeated in the song – suggests the evocation of pleasant memories of home, actually recounts Veloso's persecution and arrest by the military. The mode of enunciation is rock 'n' roll with a touch of blues, which identifies the location from which the subject voice speaks as being outside of Brazil. The musical quote from the Christmas carol "God Rest Ye Merry Gentlemen", with its string accompaniment, sets up a stark contrast with the lyrical content, particularly in the line, "Machine guns, in the hot sun of a Christmas Day", into which the quote is inserted.

The album ends with "Asa Branca" (White Wing), Luis Gonzaga and Humberto Teixeira's 1947 *toada* about drought in the North-east, which has achieved anthemic status in the history of Brazilian popular music. In Veloso's version of the song the rhythm is considerably slowed down, so that it becomes a ballad and after each verse there is a passage of nasalising which is so pronounced that it jars considerably on the quiet, contemplative mood and tone of the verses. This nasalising that has featured throughout the album is intensified here in a clear materialisation in the voice of one of the most pronounced features of spoken

Portuguese and particularly of North-eastern speech. The predominance of this sound in this last song represents a final affirmation of the subject voice's identity as Brazilian and north-eastern, and of his difference in his present environment.

If the 1971 album highlights the anguished memories of the exile attempting to recreate a past from which he has been suddenly uprooted, *Transa*, the second album recorded in London, reveals an individual coming to terms with the present and with the grief of exile. In *Transa*, the fragmented memories invoked and juxtaposed on the present are once again immediately noticeable in the contrast between the English and Portuguese languages and between Western and Brazilian music. The voice sings primarily in English, but is continually interrupted by quotes from Brazilian popular music standards. The interaction between the two languages and musical cultures points to a subject voice that has succeeded not only in recuperating its memories, but also in establishing an effective dialogue between the past and the present. References to Brazilian popular songs invade the space of exile, and go a long way towards closing the gap between past and present that is evident in the 1971 album. In *Transa* this flow of the past and the present is intensified to create a web of sampled material so dense that it requires considerable effort on the part of the listener to untangle them.

Much of Veloso's early work is based on what I call an aesthetic of sampling. This aesthetic is evident in all aspects of his Tropicalist performance (in music, instrumentation, arrangements, lyrics and visual style) and is fundamental to his "evolutionary approach" to music-making discussed in Chapter 1. Indeed, as mentioned earlier, on one occasion he makes explicit his intention to create a sampled effect with the song "Alegria, Alegria". In addition to the effect of musical sampling, its lyrics are a collage of images, a kind of visual sampling that works together with the aural effects created in the song. Veloso's status as an unknown, exiled performer in London meant limited opportunities in terms of shows or televised performances and led him to focus the aesthetic of sampling very closely around the recorded voice in the *Transa* album. The album's title is a word that suggests both a meeting-place, as well as intimate relations between two people. The album, indeed, provides a meeting-place for the Brazilian past and the London present, and sampling is the defining dynamic in the exploration of the relationship between the two places, moments and cultures. The use of English and Western musical forms suggests Veloso's physical distance from a body of national traditions that had previously served as a point of reference for confidently negotiating a way in the modern world. The English language and rock 'n'roll music encapsulate the displacement of the subject voice to the locus of an internationally dominant culture. The practice of sampling becomes a strategy of resistance that allows the performer to be reconnected to Brazilian traditions and not simply overwhelmed by Western sounds. Veloso's sampling counters the predictions of the acculturation discourse that had been dominant in the study of music of the non-Western world. The theories of transnational flows and cultural hybridity that began to replace the concern with homogenisation from the 1970s are more appropriate to an examination of the anti-essentialist approach to music-making he had been practising from the late 1960s. To these theories of cultural process, I would add the concept of sampling, as a strategy that compels interaction between different places and different times.

The deluge of samples constitutes an almost aggressive and Tropicalist approach to addressing the subject's feelings of disconnectedness and isolation. The storehouse of memory is raided in an exuberant acknowledgement of the potential of the past to elaborate new identities and forms of expression in the present. Although *Transa* learnt from Tropicalism the creative possibilities of combining and juxtaposing different genres of music, in this London album the incredible hybrids produced are not used to mock or parody. Instead, they provide evidence of the resilience of Brazilian cultural forms, even when they are confronted with Western culture in its own terrain. The process of reconciling these cultural forms and reconciling the past and the present compels the listener to shift positions continually in order to keep up with the activities of the voice. We are catapulted back and forth in time, for example, an adaptation of a 17th century poem by Gregório de Matos ("Triste Bahia" [Unhappy Bahia]) follows a song with a sample and reference to reggae ("Nine Out of Ten"), a novelty within the Brazilian music scene at that time. Celso Loureiro Chaves has highlighted the proliferation of references in this album, which include various bossa nova songs, traditional folk songs of the North-east, and the Beatles. The last song, "Nostalgia (That's What Rock 'n' Roll Is All About)", is a short, straightforward homage to rock 'n' roll in English, which Chaves describes as "a trick to disguise the chaos produced by this torrent of memory and to make the listener forget that he or she has just undergone an extremely demanding listening experience, with a record that lasts much longer, emotionally, than its chronometric time."[24]

An examination of the song "You Don't Know Me", which appears first on this album, reveals just how sampling and vocal features function in this transmission of memory and emotion. Drums and guitars accompany and are subordinate to the vocal part. The drums follow the crucial moments of the vocal part, coinciding with its melodic peaks and stressed accents, which lends increased impact to its emotive qualities. On the whole the voice is monophonous, although there is a moment when a female voice joins in, singing in Portuguese. The female voice pushes forward, ahead of the male lead, with some rhythmic variation of the melody, creating a temporary inconsistency that represents an intrusion of memory into the present. After the "contact" with the female part, Veloso resumes the line "You Don't Know Me" in a noticeably higher register, which makes the timbre of the voice much less subdued and mournful. With each insertion by Veloso of a fragment of a well-known Brazilian popular song, the tone of the voice becomes more exuberant and the vocal patterns become more liberated. As this song progresses, then, we as listeners actually experience, not through the lyrics, which in English remain the same, but through the actions and interventions of the voice, a movement from loneliness and isolation to an expansiveness and joy that come from recalling the musical traditions out of which the performer comes. This movement is further reinforced in the undulating melodic line of the song, and emotion is heightened through the use of progressively stronger accentuation placed on the main pulses of the metre.

The song "It's A Long Way" is the first on Side B of the album and bears similarities to "You Don't Know Me", the first track of Side A, thereby establishing a balance between the two parts of the album. Both songs have English titles, immediately locating the subject voice and the emotions expressed in the present. The lyrics of "It's A Long Way" also begin with a direct reference to the present: "Woke up this morning singing an old Beatles song". The song is subsequently punctuated by a series of samples from Brazilian popular songs. Apart from the musical coherence produced by weaving the sampled songs together with the original passages in English, the choice of songs sampled is interesting for other reasons. Of the four songs referenced, three were written in the Golden Age of Brazilian radio discussed earlier. These songs are, in the order in which they appear: "Sodade, Meu Bem, Sodade" (Miss You So, My Darling) – Zé do Norte; "Água com Areia" (Sea and Sand) – Jair Amorim/Jacobina; "A Lenda do Abaeté" (The Legend of Abaeté) – Dorival Caymmi (about a lake located in Veloso's home-state of Bahia that was a potent source of myth and legend for indigenous peoples). The other song sampled, "Consolação" (Consolation), by Baden Powell and Vinícius de Moraes, was recorded in 1964, the year of the military coup. While the lyrics of this song express the suffering that can come from love, its sampling here re-signifies the words to suggest love for country, and pain on account of its current situation. The samples, therefore, map the performer's personal history – his origins as a Bahian, a Brazilian and a songwriter, and locate his present predicament and private emotions within recent national history.

The voice is crucial here in weaving the threads of memory into expressions of the present. In a repetition of a vocal trick used in the 1971 London album, the first hint we have of the intrusion of Portuguese and the tradition of Brazilian popular music into the song comes in the refrain "It's a long way", in which the word "long" is nasalised and repeated in an approximation of Portuguese speech. This is followed by the first musical quote, after which the song oscillates between English and Portuguese, between the Beatles and Brazil. The voice negotiates the two seamlessly; at one point, for example, one of the lines "gives way" to Portuguese from the English: "It's a long água com areia/ Brinca na beira do mar". This means that for listeners, these juxtapositions, which may have sounded more surprising in "You Don't Know Me" on Side A, begin to be heard as a whole, as interacting facets of the emotional experiences of the subject voice. After several excursions into the terrain of memory the song ends, however, in the present, with a repetition of the first four lines in English.

The most ambitious and complex song on the album, and the longest, lasting a full 9 minutes 32 seconds, is "Triste Bahia", an adaptation of the poem by Gregório de Matos, which laments the increasing commercialisation of colonial

Bahia.[25] In keeping with the poem's baroque style the musical structure of the song is dense and layered. The song opens with the sound of the berimbau, which has immediate regional and traditional connotations, but throughout the song folk instruments and music are juxtaposed with electronic instrumentation. The movement of the song relies on a gradual proliferation of rhythms and increase in pace, which intensifies the layering of different traditions and times. This is the most intense expression in the album of the meeting of past and present, in which the lament for the degeneration of 17th century society in the poem parallels that for the degeneration of Brazilian society under the military dictatorship. The words of the poem are laced with disparate images and ideas, so that what we hear is the flow of fragmented memories in the musical flow of the song. Chaves has seen in this flow something of a Brazilian Joycean stream of consciousness *avant la lettre*, as the album preceded the publication of the Portuguese translation of *Ulysses* by two years.[26]

The fragmented character of memory is perhaps the most salient characteristic of these London albums. Prior to this period, memory was frequently represented in Veloso's work by covers of songs in their entirety. However, through its aesthetic of sampling *Transa* reveals a process of re-articulating fragments of memory as a response to conditions of the time. The clash between past and present, together with the contrast between cultures, are gradually worked out over the course of the 1971 album and of *Transa*. The latter ends with an aural trick which points to this reconciliation. After the brief and simple rock 'n' roll track "Nostalgia", sung in English, the last sounds we hear are the sounds of voices in the recording studio talking. We immediately locate these voices within London and within the present time action of the performance of the song, but significantly, they are speaking in Portuguese, the language that we have come to associate with the past and with Brazilian musical traditions.

I maintain that Veloso's extraordinary vocal plurality during this initial period of his work represents an attempt to compensate for the effects of censorship and the emptying of language in the public sphere. In addition to the creation of a language of visual style and of lyrics that rely on multiple meanings (see Chapters 2 and 4 respectively), the voice becomes vital in creating and conveying its own form of oppositional expression. This search for a multiplicity of voices and the increasingly personal nature of their communication can be seen to preview similar concerns which would be taken to extreme levels of subjectivity in the "marginal" poetry that emerged in Brazil in the mid 1970s. Political repression and state control of the publishing industry compelled these poets to take charge of the printing and distribution of their work.[27] As a result, a proliferation of individual voices emerged which sought to express social realities at an intensely personal level. For the Marginals, the representation of emotional and bodily intimacy constituted a response to the violation of private experience by public life.[28] This was a tactic extensively explored by Veloso in his performances at this stage of his career, as demonstrated in Chapter 2.

Veloso also makes full use of the voice in this representation of intimacy, for example, in the recorded version of the song "É Proibido Proibir" (Prohibiting Prohibited). The song is analysed here in its studio version, as opposed to its notorious live performance at the 1968 International Music Festival examined in Chapter 2. From the first moment that the voice enters the song, having been prefaced by electronic accompaniment, bodily presence is paramount. What we get is not a singing voice, but a heavily breathing body, which acts upon our perceptions at different levels. Firstly, the singer seems to breathe life into the song, and the life of the song and the life of the body are linked by the breathing and the sonic anaphone of a heartbeat.[29] Secondly, the breathing is an erotic sound; there is an almost palpable sense of the proximity of the singer, which brings with it an intimacy that is disconcerting in its directness, giving the impression that this sound is being made for *you*, the individual, privileged listener. The uneasy pleasure afforded by this degree of intimacy gives way to a momentary and lulling timbral tenderness, from which we are disturbed by a voice which dramatically builds up to a declamatory and inflammatory refrain. In a relatively short trajectory then and regardless of the words of the song, the voice has taken us from the erotic-intimate to a kind of exalted anger.

"É Proibido Proibir" is generally structured around these two states of emotion as conveyed by the voice and it is the voice that is responsible for the extremely theatrical movement of the song to its climax. As the shouted refrain is increasingly drawn-out, it is punctuated by cries, moans and groans, guttural sounds and growls, sounds of pain and pleasure mixed in together, with an interlude which features the speaking voice, reciting poetry by Fernando Pessoa. The effect of this is to confuse the listener's perceptions, thrown into a state of turmoil like the emotions of the singer himself, and to compel us to invest more effort in understanding the message of the song. The voice is present in this song in all its forms, from noise, to speech, to song. So too is the body in its desire for pleasure and freedom, its acts and gestures of protest, its experience of pain. At the song's end, faced with the policing of free speech, the sound of the voice becomes a cacophony, resorting to non-verbal sound as a form of denunciation and opposition.

The period examined in this chapter ends with *Araçá Azul*, an improvised, avant-garde album recorded in just one week after Veloso's return to Brazil in 1972. The album marks a moment in which Veloso takes this period of vocal experimentation to its limits. The result is a performance that by and large sacrifices the creation of pleasure, alienating and distancing the listener emotionally, and encouraging instead a more objective contemplation of the songs, or rather the "peças", or "pieces" as Veloso described them. His first piece, "De conversa" (In Conversation), is a sound collage composed of vocal utterances and words, truncated so that they are abstracted into pure sound. The utterances cover a range of non-verbal sounds, turning the words into percussive noises, including whistling, humming, noisy exhaling, laughter and moaning. The seamlessness with which the rhythms of speech become those of song, through which speech is made music, highlights the ways in which everyday speech is incorporated into song. The focus on the different accents of the voices engaged in fragmented conversation emphasises the natural musicality of the human voice and by extension, the human body. This is reinforced by the song's percussive accompaniment which the sleeve notes explain are produced by: "Caetano Veloso: layered voices, percussion on skin and bone ...".[30]

"De conversa" is a piece that repeatedly frustrates listeners' expectations as we wait for the voice to assume song as the exclusive mode of enunciation. "Gilberto Misterioso" (Mysterious Gilberto), based on a poem by Sousândrade,[31] works on the basis of a similar process of denial. The piece begins by immediately creating a sense of tension, pushing the voice to its limits by holding a note and allowing it to reverberate until the song's lyrics (consisting of one line) are vocalised. The line is repeated until the song abruptly comes to a stop. When the voice resumes, its rhythm is faster and its pitch higher and again it comes to a sudden halt after a series of repetitions (Example 4). The alternating between sound and silence is pursued more explicitly in the following piece "De palavra em palavra" (From Word to Word). The piece opens with the word "soma", split into two, so that the first sound we hear is a prolonged vocalisation of the word "som" (sound). This is followed by the heavily breathed second part of the word "-ma", so that what we are hearing, both semantically and physically, is the sound of the breathing body. Inspired by and dedicated to Concretist Augusto de Campos, the piece then continues with a palindromic word invented by Veloso, which itself has no meaning, but which is relished for its sonorous qualitites, mumured repeatedly to sound like prayer. Once again the voice materialises sound by exhaling the word "soma" and this is then contrasted with the word "silêncio" (silence), which is paradoxically made sound, first by being whispered, then spoken, then screamed. The piece ends with this paradox, with the voice murmuring, giving a form of sound to the words "Não som" (Not sound).

In *Araçá Azul* Veloso takes to its limits the concern with the communicative possibilities of the voice in popular song. He has commented that the album represented "a bid for creative freedom within the profession: I needed to lose my inhibitions in the studio, test my limits and extend my horizons."[32] However, the rejection of the album by the public and by many critics meant that it was a communicative failure. It broke the record for the greatest number of returns by dissatisfied customers to record shops and clashes with the public

Example 4 *Gilberto Misterioso*

dogged the performances of the show based on the album. Two of the most publicised incidents took place at the Museu de Arte Moderna in Rio and the Teatro Castro Alves in Salvador. The crowd vociferously expressed their dislike of experimentation with Brazilian standards such as "Asa Branca", leading to confrontations between the performer and the public. In Salvador the show was discontinued and Veloso was detained by police after "disrespecting the public" by using expletives on stage.[33] This came in response to provocation by members of the audience who accompanied the booing and pelting of cans and paper with shouts of "homosexual", "degenerate" and "thief". The audience, unconsciously perhaps, linked his plundering of and alterations to musical traditions with what they saw as his moral decadence (he appeared at these shows in full make-up and dressed and dancing like Carmen Miranda!). *Araçá Azul* had pushed the relationship between singer and listener to breaking point, the logical conclusion, perhaps, of Veloso's testing and probing of this relationship.

In addition to his determination to experiment with international musical trends, Veloso was censured by committed musicians and performers for his refusal to openly state his political position. This was bound to provoke resentment and even open hostility, given the socio-political climate at the time. Veloso opted instead for a form of critique that was directed not only at the dictatorship, but also at Brazilians living under it. His work during this period constituted a consciously cultivated attack on the public, with the aim of forcing an awareness of the contradictions of Brazilian culture and society, and which was wary of blinkered idealism, or militant simplifications. This approach offered an invitation to participate in the criticism of self and society. The voice, therefore, does not restrict itself to performing its traditional function in the singer/listener relationship by giving pleasure; it also conducts an assault on the Brazilian consciousness. To return to Veloso's comment on Chico Buarque's work which I quoted previously ("We ... wanted something that was, in some way, ugly, while Chico continued to concern himself only with what was beautiful."), it is this concern that not only the beautiful, but also the ugly and the discordant should enter his music that characterises Veloso's many voices during this period. They are voices that seek to express more fully the complexities of Brazilian identity at a particular historical moment. The albums recorded during the period examined in this chapter attempt to provoke debate on controversial aspects of this heterogeneous, changing society. They seek to change the nature of the singer/listener relationship, in order to involve the listening public in these debates. Although Veloso continued to elaborate forms of communication that drew on the strategies and concerns that had informed these early years of his work, *Araçá Azul* signalled the end of an era. By the following year Veloso would look back on this period of his career and comment: "While I don't tend to look for the easy way out, I no longer want to try and communicate at any price."[34]

Notes

1. Lomax recounts the findings of the "cantometrics" project, which used computers in an attempt to analyse and quantify the different elements of "folk" song style in his book, *Folk Song Style and Culture*. Lomax's studies were flawed in fundamental ways (see Middleton for a critique of cantometrics in *Studying Popular Music*, 149–50). However, the categories that he outlined for examining vocal style are still extremely useful for analysing vocal performance today.
2. In response to my comment to Veloso that during this period he seemed to use his voice as a form of provocation, he replied that rather than seeking to create conflict, he had hoped to create dialogue and discussion (interview with the author, see Appendix).
3. For example, Campos, *Balanço da bossa*; Vasconcellos, *Música popular*; Sant'Anna, *Música popular e moderna poesia brasileira*; Favaretto, *Tropicália*; Calado, *Tropicália*, and more recently, Dunn, *Brutality Garden*.
4. Tatit, *O Cancionista*, 263–4, 268, 275–7.
5. McClary and Walser, "Start Making Sense!", 287–8.
6. Essa busca foi sendo executada ao longo de, pelo menos, seis anos, alguns dos quais fortemente marcados por circunstâncias de exílio. E de tempos em tempos apareciam os sinais, ainda nitidamente distintos, dos dois projetos: o veio experimental que ficou de *[Tropicália] ou Panis et Circensis* e a nova canção de rádio que cada vez mais se configurava.

    Tatit, *O Cancionista*, 277.
7. Severiano and Homem de Mello, *A canção no tempo: Vol. I*.
8. Tinhorão, *Música Popular – do Gramafone ao Rádio e TV*. Tinhorão also examines the phenomenon in São Paulo, which developed in a different way, as an elite leisure activity, which was not available to the popular classes until the late 1950s and '60s.
9. See also Castro, *Chega de Saudade*, Chapters 1 and 2, for accounts of the music of this period and the organisation and activities of the fan clubs, in particular the Sinatra-Farney Fan Club; and McCann, *Hello, Hello Brazil*, 181–214, on studio programmes and fan clubs.
10. (A minha inspiração não quer mais viver apenas da nostalgia de tempos e lugares, ao contrário, quer incorporar essa saudade num projeto de futuro.) Polygram, 6328 392, 1982.
11. (porque eu não quero, porque eu não devo explicar absolutamente nada.) Philips, R765.026L, 1968.
12. (Quando Pêro Vaz Caminha decobriu que as terras brasileiras eram férteis e verdejantes, escreveu uma carta ao rei: tudo que nela se planta, tudo cresce e floresce. E o Gauss da época gravou.)
13. Pensando num velho samba de Noel Rosa chamado *Coisas Nossas*, que enumerava cenas, personagens típicos e características culturais da vida brasileira ..., imaginei uma canção que tivesse temática e estrutura semelhantes ... Com a mente numa velocidade estonteante, lembrei que Carmen Miranda rima com *A banda* (e eu já vinha fazia muito tempo pensando em bradar o nome ou brandir a imagem de Carmen Miranda), e imaginei colocar lado a lado imagens, idéias e entidades reveladoras da tragicomédia brasil, da aventura a um tempo frustra e reluzente de ser brasileiro.

    Veloso, *Verdade Tropical*, 184.

14. Veloso, *Verdade Tropical*, 186–7. (These backlands bandits, known as *cangaceiros*, roamed the hinterland of North-east Brazil until around 1930. They were ambiguous figures who rose up against landowners and the state and were considered as both heroes and outlaws by the local population.)
15. (Tinha que ser uma marchina alegre, de algum modo contaminado pelo pop internacional, e trazendo na letra algum toque crítico-amoroso sobre o mundo onde esse pop se dava.) Veloso, *Verdade Tropical*, 165.
16. Intellectual, artist and friend of film director Glauber Rocha, who designed the memorable poster for the Cinema Novo film *Deus e o Diabo na Terra do Sol*.
17. (... utilizar uma ou outra sonoridade reconhecível da música comercial, fazendo do arranjo um elemento independente que clarificasse a canção mas também se chocasse com ela. De certa forma, o que queríamos fazer equivalia a 'samplear' retalhos musicais, e tomávamos os arranjos como ready-mades.) Veloso, *Verdade Tropical*, 168.
18. (À medida que a canção avançava, eu percebia que ... havia a distância necessária para a crítica ... mas, havia a alegria imediata da fruição das coisas ... Era um modo de deixar o ouvinte ao mesmo tempo perto e longe da visão de mundo da personagem que, na canção, diz 'eu vou'.) Veloso, *Verdade Tropical*, 166.
19. Koestenbaum, *The Queen's Throat*, 51.
20. "The 'grain' is the body in the voice as it sings, the hand as it writes, the limb as it performs." Barthes, *Image, Music, Text*, 188. In Chapter 4 I discuss Barthes's concept of grain more fully in relation to the love song.
21. Frith, *Performing Rites*, 210.
22. (Nós queríamos ... alguma coisa que fosse, de algum modo, feia, embora Chico permaneceu realisando só que era bonito.) *O Estado de São Paulo*, 17/08/78. For an account of the difference in attitudes to music-making between Chico and the Tropicalists and the polemic it generated, see Meneses, *Desenho Mágico*, 28–32.
23. Cone, *The Composer's Voice*, 164 and 17.
24. (... uma brincadeira para fingir que a torrente de memória não foi desparatada e que o ouvinte não foi submetido a uma onerosa audição de um disco que dura bem mais, emocionalmente, do que o seu tempo cronométrico.) Chaves, "Memórias do passado no presente", 81. (The entire album lasts only 35 minutes, 20 seconds.)
25. Matos, *Gregório de Matos: Poesias selecionadas*, 141.
26. Chaves, "Memórias do passado no presente", 80. However, Veloso's attention was drawn to Joyce by the Concretist poets, Haroldo and Augusto de Campos, before the appearance of a Portuguese translation of *Ulysses*.
27. In the late 1970s a group of "independentes" also emerged on the music scene, composers who had opted out of or had been marginalised by the recording industry and who sought alternative means of production and distribution of their records. One such composer was Antonio Adolfo, whose aptly titled album *Feito em Casa* (Home-Made) has a cover with the same artisanal look of much of Marginal poetry. It was sold at live shows by Adolfo, who travelled all over Brazil to promote his work. [Sleevenotes: *Feito em Casa* (Artezanal, LP-A-001, 1977 and *Viralata* (Artezanal, LP-A-003, 1979)]. Adolfo's *Viralata* album was distributed by Musiquim, an independent label which called itself "uma gravadora nanica" (a miniature record company). The term was borrowed from the description "jornais nanicos", used to refer to the alternative press, such as the notorious weekly publication *O Pasquim* (The Lampoon). In a sheet which doubled as a statement of intent and a customer order form and which was inserted into the record sleeves, Musiquim declared: "The alternative press shares our intentions, and has already amply demonstrated their (and our) viability: the existence of a public which is interested in and eager for new

information and points of view in accordance with our reality." (A imprensa nanica, gêmea das nossas intenções, já demonstrou suficientemente a sua (e a nossa) viabilidade. A existência de um público interessado e ávido de novas informações e pontos de vista de acordo com a nossa realidade.) *Viralata* (Artezanal, LP-A-003, 1979). Perhaps surprisingly, the determination to produce culture outside of a system under the control of both powerful record company executives and the State did not appear to result in particularly innovative, or overtly political music-making. (Krausche, *Música Popular Brasileira*, 92).

28. González and Treece, "Voices from the Silence", in *The Gathering of Voices*, 322–33.
29. The term "sonic anaphone" is used by musicologist Philip Tagg to refer to an item of musical structure that sounds like another sound, for example in rock music an electric guitar making a sound like a motorbike. "Fernando the Flute", seminar, Centre for the Study of Brazilian Culture and Society, King's College London, 13/03/97.
30. (Caetano Veloso: vozes superpostos, percussão sobre a pele e os ossos ...) Polygram, 824 691–1, 1987.
31. The Concretists included the work of the late Romantic and pre-Modernist poet, Joaquim de Sousândrade, in their project to republish and rediscover significant Brazilian writers.
32. (... um movimento brusco de autolibertação dentro da profissão: precisava me desembaraçar no estúdio, testar meus limites e forçar meus horizontes.) Veloso, *Verdade Tropical*, 488.
33. "Caetano vaiado pára *show* e xinga a platéia", Anon., *Jornal do Brasil*, 26/11/1973, and "Caetano: é preciso dar um tempo", Souza, *Jornal do Brasil*, 12/05/1974.
34. (Não estou me preocupando com o fácil, nem quero me comunicar mais a qualquer preço.) "Um novo interlúdio em busca das reinvenções", Castro, *O Globo*, 05/06/73.

Chapter 4

Language, Meaning and Memory: The Songwriting Tradition

"Long live our futile attempts to conquer language!"[1]

Caetano Veloso's work has always been concerned with the problems and pleasures of songwriting. In 1975 he released two albums that represent his most intense exploration of this concern. The songs on these albums enact struggles in the relationship between language and meaning, exposing the processes by which artistic meaning is produced. As listeners, we accompany these processes of "becoming" of meaning at a number of different moments: the emergence of ideas, their expression in a very elemental language, the proliferation of meaning in highly textured language, and the reworking of language which has become commonplace or clichéd. The songs on both of these albums also consider the ways in which cultural memory is formed, stored and transmitted in the musical and verbal language of popular song.

Luiz Tatit compares the songwriter with the figure of the *malandro*, who playfully and opportunistically manipulates words and melody to gain the confidence of the listener. The singer/songwriter must skilfully juggle the two elements within the song: the melodic continuity which carries the flow of vowel sounds in the lyrics, and the interruption, or segmentation of that flow by the consonants, into words, phrases and narratives. Negotiating between these two elements is what produces the unique diction of each singer/songwriter.[2] For Tatit, the balance between these two was to reach its peak in bossa nova, particularly in the diction of João Gilberto, in which words were fully integrated into the musical structures of the songs. In fact, Gilberto took the blurring of verbal language with melody and harmony to the point where language functioned almost as a mere vehicle for exploring the melodic contours of the song. In songs such as "Bim Bom" and "Hô-Bá-Lá-Lá" content is sacrificed completely in favour of the sonorous qualities of the words. Protest song would react strongly against this emphasis on form over content by focusing instead on the song lyrics and their vocalisation. As David Treece has observed:

> This vocal projection, by contrast with the integrated musical-lyrical texture of bossa nova, was now foregrounded in a rhythmically uttered, almost shouted delivery that disarticulated the tight polyrhythmic patterns of the earlier style into a series of crudely stressed pulses. Musical-lyrical tension, and the ironic complexities and ambiguities it generated, was replaced by an absolute equivalence of linguistic,

melodic and rhythmic value, each simply reinforcing the other in a kind of redundancy of meaning.[3]

Treece uses as an example leading protest songwriter and singer Geraldo Vandré, who ended up stripping away any musical features which were superfluous to his political message in the protest song anthem, "Caminhando (pra não dizer que não falei das flores)" (Marching [so you'll not say I didn't speak of flowers]). Songwriters like Vandré had pared down the musical idiom to the extent that it was difficult to envisage what the future of this kind of political songwriting might be, but it was a future that was, in any case, cut short by the declaration of the repressive Fifth Institutional Act (AI–5).[4]

The problems that faced the tradition of songwriting in Brazil at this time were also dramatised at the same festival at which Vandré sang "Caminhando", with Veloso's verbal assault on the public during the performance of "É Proibido Proibir" (Prohibiting Prohibited). Songwriting in Brazil had become polarised between uncritical partisanship and incomprehension. Veloso's criticism of the public suggested a crisis in the relationship between language and melody, "which would have to return to first principles, perhaps, to start from scratch, if it was to rebuild a new song tradition."[5] With Veloso facing imprisonment and then exile a few months after this showdown, and the stream-of-consciousness experimentation of the *Aracá Azul* (Blue Araçá) album aside, Veloso would not turn his attention to a detailed consideration of this new song tradition until his next studio albums in Brazil in 1975. The concern with starting from scratch is evident throughout these albums, with Veloso returning to the basics of artistic and linguistic meaning in this phase of his work. The song lyrics are a world away from the militant pronouncements of protest song, as well as the provocative juxtapositions of Tropicália, which often brought Brazil's diverse cultural influences into confrontation with each other. Instead, these lyrics elaborate a carefully crafted poetics based on a dialogue between these influences, delicately exploring crucial and complex creative issues.

Both albums, *Jóia* and *Qualquer Coisa*, should be taken together as complementary commentaries on these key issues that Veloso seeks to address, although they adopt different approaches to illuminating the creative process. Initially the titles appear to contradict each other, a "jewel", something of value, as opposed to just "anything". The cryptic statements about the albums in the record company's catalogue, however, provide the first clue that the titles are complementary rather than contrasting. The caption for *Jóia* asks "since when can anything not be a jewel, and a jewel not be anything?", while the caption for *Qualquer Coisa* states, "Anything can be a Jewel, depending entirely and exclusively on the way you see it, or rather, the way you hear it."[6] Indeed, an analysis of the albums reveals that the titles in fact point to that precious moment in artistic creation and communication when the indeterminate "anything" comes into being, becoming "something".

Each of the albums is accompanied by a short "manifesto", and in the manifesto of the *Jóia* album artistic inspiration is conveyed in terms of both joy and struggle. The manifesto also emphasises the idea of continuous cycles of productivity, resulting partly from the efforts of the artist, but also from something that has movement and a life of its own. Two facets of songwriting are suggested: concentrated artistic endeavour and its opposite – the idea of play, of performance as a state of pure being. Despite the reference to cycles of productivity, the conventional idea of historical cycles is critiqued in the manifesto. Instead, Veloso suggests the potential for transcending a sense of time which is tied to short-term economic, social and political cycles: "inspiration means: to be completely committed to the idea of a music set against those who speak in terms of the decade and forget the minute and the millennium."[7] By contrast, he proposes a connection between the immediate experience of the minute, which underlies artistic practice, and the temporality of the epoch. This approach directly contradicts the deep sense of historical evolutionism that characterised the ideological climate of the pre-coup period and the years immediately following the coup, before the imposition of the Fifth Institutional Act (AI–5). Veloso revives the debate on cultural memory by advocating a perspective that surpasses a conventional historical view of time, in favour of a temporality that embraces a wider concept of cultural heritage. The songs on this album represent a kind of re-evaluation and dramatisation of Brazil's cultural patrimony, viewing it not as the result of a succession of historical events, but the result of the continuity of ideas in the memory.

Benedict Anderson sees the writing of history as a way of bestowing continuity on events and conditions that may otherwise be forgotten.[8] This sets up a contrast between history and memory, with the former seen as a recording and interpreting of events, often by those who have not "made" this history, while the latter suggests a transmission of the experiences of those who have participated in these events. For Veloso, it is memory that is capable of providing the link between the two – between the "minute" and the "millennium" – a theme that resurfaces regularly in the songs. Of course, the fact that it is possible to lose memory emphasises its fragility, a characteristic that informs many of the songs. The very unreliability of memory, however, also makes it difficult to control and patrol, thus making it a potentially powerful tool for the disruption of hegemonic discourses. In these albums, popular song represents a site from which cultural memory is transmitted, with all of these complexities.

Veloso's exploration of the relationship between language and memory is profoundly influenced by the discourse of cannibalist consumption in Brazilian cultural expression. Oswald de Andrade's aggressive approach to the question of Brazil's cultural relations with Europe took the form of the *Manifesto Antropofágico (Ano 374 da Deglutição do Bispo Sardinha)* (Cannibalist Manifesto [in the 374th Year since the Devouring of Bishop Sardinha]) in 1928. The manifesto attacked both a purist view of national culture and wholesale imitation of foreign models. Instead, Oswald advocated a selective devouring of elements of foreign cultures, which could then be absorbed and transformed into Brazilian cultural products. In the late 1960s the metaphor of cannibalism would be revived in the context of the increasing internationalisation of Brazilian society, as a result of the economic policies implemented by the military regime. In 1967, the same year that José Celso Martinez staged his controversial version of Oswald's *O Rei da Vela* (The Candle King), a selection of Oswald's work edited by Haroldo de Campos was published. The Concretist poets had sought out Veloso shortly after his first festival appearance to discuss points of contact between their poetry and the new sound, and crucially, later introduced him to Oswald's work, which had provided intellectual support for Tropicalist ideas. The Concretist poets would soon draw heavily on a critical discourse of cannibalism in their theorisation of the poetics of translation. Haroldo de Campos elaborated the concept of "transcreation" to describe an approach to translation that involved the "revitalisation", "reinvention" or "recreation" of the original text in a Brazilian context.[9] The "transcreative" process was underlined by a concern with reciprocity: not only should the source and target texts inform each other, but the receiving text should also transform the original. In practice, this led to unprecedented freedom for the translator. For example, in Haroldo de Campos's translation of Goethe's *Faust*, the repeated echoes of Shakespeare contained in the original were "transcreated" by creating echoes of João Cabral de Melo Neto's *Morte e Vida Severina* in the Portuguese version.[10]

Veloso maintained a close intellectual friendship with the Concretists and was undoubtedly attracted to and influenced by the idea of transcreation. In 1968 he "transcreated" five songs from the Beatles' *White Album* into Portuguese for *Veja* magazine.[11] The poetics of transcreation is also evident in Veloso's songwriting, particularly in these 1975 albums. The focus of both albums is an examination of creative expression in Brazilian Portuguese, with *Jóia* exploring more closely the miscegenated nature of the language, due to the legacies and residues of indigenous and African languages, and *Qualquer Coisa* considering the interaction between Brazilian and international language and culture.

The songs enact their own process of becoming, referencing themselves in terms of existing traditions of song and poetry. This web of references is resistant to notions of musical and linguistic purity and reflects a process of translation through which Veloso acknowledges Brazilian society's condition of alterity, while simultaneously expressing a desire to be universal. Brazil's "otherness" is exemplified in the Portuguese language, which differentiates it even within the Latin American continent and which is frequently cited by performers as an obstacle to wider dissemination of their music. The translation process evident in the tradition of Brazilian popular song and highlighted in these albums recognises that a polyvalent expression is the only possible expression of Brazilian cultural memory. The condition which Brazil does share with the rest of Latin American society, what Néstor García Canclini has called "the multitemporal heterogeneity of modern culture",[12] means that in Brazil this expression draws on fragments from the past and the present: the remnants of indigenous and African musical and lyrical traditions, as well as the influence of music from Europe and the rest of Latin America. This kind of language reflects Perry Anderson's conjunctural concept of modernity as involving "the intersection of different temporalities" to create complex cultural configurations[13] and indeed, in Veloso's songs these temporalities are not ordered chronologically, but overlap. This lack of sequence means that language and the memory that sustains it are frequently inconsistent. As a result, the language of these two albums that address the question of cultural memory operates via a dynamic of instability and inconclusiveness.

The most prominent characteristic of the album *Jóia* is the frequency of repetition in the lyrics and melodies. This is pushed to its limits in some of the songs, in which Veloso appears to be making use of reiteration in order to reveal the elemental substance of verbal and musical language and cultural memory. The use of repetition conveys the sense of precariousness marking the two albums. While overwhelming repetition runs the risk of emptying language of its meanings, it may alternatively offer a chance to revitalise it and re-evaluate these meanings. Negotiating between these possibilities is what gives these songs their tension and instability. These are also conditions central to the writing of poetry and Veloso has identified João Cabral de Melo Neto as one of the most important influences on his work. In interview he has explained his attraction to Cabral's poetry – what he describes as "those quasi-rhymes" – as "a liking for a difficult beauty", describing the poet as "a man of disquiet".[14] The notion of difficulty and precariousness is exemplified in Cabral's "Psicologia da composição" (Psychology of Composition, 1946–7), in which poetic expression is described as:

Cultivar o deserto
como um pomar às avessas:
então nada mais
destila; evapora;
onde foi maçã
resta uma fome

onde foi palavra
(potros ou touros
contidos) resta a severa
forma do vazio.[15]

(Cultivating the desert/ like an orchard in reverse/ then nothing more/ distils; it evaporates/ where there was an apple/ there remains a hunger/ where there was a word/ corralled colts or penned bulls/ there remains the harsh/ silhouette of emptiness.)

In the same interview Veloso explains that he sees Cabral's poetry as a process of stripping away the layers of language, retexturing and recombining words.

The Cabralian method of examining a word, image or idea repeatedly, until it has yielded up a range of possibilities, is a key feature of the album *Jóia*. The predominant concept of the album revolves around the image of birds and this is conveyed visually, linguistically and musically. The album cover features a nude portrait of Veloso and his family, surrounded by birds. When the album cover was censored because of the nudity, the family portrait was excised, leaving only Veloso's drawing of the birds in flight. The link between the human figures in their natural state and the birds adds to the album's recognition of music as a cultural product, the notion that the origins of music lie in nature, specifically birdsong.[16] The nudity and natural state of being symbolise the album's intention to return to basics. The songs attempt to recover memory by going back to beginnings, but the return, while pointing to the possibilities for understanding the present that lie in the past, is fraught with difficulties.

Let us consider some of the songs from *Jóia* that explore the creative possibilities, as well as the precariousness of a return to origins in language and memory. The relation between song and nature, with song portrayed as an organic entity evolving out of a symbiotic relationship with its creator, is the structuring principle of the song "Asa, asa" (Wing, wing). The song is constructed around a more or less unaltered percussive line, with no accompanying strings or keyboards. This underlines the repetition of the word "pássaro" (bird), the root of the song from which other words appear to sprout, with the vocalising of these different words adding texture to the sound and propelling the movement of the song:

"Pássaro um
Pássaro pairando
Pássaro momento
Pássaro ar
Pássaro ímpar
Parou pousar
Parou repousar
Pássaro som
Pássaro parado
Pássaro silêncio
Pássaro ir
Pássaro ritmo
Pássar voou
Passar avoou".

(Bird alone/ Bird hovering/ Bird moment/ Bird air/ Bird without equal/ Stopped came to rest/ Stopped to rest/ Bird sound/ Bird stood still/ Bird silence/ Bird going/ Bird rhythm/ Bird flew/ Bird a-flew.)

The repetition generates language and creates relationships between time and space (momento/ar), sound and silence (silêncio/som), written language and orality/memory (voou/avoou). These relationships are not stable ones, however, as many of the words have different layers of meaning. The word "pairar" is most emblematic of this instability, meaning "to hover", as well as "to be imminent", "to hesitate" and "to suffer". It is one of several verbs of movement that are held in a tense balance with other verbs that denote a halt to this movement of language and the consequent threat of silence. Additionally, "pairar" has other connotations, deriving from the Latin *pariare*, meaning "to be equal". This contrasts with "ímpar" (line 5) which suggests being "without equal" and undermines our complacency about meaning: some of these words may have similar connotations, but essentially, individual words are without equal and full of different possibilities. This idea of the shifting possibilities of language is dramatised by the addition of a prefix that confers a different meaning or adds shades of nuance to a word. "Pousar" (land) therefore becomes "repousar" (rest) and "voou" (flew) becomes "avoou", similar in meaning, but a word that is associated with popular speech. This method of "prefixing" was already explored in Veloso's rock song "Relance" (co-written with Pedro Novis) and recorded by Gal Costa on her *Índia* album:

PARE	REPARE
CITE	RECITE
SALVE	RESSALVE
VOLTE	REVOLTE
TRATE	RETRATE
VELE	REVELE ...[17]
(STOP	NOTICE
CITE	RECITE
SAVE	SAFEGUARD
RETURN	REVOLT
TREAT	RETRACT
HIDE	REVEAL)

Such songs reveal the inner workings of the language and invite us to enter into the structures of the songs. The participatory nature of this kind of creative expression is lent even more significance in 1975, during a certain relaxation of military rule that would lead to the policy of *abertura* under the Figueiredo administration. It reflects a degree of optimism in the possibilities for audience interaction with the performer. This lies at the heart of Veloso's concept of communication in popular song, the opportunity for the artist and the listener to interact and for the latter to participate in a song's creative development. In "Asa, asa", we accompany this movement and are returned to an originary point of communication, when the song ends on an inconclusive repeat-to-fade of the performer's voice imitating the sound of birdsong. This return to origins seems to invite us as listeners to recover, reinterpret and appropriate cultural memory in our own way.

Other songs on the album, such as "Gravidade" (Gravity) and "Tudo, tudo, tudo" (Everything, everything, everything), continue "Asa, asa's" exploration of the dynamic yet fragile nature of communication. The songs struggle against the threat of silence and nothingness, not only in the imagery of the lyrics, but in the pauses and disruptions in the music and vocals. The interplay between sound and silence reflects the constant threat of losing the thread of memory. However, the songs are supported by very regular rhythms: the song form of "Tudo, tudo, tudo", for example, is a lullaby, a repetitive form associated with earliest childhood memories. Faced with the precariousness of memory, rhythm here functions as a bulwark against forgetting. Many of the songs on this album have insistent and regular percussive lines that give a clear impression of the marking of time. In "Pipoca Moderna" (Modern Popcorn), the percussion is meant to evoke the sound of popcorn, as words "pop" out of nothing, but it also resembles the sound of a ticking clock. The effect is to create an acute sense of time in the present, but also of the passing of time, of the present slipping rapidly away from us, even as we are made aware of it. Within the temporal continuum of the song, this establishes a tense and transient link between the present and memory that is also evident in the song "Lua, lua, lua, lua" (Moon, moon, moon, moon).

However, while "Pipoca Moderna" is dominated by a sense of continuous movement and sound,[18] "Lua, Lua, Lua, Lua" is dominated by the very real threat of the halting of movement and of silence. In this song the relationship between silence and sound is extremely tense. The repetition of the word "lua" in the title and in the first and last lines, as well as the parallel repetition of "branca" (white, blank) do not convey the sense of the multiplying of meaning through reiteration which is evident in other songs. Instead, that repeated image of the moon's whiteness, or blankness, suggests a void that imposes itself despite the fleeting moments of communication:

> Lua, lua, lua, lua
> Por um momento
> Meu canto contigo compactua
> E mesmo o vento
> Canta-se compacto no tempo
> Estanca
> Branca, branca, branca, branca
> A minha, nossa voz atua sendo silêncio
> Meu canto não tem nada a ver
> Com a lua
> Lua, lua, lua, lua

(Moon, moon, moon, moon/ For a moment/ My song makes a [com]pact with you/ And even the wind/ Sings itself compact in time/ Stagnates/ Blank, blank, blank, blank/ My, our voice acts out silence/ My song has nothing to do/ With the moon/ Moon, moon, moon, moon)

The "pact" between the object and its artistic representation, which creates meaning, is soon dissolved, causing memory (momento, tempo) to stagnate and the expression of it (canto) to become unreliable, when the collective voice (a minha, nossa voz) is reduced to silence; this is also suggested in the melodic movement of the song, which frequently appears to have ground to a halt. In the fourth and fifth lines of this verse, the relationship between the object and its representation is exposed as being an arbitrary one, leading to a crisis of meaning.

"Lua, Lua, Lua, Lua" also considers the transient presence of song, whose performance represents a few moments in time, as opposed to the enduring presence of the written word. Song's ability to communicate – to create a relationship with the listener and be retained in the memory – is contingent upon these few, precarious moments. This provisionality makes the relationship between verbal and musical language and between memory and meaning a problematic one. The song's reflection on the materiality and immateriality of artistic language and the play on an apparent arbitrariness of meaning in the last three lines, echo some of the concerns of Concretist poetry, in particular Haroldo de Campos's "Branco" (White/Blank):

branco	branco	branco	branco
vermelho			
estanco	vermelho		
	espelho	vermelho	
		estanco	branco
white	white	white	white
red			
I stagnate	red		
	mirror	red	
		I stagnate	blank

Here the reality of the space on the page that is "branco", is juxtaposed with the arbitrariness of the written sign "branco", making the physical space not just an active and integral part of the text structurally, but also semantically, as the meaning of the verbal sign.

As early as 1966, Veloso's songwriting contribution to that year's music festivals had aroused the interest of Augusto de Campos. His relationship with the Campos brothers and Décio Pignatari was established soon afterwards, as the Tropicalists found that they shared the Concretists' need to defend themselves from the nationalistic cultural left. The influence of the Concretists' radical approach to language is evident in Veloso's work. However, Veloso's concern to create a dialogue with the reader contrasts with the didacticism evident in Concretist poetry, which often failed to involve the reader in the process of the poem's creation:

> Indeed, to read a Concretist poem ... is a disheartening experience, for one is not being invited to participate actively and critically in a process of communication. Instead, the possibilities of communication are pre-determined by the internal relationships between the various "verbivocovisual elements" of the poem. In the end the reader must accept the rules of the poem's structure and consume it, or be

excluded by it; however complex and sophisticated it is, that structure remains inert, immune to interrogation and dialogue ..."[19]

In "Lua, Lua, Lua Lua", the intimate timbre of the voice is aimed at involving the listener and we accompany the creative process in the sounds and silences of the voice and of the spare musical arrangement.

José Miguel Wisnik has made an insightful survey of the role of urban popular music in Brazil in creating a dialogue between literature and song.[20] Wisnik uses the song "A terceira margem do rio" (The Third Bank of the River [1992]) (music by Milton Nascimento, lyrics by Veloso) to exemplify the range of conditions which affect the production of popular song in Brazil. The song is inspired by João Guimarães Rosa's short story, in which silence and death are the central themes. In the story, a father builds himself a canoe and abandons the family home to float in perpetuity on a river. Death – the unspeakable – is allegorised as the flow of the river back on itself, an image that suggests both the perpetual and the provisional. The imagery and the use of repetition recall the *Jóia* songs and the song also echoes *Jóia*'s concern with the endurance of language and the word in spite of their fragility and inconsistencies: "the lyrics of the song leave their own trace on the surface of the water (parallel and interior to the rhythm and to the melody) as a place for speech, or at least for a speech which inscribes and then dissolves meanings in all their contradictions ...".[21] Throughout his career, therefore, but particularly evident in *Jóia* and *Qualquer Coisa*, Veloso uses the popular song form as a vehicle for focusing on the creation of poetic language.

The dialogue with the Modernist tradition that produces a cannibalist cultural borrowing is evident throughout these albums and additionally, there are unmistakeable echoes of Oswald's poetics in the lyrics of the song "Jóia". The song is structured like one of his highly expressive and compressed poem-vignettes, in which the traditional and the modern are juxtaposed to reveal the peculiarities of modern Brazil:

Beira de mar,
Beira de mar,
Beira de mar é na América do Sul
Um selvagem levanta o braço
Abre a mão e tira um caju
Um momento de grande amor
De grande amor

Copacabana, Copacabana
Louca total e completamente louca
A menina muito contente
Toca Coca-Cola na boca
Um momento de puro amor
De puro amor

(Sea shore/ Sea shore/ Sea shore in South America/ A savage raises his arm/ Opens his hand and picks a cashew/ A moment of profound love/ Of profound love/ Copacabana, Copacabana/ Total madness and totally mad/ A very contented girl/ Caresses her lips with Coca-Cola/ A moment of pure love/ Of pure love)

Here the idea of memory as the "minute" and the "millennium" surfaces once again. At its centre is the idea of human agency and intervention in history, in the figures of the Indian and the girl whose actions in the two scenes serve to link the moment to Brazil's epochal cultural heritage. The song expresses a view of history and development that opposes the positivist notion of linear progress as the goal of history – the precept on which the Brazilian nation was built. The pre-capitalist image of the Indian in an as yet unnamed territory (unnamed by Europeans and therefore not yet fixed in official history) contrasts sharply with the urban scene of Copacabana and the prominent icon of capitalism that is Coca-Cola. The two are presented as parallel images, reinforced by the parallel structure of the two halves of the song and the similarity of the sounds Copacabana/Coca-Cola.

The two moments may be equated as coexisting momentary experiences of the sublime. On one level, this portrayal of potentially creative, innocent moments and the tenderly intoned vocals, echo the optimism of Oswald's cultural cannibalism, with its revitalisation of culture through the dialectic between the traditional and the modern. The idea of the continuity of memory conveyed in the parallel images confers historical significance on the aesthetics of repetition underlying the album. This view of repetition as continuity and endurance is also seen for example in "Canto do povo de um lugar" (Song of a People from Somewhere) which presents a universal life cycle of joys and sorrows marked by song, tears and dance. In such songs, music is shown to tap into a different temporality which is not so much historical as ritual. Here the exercise of cultural memory does not serve to refer us back to the historical past as such, but to certain cultural forms of the past. This practice of cultural memory is problematic because it runs the risk of disconnecting the past from the context of its specific historical moment. It could be argued that while seeking to challenge the hegemonic discourses that have manipulated the past into a linear narrative, Veloso runs the risk of producing another narrativisation of the past, without sufficiently interrogating it.

On another level, the song "Jóia" can be seen as suggesting that it is futile to attempt to resolve the tension existing between these two temporalities. Perhaps the parallel is intended to invite contrast rather than comparison, with the first verse citing or referring to an over-determined discourse (of natural and colonial origins) that can then be contrasted with Veloso's own use of this discourse in the second verse.[22] This interpretation produces a tension within the song. The two verses are linked by the same rhythm and by their lyrical structure, creating an effect of continuity, yet the contrasting images of the lyrics point to radical change and disruption. The tension between the two challenges notions of the "authentic roots" of the Brazilian nation. In this reading, continuity of memory does not imply continuousness of memory, in the sense of a memory that has not been subject to repression, disruption and transformation. As Rowe and Schelling observe: "To think of a single, continuous popular memory is to indulge in mythology. And without forgetting, or the alteration of the structures of memory, there can be no invention or creativity."[23]

The album *Qualquer Coisa* focuses closely on the processes of alteration to a cultural memory portrayed as a tense series of relationships, interactions and dialogues. The title song enacts attempts at communication between two people, in which they manage to close some of the distance between them, only to see the fragile threads of meaning they have spun break and have to be rebuilt:

> Esse papo já tá qualquer coisa
> Você já tá pra lá de Marraqueche
> Mexe qualquer coisa dentro doida
> Já qualquer coisa doida dentro mexe
> Não se avexe não baião de dois
> Deixe de manha deixe de manha deixe de manha

(This chat of ours is taking shape/ But you're already way out of reach/ Something crazy's stirring inside/ Already something crazy stirs inside me/ Don't let our two-step make you mad/ Leave off the tricks leave off the tricks leave off the tricks)

In this song we accompany this process of unravelling that is artistic creation, likened to the spinning of a delicate spider's web, which breaks easily when communication creates resentment or becomes misleading. The conversation is already taking form (qualquer coisa), although the challenge to overcome the communicative distance is great (pra lá de Marraqueche). The idea has been born (qualquer coisa doida), but attempts to convey it bring frustration, as the speaker and interlocutor dance around meaning (Não se avexe não baião de dois), which can be obscured by artifice (Deixe de manha).

Whereas poetic expression in *Jóia* is extremely succinct and compressed, the *Qualquer Coisa* album is much more wordy. The title song exemplifies the multiplying of meaning when the image of the spider is introduced:

> Sem essa aranha sem essa aranha sem essa aranha
> Nem a sanha arranha o carro nem o sarro arranha a espanha
> meça tamanha meça tamanha
> esse papo seu já tá de manhã

(Without that spider weaving, weaving/ Even your wrath won't scratch the surface leave a trace on this place/ a measure so great a measure too late/ this chat of yours is out of date)

Language depends on these precarious attempts to weave meaning, but the very proliferation of words and meanings can present a threat to communication. The mutation of the words conveys the slipperiness of meaning: "aranha" (spider), associated with creative labour, becomes "arranha" (scratch), which suggests destructiveness, but which also has the second meaning, "to speak a language imperfectly", or may perhaps be a reference to the etching of ideas in memory. In these two lines words appear to metamorphose in and out of each other until they become "immeasurable", and appear as a flawed attempt to communicate, to speak a language whose meanings elude the addressee (esse papo seu já tá de manhã). The voice relishes the shifting, sliding sounds of the words, and the inconclusive nature of the problem posed is also conveyed in the music, whose melodies are circular and playfully elusive.

In addition to its linguistic profusion, the practice of cultural borrowing also forms part of the central aesthetics of the *Qualquer Coisa* album. There are many cover versions on the album, with original compositions constituting only a third of the material. These covers allow Veloso to explore the notion of transcreation in the area of popular music. The manifesto for the album emphasises the idea of artistic re-creation through interpretation of the work of others, and through a fertile crossing of the genres which make up Brazil's highly varied musical expression:

VII   jazz carioca. samba paulista. rock baiano. baião mineiro.
VIII   jazz carioca feito por mineiros. samba paulista feito por baianos. baião mineiro feito por cariocas. rock baiano feito por paulistas.[24]

(VII   jazz from Rio. samba from São Paulo. rock from Bahia. baião from Minas Gerais.
VIII   jazz from Rio made by musicians from Minas. samba from São Paulo made by Bahians. baião from Minas made by musicians from Rio. Bahian rock made by musicians from São Paulo.)

The album is a site in which not only do different artistic materials meet, but also different temporalities:

XI   a década e a eternidade, o século e o momento, o minuto e a historia.
(XI   the decade and eternity, the century and the moment, the minute and history.)

The manifesto makes explicit Veloso's concern to transcend historical time and link the "minute" and the "millennium" by experimenting with different styles and traditions. The cover versions therefore chart aspects of Brazil's musical heritage, including Chico Buarque's 1969 composition "Samba e Amor" (Samba and Love), which focuses on popular song as communication and as a way of mediating personal and social relationships. The choice of this classic of Buarque's repertoire pays homage to one of the most censored composers of the dictatorship. In the song samba creates solidarity, companionship and hope in terrible times and is a transgressive form of expression that must be conducted in secret.

By following "Samba e Amor" with another cover titled "Madrugada e Amor" (Daybreak and Love, by José Messias) Veloso immediately points to the links and continuities in the tradition of Brazilian popular music. Yet, as mentioned earlier, it is the alterations and transformations to this tradition that allow for creativity and inventiveness. The ideas and images that accrue in the memory and constitute a repository of the language of popular music, evident here in the similarity of imagery between the two songs, are always subject to elaboration or re-articulation to provide different meanings in different contexts. While José Messias's composition is a beautifully simple love song, Chico Buarque's love song has a powerful political message. In Veloso's cover version, this message is emphasised in the deliberate nature of the vocalisation, the dramatic pauses, the point at which the pitch rises so high it seems that the voice has been taken to its limits and will break, that communication will fail, as opposed to the more straightforward and upbeat rendering of the Messias cover.

The range of cover versions therefore points to diverse antecedents and influences in Brazilian popular music. Apart from traditional samba and Chico Buarque's bossa nova-influenced samba, these include Jorge Ben's fusion of rhythm and blues with samba, linking Afro-American musical expression with Afro-Brazil; the contribution of music from the rest of Latin America, evident in a Portuguese version of Eliseo Grenet's "Drume Negrita" and in the homage to Peru's La Chabuca Grande, in the rendering of "La Flor de la Canela"; and prominently, the music of the Beatles.

The inclusion of "Help" on the *Jóia* album gives a foretaste of the concern with the Beatles which is a preoccupation of the *Qualquer Coisa* album, with no fewer than three consecutive Beatles songs covered. These songs acknowledge the huge influence of the Beatles on Veloso's generation and the way in which he anthropophagically "devoured" the Beatles during the Tropicália period. Veloso was also attracted to the ways in which the Beatles manipulated language, crafting their most memorable songs out of the most quotidian and colloquial speech. Although the use of everyday language is a common feature of popular song lyricism, the Beatles' genius is often acknowledged as a heightened ability to "take a well-worn phrase and make it new again", to release "the syllables that locked a phrase up and were begging to be prodded": "The sudden shift of weight to an unexpected place continually brought the listener's attention to the language itself, engendering a startled awareness of the essentially poetic nature of the flat phrases he'd been living with for years."[25]

Veloso's interpretation of "Help" casts a different light on one of the most famous pop songs of all time. The pace is slowed right down and the timbre of the voice conveys melancholy and vulnerability, which matches more closely the lyrical content of the song. The dynamic of the original relied on a certain disjuncture between the pathos of the plea for help and the upbeat delivery and musical arrangement and playful, textured vocalisation. By stripping the accompaniment to one guitar and laying the vocals bare, Veloso foregrounds one element of the mood and message of the original, the feeling of insecurity and self-doubt, without the upbeat façade with which the subject voice in the original tries to mask the feeling of defencelessness. The idea of re-articulation, of transformation through translation is emphasised in this cover version, in which Veloso's voice and slightly accented English confer difference and a certain strangeness on a song which forms a part of the cultural memory of many people all over the world. The focus then is on the act of interpreting the Beatles, of re-creating the Beatles in the voice of someone else. This is even echoed in the design of the *Qualquer Coisa* album, which makes an explicit reference to the graphics of the *Let It Be* album.

The main concern underlying the *Qualquer Coisa* album is to point to a repository of memory and language from which the traditions and contemporary expression of Brazilian popular music emerge. Since 1975 Veloso has repeatedly returned to these considerations, most recently in the album *Noites do Norte* (2000). I choose to conclude this chapter, however, with the song "Língua" (Language) from the 1984 album *Velô*,[26] because it returns so explicitly to the chief concerns of the 1975 albums. These are summed up in the rallying cry contained in the chorus – "Minha pátria é minha língua!" (My country is my language!) – a reference to Fernando Pessoa's famous words, defiantly appropriated from the Portuguese poet. The song examines the language that has emerged and is still emerging in Brazil, as a result of the particular shaping of cultural memory. The first verse points to the historical origins of the language in Portugal and the particularities and baroque richness of Portuguese. However, Brazilian Portuguese is shown to have developed its own unique form of expression, as seen in the writing of Guimarães Rosa and the carnivalised popular expression of the Mangueira samba school:

> Gosto de sentir a minha língua roçar
> A língua de Luís de Camões
> Gosto de ser e de estar
> E quero me dedicar
> A criar confusões de prosódia
> E uma profusão de paródias
> Que encurtem dores
> E furtem cores como camaleões
> Gosto do Pessoa na pessoa
> Da rosa no Rosa
> E sei que a poesia está para a prosa
> Assim como o amor está para a amizade
> E quem há de negar que está lhe é superior
> E deixa os portugais morrerem à míngua
> "Minha pátria é minha língua"
> Fala Mangueira!
> Fala!

(I like to feel my tongue caress/ The language of Luís de Camões/ I like to be and I like being/ And I want to dedicate myself/ To creating prosodic confusion/ And parodic profusion/ That kill pain/ And steal colours like chameleons/ I like the persona in Pessoa/ The rose in Rosa/ And I know that poetry is to prose as love is to friendship/ And who dares to deny that the latter is superior?/ And leave the Portuguese to languish/ "My country is my language!"/ Tell them Mangueira!/ Tell them like it is!)

The delivery and format of the song is rap, a song form whose use of the vernacular as the basis for highly inventive verbal contests marks out and celebrates difference, while simultaneously protesting against social exclusion. Veloso cannibalises rap, mixing it with samba, which had historically exercised similar functions in Brazilian society, and had suffered first censorship, then appropriation and officialisation by the state. The fusion of rap and samba in "Língua" suggests that contemporary Brazilian language is the result of a criss-crossing of cultural forms and frontiers. The interaction and dialogue of cultures is reiterated in the chorus, sung by the sambista Elza Soares, which points out that Brazilian Portuguese has a past which goes back to the ancient territory of Latium, but that the language has been reinvented and re-articulated in Brazil to create new words, new forms of expression, new possibilities:

> Flor do Lácio Sambódromo
> Lusamérica Latim em pó
> O que quer
> O que pode
> Esta língua?

(Flower of the Latium Sambadrome/ Pulverised Lusoamerican Latin/ What does this language want?/ What can it do?)

This creative translation of continental Portuguese is explored in the second verse, in which Brazilian Portuguese is shown to exist not as a monolithic whole, but as a process of constantly proliferating variants, including that of the regional (São Paulo), youth culture (surfers), self-parody (Carmen Miranda), the marriage of traditional and modern (Chico Buarque's sambas), and media speak (TV Globo).

The final verse opens with an ironic comment on the extraordinary role played by popular music in Brazil as a site for the development and exchange of ideas. Following on from the idea of the diversity of language, in this verse Veloso revises some of the institutionalised ideas of Brazil's cultural patrimony. The song calls for a recognition that the relationship between different aspects of Brazilian cultural expression is far more complex than is evident in official portrayals. It is necessary to acknowledge this complexity (prosa caótica [chaotic prose]), which includes Brazilian creative forms with an international outlook, such as Concrete poetry, for a long time not accepted by Brazilian cultural critics, and international influences such as rap, with its political, racial agenda. Additionally, Veloso pays homage to slang as an expression of shared identity and as a means of rapid communication among marginalised groups. The song ends with a tongue-in-cheek acknowledgement and celebration of the vitality of the transformations of language produced by new socio-historical conditions, the reach of the mass media and new technologies:

> Se você tem uma idéia incrível
> É melhor fazer uma canção
> Está provado que só é possível
> Filosofar em alemão …
> A língua é minha pátria
> E eu não tenho pátria: tenho mátria
> E quero frátria
> Poesia concreta e prosa caótica
> Ótica futura
> Tá craude brô[27] você e tu lhe amo
> Qué queu te faço, nego?
> Bote ligeiro
> Samba-rap, chic-left com banana[28]
> Será que ele está no Pão de Açucar
> Nós canto-falamos como quem inveja negros
> Que sofrem horrores no Gueto do Harlem
> Livros, discos, vídeos à mancheia
> E deixa que digam, que pensem, que falem!

(If you have a great idea/ It's always best to express it in song/ There's proof it's only possible/ To philosophise in the German tongue …/ My language is my fatherland/ but I don't have a fatherland: I have a motherland/ And I want a brotherland/ Concrete poetry and chaotic prose/ Vision of the future/ It's cool bro' love ya baby/ What-can-I-do-for-you, my man/ Chill out/ Samba-rap, chic-Left with bananas/ And we find all this on the Sugar Loaf Mountain?/ We sing-speak like we envy blacks/ Who suffer horrors in the ghettoes of Harlem/ When we have so many books, records, videos of our own/ Let them tell it, let them think, let them speak!)

The hybrid and continually mutating language portrayed in "Língua" reflects Veloso's perception of the way in which cultural memory works. It was a perception that split the Brazilian music scene in the highly charged atmosphere of the late 1960s, only allowing for considered reflection when the nationalist debate had cooled. The legacy of his approach to memory and tradition is perhaps evident in some of the most vibrant musical forms and movements in Brazil in recent times. For these movements, such as hip hop in São Paulo and Rio, or manguebeat in the North-east, the question of the relationship of cultural memory to national and international traditions continues to be central to contemporary Brazilian musical expression. Veloso's concern to create a dialogue between the national and the international, and between memory and the present, played a major role in legitimising musical hybridity as a means of articulating cultural identity in the face of the changing conditions of Brazilian society.

Notes

1. (Viva as inúteis conquistas da linguagem!) Veloso, from sleeve notes for album *Barra 69*, reprinted in Salomão (ed.), *Alegria, Alegria*, 28.
2. Tatit, *O Cancionista*, 9–11.
3. Treece, "Rhythm and Poetry", 34.
4. Treece, "Rhythm and Poetry", 36.
5. Treece, "Rhythm and Poetry", 37.
6. (desde quando qualquer coisa não é jóia, e jóia não é qualquer coisa?) (*Qualquer Coisa* pode ser *Jóia*, dependendo única e exclusivamente do ponto de vista; ou melhor, do ponto de audição.) Philips Catalogue, 09/1975.
7. (inspiração quer dizer: estar cuidadosamente entregue ao projeto de uma música posta contra aqueles que falam em termos de década e esquecem o minuto e o milênio.)
8. Anderson, *Imagined Communities*, 204–5.
9. Vieira, "Liberating Calibans", 96.
10. Vieira, "Liberating Calibans", 106–7.
11. See Fonseca, *Esse Cara*, 74–7 for these "transcreations".
12. (la heterogeneidad multitemporal de la cultura moderna) Canclini, *Culturas híbridas*, 67.
13. Anderson, "Marshall Berman: Modernity and Revolution", 34.
14. "Música Popular Brasileira: Entrevistado – Caetano Veloso", cassette, 13/02/87, from a series of interviews, Museu da Imagem e do Som, São Paulo.
15. Cabral, *João Cabral de Melo Neto: Antologia Poética*, 187–8.
16. See Storr, *Music and the Mind*, 3–7 for a summary of some of the arguments for and against the idea that human music originated in the imitation of birdsong.
17. Philips, 6349.077, 1973.
18. Christopher Dunn sees the popping of corn in this song as a reference to the eruption of irrepressible forms of opposition to military rule. *Brutality Garden*, 187.
19. González and Treece, *The Gathering of Voices*, 245–6.
20. Wisnik, "The Gay Science", 191–202.
21. Wisnik, "The Gay Science", 201.
22. I wish to thank William Rowe for drawing my attention to the presence of this over-determined discourse in the song.
23. Rowe and Schelling, *Memory and Modernity*, 233.
24. Veloso, *Alegria, Alegria*, 165.
25. Clive James, quoted by Frith, *Music For Pleasure*, 122.
26. In addition to being part of Veloso's surname, "Velô" was contemporary slang for "velocidade". In "Língua" the length and wordiness of the lyrics call for flexibility and speed in the rap vocalisation and in the song Veloso refers to the "velô da dicção choo choo de Carmem Miranda" (the speed of Carmen Miranda's 'choo-choo' diction).
27. From English "crowd" and "brother".
28. Reference to the 1959 samba-bop "Chiclete com Banana" (Chewing-gum with Banana, by Gordurinha [Waldeck Artur de Macedo] and Almira Castilho) first made famous by Jackson do Pandeiro and recorded by Gilberto Gil in 1972. The song is a light-hearted reaction to the influence of American music on Brazilian: "Eu só boto

be-bop no meu samba/ Quando o Tio Sam tocar um tamborim/ quando ele pegar num pandeiro e num zabumba/ quando ele aprender que o samba não é rumba/ aí eu vou misturar Miami com Copacabana/ chiclete eu misturo com banana ..." (I'll only put some be-bop in my samba/ When Uncle Sam starts beating on a drum/ when he picks up a tambourine and a *zabumba* (bass drum)/ when he learns that samba is not the same as rumba/ Only then will I mix Miami with Copacabana/ chewing-gum I'll mix with banana ...).

Chapter 5
The Tradition of the Love Song in Brazil

> young men and ladies sang love songs so immodest, that I blushed with shame as if I had suddenly found myself in a brothel, surrounded by women of ill-repute. In the old days our young people listened to and sang songs of war, which inspired boldness and courage. Today, however, one hears only sighing love songs, about dalliances, flowery courtships and dandies. This plague is widespread these days since Caldas began to perform his romantic ballads, and compose verses for women.[1]

When the mulatto songwriter Domingos Caldas Barbosa arrived in Lisbon from Rio de Janeiro in 1775, he brought with him a song form that caused a stir in the court of Queen Maria I. The *modinha* – a Brazilianised version of the Portuguese *moda* – brought a new tone of directness to discourses of love, and a freedom which was associated with colonial society, but which struck a responsive chord in a courtly scene animated since the mid 18th century by the increasing number of great families gaining wealth from Brazilian gold mines, and after a prolonged period dominated by the strict moral codes of the Inquisition.[2] The popularity of the Brazilian *modinha* in Portugal in the late 18th century represented a kind of "invasion" of the metropolis by the romantic sensibilities of the colony, which were associated with a particularly Brazilian sensuality. Writing in the 1960s, Brazilian musicologist Mozart de Araújo commented on the legacy of the *modinha*: "They say that the *modinha* is dead. I disagree, because it has transcended the song form, it has become our very soul. It is present in the very essence of who we are as Brazilians."[3] In somewhat less exalted terms, critic Bruno Kiefer described the urban *modinha* as a "a way of being which is particular to our (Brazilian) romantic sensibility."[4] Both claims for the *modinha* touch on questions of identity, both statements link existential states with national feeling. These statements recognise the *modinha*'s language of love as a means of dealing with an aspect of social identity.

José Ramos Tinhorão has observed that the new, direct treatment of love in song was facilitated by an unprecedented interaction between men and women in public and represented the creative projection of the changes occurring in society as a result of urbanisation. Tinhorão also claims that being less influenced than the metropolis by the weight of behavioural norms and conventions, Brazilian colonial society was somewhat more dynamic in terms of class interaction, and its cultural forms reflected this.[5]

The singing of *modinhas* became a prominent feature of a very incipient middle sector of society. The development of the *modinha* from the mid 18th century represents the first case in which a musical form acts as a vehicle of both popular and erudite expression in Brazil, "and a new kind of urban, bohemian *modinha* singer, who specialised in serenades would give a voice to this romantic sentiment, definitively popularising the new form with his mulatto irreverence."[6] The mediation between high and popular forms was enhanced further from the mid 19th century by a generation of Romantic novelists and poets based in Rio de Janeiro, including José de Alencar, Gonçalves Dias, Gonçalves de Magalhães and Laurindo Rabelo. Part of a circle of intellectuals grouped around the figure of the mulatto poet and publisher Francisco de Paula Brito, the Romantics sought out and collaborated with street musicians, creating partnerships between romantic lyric-writing and the music of popular composers. The poetics of the *modinha* at this time left its legacy on the form long after the involvement of these intellectuals, as popular *modinha* performers sought to imitate the language of the Romantics. The use of ornate and complex language, in particular, reflected the social and cultural aspirations of these predominantly mulatto performers in urban centres across Brazil.[7]

Studies of the *modinha* tend to assume that what can be said within this form is quite unambiguous. Indeed, a number of clear themes emerge repeatedly, such as scenarios of desperate, unrequited love and idealisation of the object of love, as does a fairly stock romantic imagery, frequently derived from nature and from religious suffering and exaltation. However, while *modinha* lyrics may in general seem hyperbolic and clichéd to us today, they were frequently considered quite risqué by the form's contemporary public. Additionally, the manner in which they were performed also imbued the songs with an intense sensuality. Examining *modinha* performance allows us to understand how romance, love and questions of gender are problematised in the form, even as it expresses the predefined ideologies of the patriarchal society out of which it arose. How, then, did the *modinha* facilitate the translation of social and cultural rhetoric into an individual emotional experience?

One answer to this must surely lie in the vocal styles and gestures of *modinha* singers. Despite the lingering influence of *bel canto*, the tone of the *modinha* was for the most part one of "simplicity, intimacy, sweetness and longing".[8] A 1787 account by Lord Beckford, England's ambassador to Portugal at a time when Caldas Barbosa was popularising the form in Lisbon, highlights the effects of the corporeality of *modinha* performance on the listener:

> They consist of languid, interrupted rhythms, as if an excess of rapture had made the singer short of breath and as if the soul longed to be joined with its mate, the object of its affections. With innocent ease, they insinuate themselves into your heart, before it has had time to defend itself from their seductive influence; imagine, if you will, sipping milk, when in fact it is the poison of voluptuousness which is penetrating the most intimate recesses of your being.[9]

This quotation highlights very effectively the extent to which the rhythm of the *modinha* is subordinate to the vocalisations of its performance. Additionally, Lord Beckford's observations also point to the fact that the sensual and the sublime are not mutually exclusive, that music with a slow pace, which focuses on melody, can be as erotic as more rhythmic music, such as the *lundu*. This idea is reinforced by Modernist poet, ethnographer and musicologist, Mário de Andrade, in the quotation used under the entry on the *modinha* in his *Dicionário Musical Brasileiro*:

> In the silence of the night the tender couplets floated on the weeping chords of the guitars. The melancholy and longing spread over the velvety sound of the bass in the minor key. The amorous joy was accompanied by arpeggios and accidentals of such intense eroticism that it made the whole audience sigh with sensual pleasure.[10]

Secondly, it is impossible to remove the *modinha* from its contemporary performance context, especially since, as previously mentioned, the *modinha* articulated for its public nascent forms of social conduct in urban Brazil, such as the increased visibility of women and approximation between the genders in public places. From the second half of the 19th century one of the main performing spaces for the *modinha* was the street, in the form of the serenade. The serenade constitutes an exposé of male sentimentality; not only is the irrational, emotional language conventionally associated with women taken on by male voices, but these private desires are made very public by their performance in the street. Additionally, it constitutes a moment when the organisation of social space into house and street is complicated, as the woman temporarily inhabits an intermediary zone which is the balcony, or the window, positions which are still within the house, but from which she can publicly acknowledge the declarations of love made in the street.

Gender relations in the *modinha* at this time are, therefore, not as straightforward as they seem, although there are constants. The "I" of the speaker, for example, is readily identifiable as male and the lyrics are not interchangeable, that is, it is not possible to imagine the speaker being a woman. Women are clearly addressees, objects of male fantasies, desires and romanticisations. The *modinha* is thus a space for the imagining of the other in terms of the expectations of a male-dominated society. However, despite the affirmation of patriarchal dominance in the romantic discourse of the *modinha*, in its narratives and scenarios of love women can exercise an enormous influence over the happiness of the desperate male lover. The withholding of affection makes romance the only realm, albeit a creative or imagined one, in which the woman can wield power. The *modinha* reinforces conventional views on femininity, but at the same time the hyperbolic, sentimental posturing of its male subjects unsettles the conventional views of masculinity and highlights the vulnerability of the man in love.

Until the 19th century, the salon *modinha* in a *bel canto* style coexisted alongside the more lively street *modinhas* of the serenade. However, during the second Empire (1840–89) these styles were transformed into two genres, sentimental *modinhas* and sensual *lundus*. The *lundu* was a dance form accompanied by songs based on heavily percussive rhythms, brought to Brazil by Bantu slaves. The dance enacted a process of seduction of the female partner and was regarded as a shameless display of raw sexuality by polite society at the time. The song form of *lundu* was thus viewed as the vehicle for rhythms that expressed the primitive and the sexual, as opposed to the *modinha*, which was seen to express the sublime face of romantic love. Composing from Lisbon, Domingos Caldas Barbosa refers to the distinction made between music of the body and music of the mind, between nature and culture in his "Lundum em Louvor de uma Brasileira Adotiva" (*Lundum* in Praise of an Adoptive Brazilian Woman):

> Os respeitos cá do Reino
> Dão a Amor muita nobreza,
> Porém tiram-lhe a doçura
> Que lhe deu a Natureza.[11]

(The esteemed natives of this Kingdom/ Confer great nobility on Love/ But they rob it of the sweetness/ That Nature herself bestowed upon it.)

By the second quarter of the 19th century, however, this perceived split was complicated by the fact that the *lundu* had been removed almost entirely from its original performance context, the dance, and transformed into a *lundu de salão* (drawing-room *lundu*). The high-society taste for *lundu-canção* (*lundu*-song) had begun in the late 18th century, a taste fuelled by Caldas Barbosa, who combined the *lundu* with elements of the court aria cultivated in Portugal. In the 19th century, therefore, the *lundu* had become a genre altered by its adaptation to salon tastes. It would appear that the rhythmic drive of the *lundu* was sacrificed, while elements of the language associated with the dance of seduction were incorporated into the new hybrid *modinha-lundu* style. At this time there is a great deal of confusion between the genres of *modinha* and *lundu*. Researchers have identified a mixture of the two in the collection entitled *Modinhas do Brasil*, as well as collections in which a song that may be classified as a *lundu* has the musical form of a *modinha*.[12] For example, José Ramos Tinhorão quotes a song containing lyrics that speak of actual physical contact between a man and woman: "Ponha a mão sobre o meu peito/Porque as dúvidas dissipe/ Sentirá meu coração/ Como bate, tipe, tipe"[13] (Place your hand upon my breast/ Because for doubt it leaves no room/ There you will feel my heart/ As it beats, boom, boom). (Curiously, its colloquial tone would not look out of place in the lyrics of a bossa nova composition 130 years or so later!) Tinhorão identifies the song as a *modinha*, yet it appears in Caldas Barbosa's *Viola de Lereno*, under the title "Lundum de cantigas vagas". This new, cross-fertilised song form placed two ways of articulating desire into dialogue:

the *lundu*'s more explicit, sexually charged expression, with the *modinha*'s sensibilities of courtly romance (no less erotic, albeit in a different way, as the examination of its performance rhetoric has shown). Already the two central discourses of the popular love song meet – romance and sex, love as the sublime and love as the sensual.

Lyrically, the *samba-canção* genre which emerged in the late 1920s, and which represents the next key moment in *música romântica* in Brazil, did not differ vastly from the more traditional sentimental *modinha*'s high lyricism. Indeed, one of Brazil's best-known exponents of the love song, Vicente Celestino, began his career in popular music singing *modinhas* and his first album contained the songs of the famous *modinha* composer, Catulo da Paixão Cearense. Later, Celestino was to become associated with a kind of *samba-canção* that made use of the virtuosity of his operatic voice, with the emphasis on vocal technique and imbued with the drama of the tango and *bolero* styles that became widely disseminated due to the expansion of the international phonographic market in the late 1940s. The key themes of Celestino's songs were ingratitude, betrayal, pain, madness and occasionally crime – dark and unrelenting passions – delivered in a *bel canto* style. The voice swells, syllables are prolonged melismatically and embellished, and 'r's are rolled, all according to the conventions of a classical style of delivery. However, there is a materiality in Celestino's voice that recalls Barthes's concept of "grain", or signifying weight. Barthes compared the classical singers Fischer-Dieskau and Panzera: the first conforms to all of the expected norms of this style of vocal music, with duly dramatic diction, pauses and disciplined breathing, and answers the demands of listeners who want music to be clear, have a predefined meaning, to reduce pleasure to known, coded emotions. Barthes asserted, however, that Panzera did not belong to this culture, which he calls an average and mass culture, and could not have done, as he preceded the coming of the microgroove record.[14] Like Panzera, Vicente Celestino sang with his whole body and one can hear the throat, the nose, the glottis in his performances. This is evident early in his career in particular, because the sheer power of his voice was at odds with conditions of contemporary recording and Celestino was obliged to sing five metres away and with his back to the microphone! Celestino explains:

> They said that the timbre of my voice, a tenor, kept damaging the more sensitive sound recording equipment, like the crystal and the wax. Only in the 1930s, when I signed to RCA Victor, after I'd been with other record companies, Odeon, Columbia, ... did I start recording facing the microphone about a metre away, just one metre, and so my voice became clearer, cleaner.[15]

On the day that he died, Celestino was about to join Caetano Veloso for a performance in the studios of TV Record in São Paulo, bringing together the old and the new in Brazilian romantic music. The very fact that Veloso chose to record Celestino's "Coração materno" (A Mother's Heart) on the *Tropicália* album highlighted the continuity of tradition in *música romântica*, and his soberly dramatic, contemporary version of the kitsch ballad served as a commentary on the imposition of taste on individual aesthetic sensibility:

> In 1967 Vicente Celestino was practically forgotten and his style – the complete opposite of what eventually gave rise to bossa nova – was indefensible. The melody of "Coração Materno", like all of Celestino's melodies, sounded to us like a mere pastiche of an Italian aria. It occurred to me to record that song because it was a radical example of aesthetic norms to which we believed ourselves infinitely superior.[16]

One *samba-canção* singer-songwriter who developed distinctive vocals and an idiom that differed from the *tango-canção* and foreshadowed the direction popular music was to take with bossa nova, was Lupicínio Rodrigues. In an interview published in the satirical magazine, *Som do Pasquim*, when asked to give his opinion on the contemporary music scene in Brazil and situate himself within the tradition of Brazilian popular music, Rodrigues answers unequivocally: "I've got nothing to do with the Brazilian arts scene. I'm not a musician, I'm not a composer, I'm not a singer, I'm not anything. Just a bohemian." Pressed by the *Pasquim* interviewer, Rodrigues insists: "My thing is being like I am now with my guitar at my side, in a bar, with you all, having a few drinks and singing. It's not a business for me."[17] These statements seem to me to be fundamental to his treatment of the *samba-canção*; the way in which he performed it and the poetics he developed for the form. As a non-professional composer, Rodrigues's songs were written for spontaneous performance, in informal social settings, rather than for recording. His songs were originally disseminated throughout Brazil by sailors passing through his home city of Porto Alegre and his first hit "Vingança" (Vengeance) was recorded by Linda Batista without his prior knowledge. Rodrigues's intended audience consisted of his bar room contemporaries, self-professed bohemians like himself.

From February 1963 to February 1964, Rodrigues wrote a regular Saturday column for the Porto Alegre daily *Ultima Hora*, beginning with an article entitled "O que é um boêmio?" (What is a Bohemian?), which outlined the main concerns of his notorious wine, women and song lifestyle. In the column, he consistently made outrageous statements about the position of women in society[18] and his lyrics reflect these views, making a clear distinction between two types of women, the homemakers and the "mulheres boêmias", or female bohemians. The two opposing stereotypes are reminiscent of the martyr/*malandra* dichotomy found in early samba lyrics. The subject of Rodrigues's songs, however, tends to be more the bohemian than the woman in the home. Interaction with the *mulher boêmia* takes place in public places, in the street, bars and clubs, under the cover of the night. The presentation of this particular kind of woman contributes to Rodrigues's radical reworking of the *samba-canção* genre. Unlike the homemaker, the *mulher boêmia* meets, and can even supplant the man in a masculine dominated space. She appears free to form and dissolve relationships and the majority of his song lyrics contain vitriolic attacks on women who have abandoned or betrayed him. The rancour and violence of the language used to condemn such women reflect profound insecurities about the changing role of women at the time, in a traditionally male-dominated society.

Getúlio Vargas's rise to the presidency in 1930 was followed by a developmentalist drive characterised by increased industrialisation and urban expansion in Brazil. This led to fundamental changes in social and demographic configurations, with many patriarchal families abandoning the country or outskirts of the city for city centre apartments, accompanied by the growth of an urban middle class. Urban life at this time became more permissive than in the rest of the country, as Bradford Burns has noted: "Urban women enjoyed far more freedom than their rural counterparts. The granting of the vote to working women in 1932 announced their political emancipation. The presence of daughters of the middle class in the universities became more pronounced and not a few took their place as lawyers, judges, professors, and doctors".[19] Rodrigues would have been eighteen, just emerging into manhood, when the Electoral Code extended suffrage to working women in 1932. However, while the profile of women in public and professional life as a result of Vargas's reforms was rising, one has to bear in mind the peculiar character of such reform, part of a wide-ranging body of social legislation imposed from above in order to cultivate support for the paternalist state.[20] In a sense, then, the state under Vargas was assuming the patriarchal power of the old coffee oligarchy whose influence it had diminished.

This state of ambivalence is evident in Rodrigues's treatment of women in his songs. While his chronicles for *Ultima Hora* emphasise the role of the woman as romantic creative muse, the predominant sentiments of his songs are vengeance and anger at the betrayal of love and an implied condemnation of the new freedom exercised by women. Desire is therefore expressed without exalted language and sublime romantic imagery, and is instead articulated in terms of a masculine honour that is linked to sexual conquest. Narratologically, the movement of the songs frequently depends on the transient reappearance of the woman in his life after her departure, or an appeal (to the woman, or to divine intervention) for her return ("Castigo" [Punishment], "Judiaría" [Cruelty], "Loucura" [Madness], "Se é Verdade" [If It's True]). The vast majority of the songs enunciate an emotional state or a response to a situation that results after the woman has called the shots. "Pra São João Decidir" (Saint John's Decision), for example, is a dramatisation of the man's lack of agency in love – the choice of another suitor over the singer is made completely arbitrarily by the woman, with the counsel of St John. The event is recounted in typically direct style, relying on colloquial expressions and with a simple narrative structure, all of which give the impression of the communication of a real event. The question of veracity in Rodrigues's songs was always a central concern and the narrating of real events and circumstances of his life was cited time and time again as the legitimation of his songwriting art.

The emphasis on reality provides the means by which Rodrigues radicalises the genre of the love song. As Augusto de Campos indicates, Rodrigues's songs represent an explosion of the obvious, of vulgarity and the commonplace. In contrast to the ornate language of the mainstream *samba-canção*, "Lupicínio wades straight into all of the clichés of our language and achieves unusual effects by making use of what others reject; he achieves the new through the redundant, dislocated from its context."[21] The rendering of new information via the de-contextualised familiar is evident in "Caixa de Ódio" (Box of Hatred), which recounts a woman's indiscretion in terms of a very pedestrian image: "Até num coqueiro às vezes trepamos/ Depois não achamos por onde descer" (Sometimes we climb a coconut palm/ Then we find we can't get down). (The verb "trepar", to climb, is also used colloquially for the sexual act.) The irreverent and humorous treatment of matters of the heart gives Rodrigues's songs a very accessible and spontaneous dimension, which rescues his often stereotypical formulations of love and loss.

His performance style is vital to creating this accessibility and to the projection of his songs as lived experiences. Augusto de Campos hails his rediscovery of the "voz humana" (human quality of the voice) as representing "the rupture with an alienating vocal formula that placed all the importance on the singer's skill, devaluing the experience of the music and lyrics."[22] The qualities of this reworking of the genre of the *samba-canção* are all in evidence in the song "Loucura". The overall message of the song is one of sensational existential agonising, while the language manages to remain earthy and conversational. The song has a confessional quality and begins as if in mid-conversation with an imagined interlocutor: "E aí, eu começei a cometer loucura/ Era a um verdadeiro inferno, uma tortura/ O que eu sofria por aquele amor/ Milhões de diabinhos martelando/ Num pobre coração que agonizando/ Já não podia mais de tanta dor." (And so, I began to do crazy things/ It was a real hell, a form of torture/ What I suffered for that love/ Millions of little devils pounding/ On my poor tormented heart/ I couldn't take that pain any more.)

For a song that speaks of suffering, insanity and pain, the timbre of the voice is very measured and conversational, and the tone is even. This means that the carefully timed vocal gestures which depart from the overall texture of the song appear almost as inadvertent expositions of emotion – a "real" feeling that the singer has let slip: the tremulant melisma on "agonizando", deliberately stressing the second syllable instead of the penultimate to create an unexpected effect on the ear; the stress on "tanta" dor; the drawn-out syllable "-dor" (pain) in "sonhador" (dreamer); the groaned appeal of the word "Faça" ("ela voltar de novo pra meu lado") (Make [her return to my side]). This song also explicitly links the processes of Rodrigues's musical creation to the experience of betrayal: "E aí, eu comecei a cantar verso triste" (And so, I began to sing sad verses). This is the first line of a verse which constitutes an indignant affirmation of the veracity of his songs: "Como é que existe alguém/ Que ainda tem coragem de dizer/ Que os meus versos não contém mensagem/ São palavras frias, sem nenhum valor" (How could there be anyone/ Who still dares to say/ That my verses have no message/ That they're cold words, which mean nothing). However, when this verse is repeated, the fairly banal lyrics take on a different complexion, the voice trembles to the point where it almost breaks down in the first line, altering the tone to one of emotional appeal and vulnerability and the message to a lover's lament.

The late 1940s and '50s represent a bridge between the traditional and the modern in Brazilian popular music. Composing and performing during this period were both veterans of the *Época de Ouro* (Golden Age) of music history at the end of their careers, and novices, some of whom who would end up participating in the bossa nova movement. The 1950s saw improvements in recording techniques that dispensed with the need for sheer vocal power and this created the conditions for changing interpretative styles in *samba-canção*. This enabled the development of intimate, colloquial styles such as that of Tito Madi and Dolores Duran, both precursors of bossa nova. Madi was the idol of the next generation of bossa nova musicians, and a mentor and friend to the young João Gilberto. Despite the proximity of his style to what would later become bossa nova, he refused to continue participating in the early meetings of practitioners of the new genre held at singer Nara Leão's apartment. However, were it not for her sudden death at age 29, Dolores Duran would very likely have embraced bossa nova as a development of her own tender lyricism and restrained delivery, also encouraged perhaps by her songwriting partnership with Tom Jobim.

Duran represents a very important development in the tradition of romantic music; as a composer, writer of lyrics and performer, she opened up within the genre a new, female perspective on relationships, love and loss. The Copacabana of the 1950s was characterised by a tension between traditional and modern values and had become a space in which the increasing acceptance of models of *conjugalidade* allowed for alternative personal relationships, and where moral double standards that favoured men were beginning to be questioned. Duran's work clearly communicates the ambivalence of the new multifaceted roles emerging for women in this environment. While her songs allow her to speak of her most intimate feelings and to link emotion to the idea of choice, they also express the frustration of aspiring to an independent lifestyle in a society still rooted in conventional values. In her songs men are rarely condemned for their lapses, while women, ever ready to forgive, take on the guilt for the failure of a relationship. While men are ruled by honour, women are governed by passion, more often than not leading to rejection and abandonment. The woman's solitude is deeply ingrained in the idea of romantic love, a space of fantasy and frustration. Indeed romantic love is articulated in terms of a constant search for the fulfilment of desire and pleasure. Their absence creates a condition of waiting, of sublimated desire and pleasure as possibility.[23] The 1956 song "A Noite do Meu Bem" (My Beloved's Evening) encompasses the waiting woman's hopes and needs and her vulnerability to disillusionment and disappointment, with a beauty and delicacy that anticipates somewhat the lyricism of bossa nova:

Hoje, eu quero a rosa mais
Linda que houver
E a primeira estrela que vier
Para enfeitar a noite do meu bem
Hoje, eu quero paz de criança dormindo
E abandono de flores se abrindo
Para enfeitar a noite do meu bem
Quero a alegria de um barco voltando
Quero ternura de mãos se encontrando
Para enfeitar a noite do meu bem
Ah! eu quero amor
O amor mais profundo
Eu quero toda a beleza do mundo
Para enfeitar a noite do meu bem
Ah! como esse bem
Demorou a chegar!
Eu já nem sei se terei no olhar
Toda a pureza que quero lhe dar.

(Today, I want the prettiest/ Rose there is/ And the first star to appear/ To adorn my beloved's evening/ Today, I want the peace of a sleeping child/ And the abandon of flowers opening/ To adorn my beloved's evening/ I want the joy of a ship returning to port/ I want the tenderness of hands entwining/ To adorn my beloved's evening/ Ah! I want love/ The most profound love/ I want all the beauty of the world/ To adorn my beloved's evening/ Ah! How slow/ My beloved is to arrive/ I no longer know if he has in his eyes/ All the goodness I want to bestow upon him.)

The prevailing modality, therefore, for writing and performing the *samba-canção* tended early on towards melodrama and operatic delivery. The rawness and violence of Lupicínio Rodrigues's idiom, however, set a trend in the use of more direct, colloquial language, which the more understated forms of expression of the 1950s transformed into a simple and beautiful poetics. This anticipated the transformation in vocal style and lyrics that would take place in Brazilian popular music with the advent of bossa nova.

Bossa nova took up the traditional romantic themes that had dominated the *sambas-canção*, boleros and tangos and explored them in a language of consummate grace and refinement. The new musical form's lyrical power resulted from the blending of the timeless literary language of the love poem with urban *carioca* colloquialisms of the moment. Bossa nova made a banal conversation, an argument, a moment of appreciation of beauty or transcendence into valid subjects for the most exquisite love songs, in so doing making discourses of love both beautiful and accessible. Part of this accessibility also resulted from the way in which expressions of love were worked out lyrically and musically within the space of the song, enabling listeners to accompany and involve themselves fully in its trajectory. This is crucial to bossa nova style because of the music's self-reflexiveness, emphasised in performance by the quiet, intimate delivery of the songs, suggesting an individual, personal communication. Bossa nova engaged in commentary on its own forms and structure, often through the idiom of love and romance, a quality, as we shall see, which was inherited by Caetano Veloso. Whereas previously popular music had provided a way of talking about love, bossa nova presented love as a way of talking about music. In the classic bossas "Samba de uma nota só" (One-Note Samba) and "Desafinado" (Off-Key) (Tom Jobim and Newton Mendonça), the subject of the compositions, ostensibly love and relationships, is actually the composition itself. As David Treece observes in his analysis of the former song:

> The two reiterated notes of the first section, D and G, supported by descending harmonic modulations ... offer a melodic representation of the constancy of two lovers in their exclusive mutual attraction ... This is counterposed to the "promiscuous" scales of the middle section, in their futile search for melodic variation ... In the final section, the reprise of the initial theme concludes by resolving the harmonic progression and the melodic "journey" into the single note and key of G, confirming the relationship proposed at the outset.[24]

Bossa nova made several important changes to the way in which popular music in Brazil had been communicated up until that time. Previously, narrative music had prevailed in the popular music scene in the form of the sentimental ballads discussed above, which demanded clearly delineated characters and specific ideas of time and place to create the desired dramatic effects. Bossa nova, however, was situational music, with no linear narrative, seeking instead to suggest and single out a moment or a feeling.[25] Bossa nova also offered the listener the opportunity to intervene in the love song to an extent which conventional *sambas-canção*, boleros and tangos had not previously facilitated. This involvement was created in large part through a strategic use of "shifters", words (particularly pronouns) which are important to the question of address in songs, and "whose property of reference varies according to who is speaking, when and where".[26] Until Lupicínio Rodrigues, popular love songs tended to make more use of the third person, with fewer direct addressees. Bossa nova, however, made particularly extensive use of first and second person pronouns, drawing the listener into a process of identification with the "Eu" of the singer, or the "Você" of the second person addressee. The Eu/Você exchange counters the musical formalism of bossa nova, investing the song-form with emotion while allowing for the rigour of its musical structures.

Bossa nova's unexpected shifts in tone, altered and inverted chords, the movement of ascending and descending harmonic progressions and melodic leaps conveyed a modern feel, in keeping with the confidence that a new age of progress was dawning in Brazil. This mood of optimism was encouraged by the frenetic development initiated by the government of Juscelino Kubitschek (1956–61), leading to the expectation that Brazil would soon be taking its place on the world stage, and made it easier to ignore some of the harsher realities of contemporary life. The lyrics were playful, simple and sometimes nonsensical and a more complete contrast to the deeply serious, heavy lyrics of the *samba-canção* could not be imagined. Take a prime example from João Gilberto's repertoire: "Bim bom, bim bim bom bom, bim bom bim bim bom, bim bim/ Eis aqui o meu baião e não tem mais nada não ..." (Bim bom .../ Here you have my simple song and that's all there is to it now). In his fascinating and detailed examination of the bossa nova scene Ruy Castro describes the meeting of the famous composer-lyricist partnership, Roberto Menescal and Ronaldo Bôscoli:

> They both cultivated the most intense dislike for that kind of sombre lyric which was typical of the time, like in a *samba-canção* called "Night-Time Bar", which went, "Waiter, switch off that light/ I just want to be alone". In another song, a bolero called "Suicide", the singer simply fired a shot during the recording. They had no patience even with Antônio Maria, much-loved by the forty-something year old crowd for having written: "No one loves me/ no one cares for me/ No one calls me/ Their true love" and "If I died tomorrow/ No one would feel the loss of me". ... In the flower of their youth, sports-mad and brimming with good health, the two beach bums found it impossible to identify with the bleak atmosphere of those *samba-canção* songs, full of fallen women, who betrayed their men and led them to their deaths.[27]

Vicente Celestino had admitted grudgingly that bossa nova was inevitable and said of its radical quality, "A generation doesn't affirm itself by copying the previous one, but by rejecting it". He was less kind, however, about *iê-iê-iê*, or Brazilian rock: "I feel that *iê-iê-iê* is killing Brazilian music. I hope that the 'Young Guard' stops clowning around like overgrown schoolboys and realises that music is serious business ... .[28] However, Roberto and Erasmo Carlos and the other exponents of *iê-iê-iê* ended up presenting the greatest challenge to bossa nova for pre-eminence on the Brazilian music scene, a challenge played out on television with the competing programmes *Jovem Guarda* and *O Fino da Bossa* (The Best of Bossa) in the mid 1960s. The music of the *Jovem Guarda* was the music of young love, and the idea of youthful love was pivotal to the staged rebelliousness and allowed transgressions of its performances, to its use of foreign musical forms and electric guitars, as well as to its romantic discourse.

Iê-iê-iê represented one of the first organised and industrialised attempts to make a Brazilian product out of rock music – a product aimed at youth and generally considered to have been consumed by the middle classes. A couple of significant statements, however, indicate a substantial working-class public for *iê-iê-iê*. Music journalist Ana Maria Bahiana observes that *iê-iê-iê* was: "A product which was sold to groups of young people who were not as privileged as is generally believed: at that time young university students were listening to the latest bossa novas and early MPB."[29] Reflecting on the lyrics of their songs, Erasmo Carlos has commented:

> Looking back on it today ... it was a very simple thing, you know? Very ingenuous, we just talked about what we knew, really. We didn't go to university. We didn't know how to talk about other things. They were our problems, girls, cars ... I'd only

been to secondary school, I was from the North Zone (of Rio de Janeiro) ... And the majority of our audience was like this too, made up of people who identified with us. We were just humble people.[30]

In Brazil, the developmentalist nationalism that involved ambitious and much-touted programmes for economic development and accelerated modernisation had not filtered down to the average man in the street. While the majority of the population lacked the means to consume the products of modernisation, it was still possible to feel that one could participate in its processes, through embracing a musical form that originated in the developed countries of Europe and North America. Erasmo Carlos also commented on the social mobility of *iê-iê-iê* in Brazil "I can't think of any other movement which had such humble origins and which rose to such heights ...".[31] Part of the appeal of the *Jovem Guarda* to its working class following, therefore, would surely have been in the dream of having access to the lifestyle choices created by the distant modernising process. The blatant consumerism of the movement[32] and their lack of interest in directly addressing the national question made it the object of attack from advocates of an "authentic" Brazilian culture, who saw it as a sell-out. If it was the case, however, that *iê-iê-iê* had a substantial working-class fan base, then the mouthpieces for working-class interests and "popular" cultural expression who attacked it were misreading the feeling of those on whose behalf they sought to speak. For its working-class fans, not only were the members of the *Jovem Guarda* confronting the realities of a changing urban society, but they were also refusing, at least symbolically, to stand aside and be left behind by it. The spirited defiance of daring to aspire to the modern was not lost on Caetano Veloso, who would later seek to incorporate this into the Tropicália movement.

The *Jovem Guarda* placed the city at the centre of their romantic imagination. The language and imagery of their songs were derived from a contemporary urban scene, suggesting a modernity that must have represented a locus of desire as great as that occasioned by the longings of love. The music of the *Jovem Guarda* presented to its public a way of living within a capitalist city, a way of experiencing and interrogating the diverse socio-cultural currents of the city. Caetano Veloso recalls that in 1967 he was "a young man in his early twenties living in the most cosmopolitan city in the continent (São Paulo), breathing the air of the factories, the world of TV, comics, advertising, and above all, living in a place where the sound of electric guitars was always in the background."[33]

In the 1950s and 60s rock music played an important part in conferring identity to young people during the transition to adulthood. Brazilian rocker Raul Seixas has acknowledged the function of rock in this regard and also its influence in instilling peer-group values as more important than those of adult society:

> Because before young people just followed the norms of adults, playing at being adults, with no identity of their own. But when Bill Haley arrived with *Rock Around the Clock*, the film, I remember, made me crazy. We smashed up the whole cinema, it

was freedom, my way out, my time to speak, to get up on a seat and make my presence felt. I felt that there was going to be an incredible revolution. At the time I thought that young people would conquer the world.[34]

The values being embraced by Brazil's young rock fans were modernity, fun and rebellion, evident in this statement by Veloso:

> Bossa nova had lost its libertarian impulse, turning into an almost academic type of music in its attempt to influence popular consciousness, but people were much more concerned with the latest trends. Like the Beatles or Roberto Carlos, for example. At that point, no one realised that the evolution hadn't stopped, that Roberto Carlos was the João Gilberto of the *Jovem Guarda*. The members of the *Jovem Guarda* were, therefore, resisted as if they were a plague, or a heresy. Well-to-do young women tried to put on a Northeastern accent to show their concern for the lack of agrarian reform. They were fixating on a detail, while Roberto Carlos and young people in general were already "sending everything to hell" [Reference to title of a song by Roberto and Erasmo Carlos, see below]. *Roberto smashed up the established norms, he made official the inherent, Brazilian tendency to irreverence in the face of authority. His role was to impose freedom of taste and consequently, freedom of expression.*[35]

The latter part of this quote also highlights the uses to which *iê-iê-iê* was put by performers and fans. Iain Chambers maintains that pop can "transform the seeming 'obviousness' of popular culture into an imaginative conquest of everyday life", something the earnest, almost academic strain subsequently developed by bossa nova seemed to have forgotten. Pop music provides an alternative knowledge to that of high or academic culture, and its transformation of official realities and the opportunity it offers for the performers' and fans' own explanation of social experiences, demonstrate "the unexpected promise of popular culture: the possibility of change in a changeable reality through the continual fusion of the imagination and the lived."[36]

This fusion is what Roberto and Erasmo Carlos expertly achieved and which is responsible for much of the affective magnetism of their music. Despite the simplicity of their lyrics, Roberto and Erasmo were adept at using the language of contemporary culture in apparently private expressions that had the tendency to resonate in the wider social sphere. The most famous example was "Quero Que Vá Tudo pro Inferno" (Everything Can Go To Hell), an exclamation ostensibly in response to a lost love, which became a defining phrase throughout the country in the year after the military coup. A large part of the imaginative power of Roberto Carlos's music derived from the way in which he articulated romance, so that the world of dream is brought into dialogue with that of everyday realities and relationships. This is perhaps nowhere more evident than in "Detalhes" (Details), one of Carlos' biggest hits, which, as the title suggests, attempts to prolong the memory of a lost love through the minutiae of daily life: "Se um outro cabeludo aparecer/ Na sua rua/ E isto lhe trouxer saudades minhas/ A culpa é sua/ O ronco barulhento do seu carro/ A velha calça desbotada/ ou coisa assim/ Imediatamente você vai/ Vai lembrar de mim" (If some other long-haired guy appears/ In your street/ And this makes you long for me/ It's all your fault/ The noisy roar of his wheels/ His old, faded jeans/ Or something like that/ And suddenly/ You'll remember me).

The imagery with which the singer identifies himself is immediately associated with youth, as in another of his hits, "Sua Estupidez" (Your Stupidity), which combines an expression of dream and desire with youthful petulance. The lyrics of the song are full of the redundancies of colloquial expression and lend themselves superbly to the naturalness and clarity of Carlos's vocal style, which Augusto de Campos considers as closer to that of João Gilberto, than say, the increasingly theatrical bossa nova as interpreted by Elis Regina.[37] Additionally, one of the prominent features of American rock at the time was its so-called "natural" singing – singing off beat and slurring syllables across beats, borrowed from black music, which highlighted the presence of the singing voice. Although Roberto Carlos's natural style may be linked to João Gilberto's, Luís Tatit points out that Carlos's voice is a subjective one, flagging the owner of the voice repeatedly, as opposed to merging with the musical forms, early bossa nova-style. Tatit talks of Roberto Carlos's "presença romântica" (romantic presence) in "Quero Que Vá Tudo pro Inferno", marked by pauses in which the voice trembles and vibrates. He sees Carlos's voice as the "voice of youth", marking a change from the previous tradition of *música romântica* and the baritone's "platonic romanticism". Instead, the voice of the "boy singer" acts as an extension of the body, "Breathing sensuality and suggesting physical contact which television at the time reinforced with every programme."[38]

While Carlos may have been communicating sensuality in his performances, the lyrics of his songs were not based on a direct sexuality, but on a male romanticisation of sex. The dominant romantic images were part of what Iain Chambers has described as the "typically masculine influenced romanticism of night streets and rear-view mirror scenes, of motor-bikes and cars ...",[39] exemplified in "As Curvas da Estrada de Santos" (Those Bends on the Santos Highway), the song which moved Caetano Veloso to tears in exile in London, where Carlos first sang it for him ("Eu prefiro as curvas da Estrada de Santos/ Onde tento esquecer/ O amor que eu tive/ E vi pelo espelho, na distância a se perder" [I prefer those bends on the Santos Highway/ Where I try to forget/ The love I once had/ And I saw disappear in the distance in my rear-view mirror]). The imagery of cars[40] and speed together with the stridency of the brass instrumentation, suggest the brashness of male youth, underlined by secret feelings of vulnerability and solitude and a subdued electric keyboard: "Se você pretende saber que eu sou/ Eu posso lhe dizer/ Entre no meu carro, na Estrada de Santos/ E você vai me conhecer/ Você vai pensar que eu não gosto nem mesmo de mim/ E que na minha idade só a velocidade anda junto a mim" (If you want to know who I am/ I can tell you/ Get into my car, on the Santos highway/ And you'll soon get to know me/

You'll think I care about nothing in this world/ And that at my age all I need is speed). As in other Roberto Carlos songs, "As Flores do Jardim da Nossa Casa" (The Flowers in the Garden of Our House), for example, a resolution of the problem occurs at the end of the song, accompanied by a flourish of dramatic music: " Mas o amor que eu perdi eu novamente vou encontrar/ As curvas se acabam e na Estrada de Santos eu não vou mais passar" (But the love I've lost I'll find again one day/ I've run out of bends and I'm done with driving on the Santos highway).

The song almost seems to be addressing and reassuring the older generation, explaining that despite a superficial rebelliousness, the needs of the young ultimately lie in romantic fulfilment – no wonder then, that the songs of the *Jovem Guarda* also found favour and popularity across all age groups. Indeed, a statement by Erasmo Carlos portrays Roberto as a reluctant rebel and highlights the links between the "Rei da Juventude" (King of Youth) and the previous generation of *samba-canção* performers: "Roberto grew up listening to Dolores Duran, Tito Madi, a lot of *samba-canção*. So he's very much like that, romantic. OK, he listened to rock, he enjoyed it, mostly because of me. But his thing is really romance, women, love, family ..."[41]

Carlos represents an important precursor to Veloso not just for his willingness to absorb external musical influences, but also for his status as Brazil's first pop star. "I think that defining your own style is an extremely important thing", he commented in a *Pasquim* interview in 1970 and fully one half of the interview is composed of questions geared around his image, clothes, (denial of) drug use and consumption of alcohol, his marriage and its effects on his female fans, that is to say, his lifestyle.[42] His statements and the focus of the questions underline Carlos's presentation of himself as a product to be consumed, a site of dream, desire and aspiration, and the aggressive way in which he was pursued by female fans challenged the conventional practices of male/female courtship rituals.

Carlos's flamboyant and ambiguous style contributed to the notions of masculinity that he articulated in his songs. Carlos confessed to modelling himself at the start of his career on Elvis, whose performances famously problematised male sexuality.[43] Carlos also relativises conventional masculinity by linking it to freedom of choice and individuality. His long hair and ostentatious jewellery and clothing presented the image of a rock 'n' roll rebel: "I dress like this because I consider myself a guy who's free to dress as he wants. Perhaps this may be a form of protest against the conservatism of a certain way of dressing and against other conventions."[44] This style, however, contrasted with the public persona that Carlos presented, playing the resigned victim in the fallout of broken love affairs and wearing his vulnerability on his sleeve. The words "magnetismo" (magnetism) and "fenômeno carismático" (charismatic phenomenon) were repeatedly used to try and account for his huge appeal. The interest was due to the fact that Roberto Carlos offered an altered image of the modern Brazilian male. On the surface he used the potent symbols that generated key ideological values associated with rock 'n' roll: freedom, youthful rebellion and a raw sexuality. However, contemporary commentators noted that in public he was modest, demure and unthreatening. It is significant that in the interview quoted on the preceding page, Erasmo Carlos ascribes Roberto's magnetism to his musical background, to his love of the sentimentalism of the *samba-canção*.

In this comment which links sexual appeal and romantic sensibility, Erasmo inadvertently highlights two key notions underlying the tradition of *música romântica* examined in this chapter. Within the space of the popular love song the relationship between the sexual and the romantic is often played out. This forms the basis for the articulation of desire in this tradition. As we have seen, frequently they do not merely oppose each other but are often combined and comment on each other. This kind of dialogue constitutes an illuminating dramatisation of individual desire, which as I have indicated, is situated in contemporary social conditions. In the context of 21 years of dictatorship and the pressures placed on forms of artistic expression during that time to engage in overt political commentary, Caetano Veloso remained acutely aware that the love song represents, not an escape from reality, but, to borrow from Iain Chambers once again, "an interrogative exploration of its organising categories", so that "imagination and 'reality' are brought together in a significant friction and exchange".[45] The following chapter will examine this interaction between imagination and reality in Veloso's own love songs.

Notes

1. cantaram mancebos e donzelas cantigas de amor tão descompostas, que corei de pejo como se me achasse de repente em bordéis, ou com mulheres de má fazenda. Antigamente ouviam e cantavam os meninos cantilenas guerreiras, que inspiravam ânimo e valor; ... Hoje, pelo contrário, só se ouvem cantigas amorosas de suspiros, de requebros, de namoros refinados, de garridices. Esta praga é hoje geral depois que o Caldas começou de pôr em uso os seus romances, e de versejar para as mulheres.

    18th Century observer, cited in Kiefer, *A modinha e o lundu*, 10.
2. Tinhorão, *Pequena história da música popular*, 13.
3. (Dizem que a modinha morreu. Ela não morreu porque já não é mais uma canção, mas um estado de alma. Ela está na própia essência emotiva da nacionalidade.) Mozart de Araújo cited in Kiefer, *A modinha e o lundu*, 29.
4. um modo de ser especificamente nosso em termos de sentimento amoroso.) Kiefer, *A modinha e o lundu*, 23. Consider the following *modinha* by Caldas Barbosa performed in Portugal:

Ah nhanhá venha escutar	Ah young miss come and listen to
Amor puro e verdadeiro,	Love pure and true
Com preguiçosa doçura	With indolent sweetness
Que é Amor de Brasileiro.	That is love Brazilian-style
Gentes, como isto	Ladies and gents, whereas here
Cá é temperado	Love is seasoned

Que sempre o favor	So that its favours always
Me sabe a salgado:	Taste salty to me
Nós lá no Brasil	Over there in Brazil
A nossa ternura	Our tenderness
A açúcar nos sabe,	Tastes of sugar
Tem muita doçura,	It is so sweet
Oh! Se tem! Tem.	Oh! So sweet, so sweet
Tem um mel mui saboroso	Like a very tasty honey
É bem bom, é bem gostoso.	It is so good, so appetising.

5. Tinhorão, *História social da música popular brasileira*, 93.
6. (e quem daria voz a essa sentimentalidade romântica, popularizando definitivamente a nova forma com o pernosticismo mestiço, seria a nova espécie urbana dos boêmios cantores de modinhas, especialistas em serenatas.) Tinhorão, *História social da música popular brasileira*, 95.
7. Tinhorão, *Pequena história da música popular*, 30.
8. (singeleza, intimismo, doçura e saudade) Kiefer, *A modinha e o lundu*, 24.
9. Elas consistem em lânguidos e interrompidos compassos, como se, por excesso de enlevo, faltasse o fôlego e a alma anelasse unir-se à alma afim, do objeto amado. Com uma inocente despreocupação, elas se insinuam no coração, antes de ele ter tempo de se resguardar contra a sua sedutora influência; imaginais saborear leite, mas o veneno da voluptuosidade é que vai penetrando nos recessos mais íntimos do ser.

    Cited in Kiefer, *A modinha e o lundu*, 13.
10. (No silêncio da noite as coplas enternecidas voavam nos acordes soluçantes dos violões. As melancolias e saudades estendiam-se no aveludado dos bordões em tom menor. Os júbilos amorosos se acompanhavam de arpejos e acidentes de tão viva expressão erótica que fazia suspirar de gozo o auditório sensualizado.) Andrade, *Dicionário Musical Brasileiro*, 471. The quote is taken from page 121 of *O feiticeiro*, by F. Marques (1922).
11. Cited in Kiefer, *A modinha e o lundu*, 37. Definitively refuting the simplistic equation of highly rhythmic music such as African-influenced music with the sexual body, Simon Frith emphasises that in such music the significance of rhythm lies not in some kind of inherent "physical expressivity, but (in) its communicative subtlety." Far from provoking a loss of control, strong rhythms impose a sense of order on and control over the body, which enables listeners to experience music in both a bodily and mental way. *Performing Rites*, 135.
12. Kiefer, *A modinha e o lundu*, 35 and 42; Baptista Siqueira, *Modinhas do Passado*, 317–21.
13. Cited in Tinhorão, 1990, 93, taken from Volume 2 of *Viola de Lereno*, published in Lisbon in 1826.
14. Barthes, 'The Grain of the Voice', 293–300.
15. Dizia-se que minha voz, pelo seu registro de tenor, danificava facilmente os materiais mais sensíveis de reprodução sonora, como o cristal e a cera. Somente na década de 30, quando me transferi para a RCA Victor, depois de passar por outras gravadoras, a Odeon e a Colúmbia, ... passei a gravar de frente para o microfone e à distância de um metro, apenas um metro, e aí minha voz ganhou em clareza, em limpidez.

    Cited in Guerra, *Vicente Celestino*, 161–2.

16. Em 67 Vicente Celestino estava praticamente esquecido e seu estilo – o extremo oposto do que viera dar na bossa nova – era indefensável. A melodia do "Coração Materno", como todas as outras de Celestino, era para nossos ouvidos um mero pastiche de ária de ópera italiana. A idéia de gravar essa canção me ocorrera por ela ser um exemplo radical do clima estético acima do qual nós nos julgávamos alçados altamente.

    Veloso, *Verdade Tropical*, 293.
17. (Eu não tenho nada com o ambiente artístico brasileiro. Eu não sou músico, não sou compositor, não sou cantor, não sou nada. Eu sou boêmio. ... O meu negócio é estar assim como estou agora com o violão do lado, dentro de um bar, com vocês, e tomando as minhas britas e cantando. Não faço comércio.) *O som do Pasquim*, 1975, 73.
18. From the article "Boêmio deve casar?" (Should a Bohemian Marry?) comes this observation and counsel:

    If we made a rough calculation, we would see that single bohemians rarely reach the age of forty, while the married ones live to a ripe old age, at least when they have the good fortune to find a second mother in the woman they marry, as our wives should be a substitute for our mothers. It's their duty to make us a cup of camomile tea and a bit of soup when we're hung over, and tell us off when we go too far. But this should be done affectionately as our mums would do, and not by fighting, as you won't win our hearts with fighting and shouting. (Se fizermos um média, vamos ver que os boêmios solteiros raramente atingem os 40 anos, enquanto os casados morrem de velhos, isto quando tiveram a sorte de encontrar no casamento a sua segunda mãe, pois nossas esposas devem subtituir nossas mães. A elas cabe a função de nos fazer chazinho de marcela e nossa sopinha quando estivermos de ressaca, e também nos passar uma carraspana quando andarmos abusando. Mas isto deve ser feito com carinho como fazia nossa mãezinha, e não com brigas, pois não é com brigas ou gritos que se prende um coração.)

    Re-printed in Rodrigues Filho (ed.), *Foi Assim*, 25–26.
19. Bradford Burns, *A History of Brazil*, 412.
20. Bradford Burns, *A History of Brazil*, 416.
21. (Lupicínio ataca de mãos nuas, com todos os clichês da nossa língua, e chega ao insólito pelo repelido, à informação nova pela redundância, deslocada do seu contexto.) Campos, *Balanço da bossa*, 222.
22. (a ruptura com um formulário vocal alienante, que só valorizava o estrelismo do cantor em detrimento da experiência da música e do texto) Campos, *Balanço da bossa*, 223.
23. Matos, *Dolores Duran*, 145–7.
24. Treece, "Between Bossa Nova and the Mambo Kings", 65–6.
25. Sant'Anna, *Música popular e moderna poesia brasileira*, 218.
26. On "shifters" see Durant, *The Condition of Music*, 202.
27. Ambos cultivavam a maior antipatia por aquele tipo de letra penumbrosa que era o forte da época, como a de um *samba-canção* chamado *Bar da noite*, que dizia, "Garçom, apague esta luz/ Que eu quero ficar sozinho". Em outra música, um bolero chamado *Suicidio*, o cantor simplesmente dava um tiro na gravação. Não tinham paciência nem para com Antônio Maria, admiradíssimo pelos quarentões por ter escrito "Ninguém me ama/ Ninguém me quer/ Ninguém me

chama/ De meu amor" e "Se eu morresse amanhã de manhã/ Minha falta ninguém sentiria". ... Na flor do tesão, fazendo esporte e vendendo saúde, os dois moleques da praia achavam impossível identificar-se com o clima pesado daqueles sambas-canção, cheios de mulheres perversas, que traíam os homens e os levavam à morte.

Castro, *Chega de Saudade*, 131.

28. (Uma geração não se afirma copiando a outra, mas negando-a.; ... eu penso que a música brasileira está sendo assassinada a golpes de iê-iê-iê. Espero que a Jovem Guarda esqueça essa brincadeira de rapazolas e descubra que música é coisa séria ...) Quoted in Guerra, *Vicente Celestino*, 173 and 176.
29. (Um produto que foi vendido a setores não tão privilegiados da juventude como em geral se supõe: nessa época os jovens universitários ouviam as últimas da bossa-nova e as primeiras da MPB.) Bahiana, *Nada será como antes*, 72.
30. Hoje eu vejo ... era muito simples, não é? Muito ingênuo, mas a gente falava das nossas coisas, mesmo. A gente não era universitário, não. Não sabia falar de outras coisas. Eram os nossos problemas, garotas, carros ... Eu só tinha o ginásio, vinha da Zona Norte ... E o grosso da nossa platéia era assim também, era feito a gente, se identificava conosco. A gente veio do povo mesmo.

Cited in Bahiana, *Nada será como antes*, 79.

31. (não me lembro do outro movimento que tenha vindo do povo e subido tão alto ...) Cited in Bahiana, *Nada será como antes*, 79.
32. Following the example of the merchandising created around the Beatles, the advertising agency Magaldi, Maia & Prosperi launched a number of products based on the image of Roberto, Erasmo and their co-host on the *Jovem Guarda* TV programme, Wanderléa. Brand names were created around their television personae, Calhambeque, Tremendão and Ternurinha respectively and used to market everything from dolls to clothes. *Enciclopédia da Música Brasileira*, 411.
33. (um jovem de vinte e poucos anos morando na cidade mais cosmopolita do continente, respirando o ar das fábricas, o universo da tevê, das histórias em quadrinhos, da propaganda, e sobretudo, vivia num lugar que tinha como fundo musical o som das guitarras elétricas.) Bar, *Acontece que ele é baiano*, 195.
34. Porque antes a garotada não era garotada, seguia o padrão de adulto, aquela imitação do homenzinho, sem identidade. Mas quando Bill Haley chegou com *Rock Around The Clock*, o filme, *No balanço das horas*, eu me lembro, foi uma loucura pra mim. A gente quebrou o cinema todo, era uma coisa mais livre, era minha porta de saída, era minha vez de falar, de subir num banquinho e dizer que eu estou aqui. Eu senti que ia ser uma revolução incrível. Na época eu pensava que os jovens iam conquistar o mundo.

Bahiana, *Nada será como antes*, 85.

35. A Bossa Nova tinha perdido seu sentido libertário, partindo para um tipo de música quase acadêmica, buscando dessa forma sensibilizar o povo que estava mais preocupado com coisas novas. Como os Beatles ou Roberto Carlos, por exemplo. Então, ninguém se dava conta de que a evolução nao parará, que Roberto Carlos era o João Gilberto da Jovem Guarda. Essa, então, era combatida como se fosse uma praga ou uma heresia. A meninada procurava arrumar um sotaque nordestino para lastimar a falta da reforma agrária. Eles se preocupavam com um detalhe, ao passo que Roberto Carlos e a juventude em geral já mandavam para o inferno. *Roberto derrubou padrões estabelecidos, oficializando a tendência irreverente do*

brasileiro em relação a aparência dos chamados homens sérios. Ele vinha para impor um gosto livre, conseqüentemente um uso mais livre.

      Quoted in Bar, *Acontece que ele é baiano*, 193. Emphasis mine.
36. Chambers, *Urban Rhythms*, 211–12.
37. Campos, *Balanço da bossa*, 55.
38. (Transpirando sensualidade e insinuando um contacto físico que a tevê da época reforçava a cada programa.) Tatit, *O cancionista*, esp. 186–92.
39. Chambers, *Urban Rhythms*, 207.
40. Under the Kubitschek administration (1956–61), 11,000 roads and highways were opened, the number of automobiles and trucks doubled and the number of buses tripled. The State also encouraged the creation of a new automotive industry and by 1962 Brazil was the world's seventh largest automobile producer. Bradford Burns, *A History of Brazil*, 460, 462.
41. (O Roberto se criou ouvindo Dolores Duran, Tito Madi, muito *samba-canção*. Então ele é todo assim, romântico. Tá bom, ele ouviu rock, curtiu rock, muito por minha causa. Mas a coisa dele é romântico mesmo, mulher, amor, família ...) Cited in Bahiana, *Nada será como antes*, 80.
42. (eu acho que definir um estilo é um negócio ultra importante) *O Som do Pasquim*, 1975, 146.
43. For a discussion of feminisations of Elvis with regard to a Mexican context, see Zolov, "*Rebeldismo* in the Revolutionary Family", 201–16. Also Zolov, *Refried Elvis: The Rise of the Mexican Counterculture*.
44. (Eu me visto assim porque eu me considero um cara com a liberdade de me vestir como eu quero. Talvez isso seja uma forma de protestar contra o convencionalismo de certas roupas e de outras coisas mais.) *O Som do Pasquim*, 1975, 145.
45. Chambers, *Urban Rhythms*, 209.

Chapter 6
Unidentifiable Objects of Desire: Caetano Veloso's Love Songs

Eu vou fazer uma canção pra ela	I'm going to write her a love song
Uma canção singela, brasileira	A simple, Brazilian song
Para lançar depois do carnaval ...	To release after carnival ...
Eu vou fazer um iê-iê-iê romântico	I'm going to write a romantic rock song
Um anticomputador sentimental ...	A sentimental anti-computer song ...
Para lançar no espaço sideral ...	To release into outer space ...
Como um objeto não identificado ...	Like an unidentified flying object ...

In the previous chapter, the account of the key moments in the history of the love song in Brazilian popular music points to certain continuities within this tradition, such as the use of romantic music to articulate relations between men and women in given periods of Brazilian social history. Additionally, it demonstrates that the love song is perhaps the most significant popular song form in terms of the elaboration of the relationship between performer and listener. I will now turn my attention to how Veloso engages with *música romântica*, both drawing on it and challenging it, in order to make his own contribution to the tradition.

A number of Veloso's songs reflect on the legacy of bossa nova and *iê-iê-iê*, the two most popular forms of *música romântica* when he started his songwriting career. Veloso's 1968 bossa nova composition, "Saudosismo" (Nostalgia), provides a succinct and perspicacious commentary both on bossa nova's contribution to music-making in Brazil – as a musical revolution which imposed an aesthetic of experimentation and innovation – as well as on its limitations. The very first line refers to the question of address, which altered the performer/listener relationship in *música romântica*, creating an unprecedented level of intimacy: "eu, você, nós dois já temos um passado meu amor" (I, you, we two already have a past my love). The song goes on to highlight the presence of and identification with the singer's voice as a personality in the listener's imagination: "Eu, você, João [Gilberto] girando na vitrola sem parar" (I, you, João [Gilberto] spinning non-stop on the record player). It ends with the intimately intoned first two pronouns, "eu, você ...", with the voice trailing off on "você". In the song the ephemeral happiness of a *carioca* good life created by the optimism of the Kubitschek years, recalled in the musical quotation from the Jobim/Lyra composition "Felicidade" (Happiness), rings hollow in the light of later social and political events: "Quarta-feira de cinzas no país/ E as notas dissonantes se integraram/ Ao som dos imbecis" (Ash Wednesday all over the country/ And the dissonant chords [of bossa nova] merge/ With the sound of the imbeciles). The song recreates the genre's stylistic features, such as its sonorous playfulness (with another musical quote, for example, "Lobo lobo bo-bo ..."[1]), acknowledging the freedom it brought to Brazilian music, but stressing the need to continue elaborating paths for the development of popular music in the future, a "saudosismo do futuro" (nostalgia for the future) rather than for the past: "Mas chega de saudade a realidade/ É que aprendemos com João/ Pra sempre a ser desafinados" (But enough of this longing the truth/ Is that we learnt from João/ To always be off-key). The reference to "chega de saudade", as to the other defining songs of the bossa nova era, is masterful. Ending with what is perhaps bossa nova's most famous phrase, the immediate association with longing for lost love is re-contextualised as a statement on the development of Brazilian popular music. While recalling the phrase links Veloso's song to its bossa nova past, the pleasure for the listener in the familiarity of these words is disrupted by a vocalisation purposefully distinct from the unforgettable vocalisation of João Gilberto. The stresses are placed at the beginning of the words and the speed is more hurried. This re-articulation points Veloso's song in the direction of the future, emphasising his commitment to continuing the "linha evolutiva" (evolutionary line) he viewed as necessary to Brazilian musical production. "Saudosismo" then, is a song about how new relationships between existing traditions of songwriting and the changing conventions of musical creation were being worked out.

Veloso's performance of "Saudosismo" at the series of shows at Rio's Sucata nightclub in October 1968 underlines this link between old and new musical traditions. Lulling the audience into a false sense of security by beginning with an intimate, typically bossa nova style delivery, he ended the song shouting, screaming, grunting and whistling, vocal gestures which Gilberto Gil had introduced into that year's Song Festival and which had irritated audience, press and jury alike, resulting in him never making it past the preliminaries. The performance purposely frustrated the public's expectations of a love song and it was a clear statement by Veloso that popular music needed to reflect changing times. Bossa nova's focus on the "eu" and "você" and the notion of completion of the self in the other may have been appropriate in the context of the optimistic late 1950s in the affluent Zona Sul. However, the conditions of 1968 Brazil obliged the composer-performer to be less introspective, to contemplate the self in relation to society.

After this early appraisal of bossa nova, Veloso has gone on to cover several famous numbers in concerts and on albums, in a more straightforward homage to the style that taught him so much about the importance of the intimate, private space of the love song. For example, he has interpreted "Eu sei que vou te amar" (I Know That I will Love You) (Tom Jobim and Vinícius de Moraes) on two albums. Firstly on *Muito* (*A Lot*) (1978), a version fairly faithful to Jobim's well-known rendering of the song, in which the vocals take on some of the qualities which almost suggest a speaking voice, in the typical colloquial delivery of bossa nova.

Veloso's second version (on *Caetano Veloso* [1986]) is prefaced with a brief extract from "Dindi", by Jobim and Aloysio de Oliveira. In this particular cover the voice is somewhat more unrestrained and lingers melismatically over the words, also at times rising to the point of almost breaking down. Suddenly, what is actually stock romantic language becomes imbued with exquisite beauty. The performance gives the song a sublime quality, but this is combined with a bodily presence lent by the sounds of breathing and the occasional phrase that is almost groaned. The sentimental and the corporeal are thus combined in the song, creating a climate of intimacy that moves the listener to take up a position with regard to the subject voice. Whether identifying with this voice, appropriating it as one's own, or experiencing the impression that one is present at another's intensely private declaration of love, this version of the song has an imaginative resonance that invites involvement and response.

This complex question of positioning and identification that clearly varies according to the private experience of the listener is one of the questions that Veloso considers in his "trilogy" of songs composed in 1978 by way of homage to Roberto Carlos. A contemporary review of Veloso's 1978 concert based on the album *Muito* reports:

> Caetano's praise was even more effusive for Roberto Carlos, with the songs that he wrote for the former leader of the *Jovem Guarda*, which 'form a trilogy'. 'Two plus Two', 'Very Romantic' and 'Mysterious Force' are, according to the Bahian composer, 'like photographs of Roberto Carlos taken by me or *taken by him through me*'.[2]

The highlighted phrase points to the continuity of tradition from Carlos to Veloso. "Muito romântico" provides a commentary on the relationship created by the love song between the composer and the listening individual in society. Given its title, the song form is a surprise – a religious canticle – which does not even make use of typical romantic discourse, but does appear to recount a relational misunderstanding between two people, "Eu não consigo entender sua lógica" (I just don't get your logic), a reference perhaps to early critics of Roberto Carlos's Brazilian rock 'n' roll. The ambiguities of this relationship are addressed again in "Como dois e dois", in which the singer advises his audience or potential lover: "não conte comigo" (don't count on me), "estou longe e perto" (I'm distant and near), and emphasises the lack of certainty in the relationship: "Tudo certo como dois e dois são cinco" (Everything's fine as sure as two and two are five). The title of the song also recalls the song "Como dois e dois são quatro" (As sure as Two and Two are Four), made famous by the voice of Nara Leão. The latter song dates from after the peak of bossa nova, during the protest song era and is an earnest affirmation of the certainties of life, in spite of economic hardship and social oppression: "Como dois e dois são quatro sei que a vida vale a pena/ Embora o pão seja caro e a liberdade pequena" (As sure as two and two are four I know that life is worth the tears/ Although freedom may be scarce and the bread we eat so dear). The song's lyrics and delivery assume a completely different, more didactic relationship with the audience, characteristic of much of protest song.

The lyrics of "Muito Romântico" allude initially to the shock value attached to Roberto Carlos's music in the early stages of his career: "Minha palavra cantada pode espantar/ E aos seus ouvidos parecer exótica" (The words I sing may scare you/ And sound exotic to your ears). The song suggests the importance of the love song as the right to personal expression: "Nenhuma força virá me fazer calar" (No force will ever silence me); the role of this popular song form in offering the possibility of transcendence: "Faço no tempo soar minha sílaba" (I make my syllable sound through time); the social role it fulfils: "Canto somente o que pede pra se cantar" (I sing only what needs to be sung); and the opportunity it offers for talking about identity: "Sou o que sou, eu não douro pílula" (I am what I am, I don't dress things up). The canticle form has Veloso as lead voice with male and female choruses echoing and reinforcing him in their "dialogue" with him and between the genders. The consecration of *iê-iê-iê* in hymn form is also particularly ironic, given early fears that it would corrupt the young.

"Força estranha" is a more straightforward homage to Carlos, which focuses exclusively on the idea of songwriting superseding the finite, time and even death. In this song Veloso considerably romanticises the role of the composer, seeing an ineffable mystery of musical creation, or "mysterious force", as the motivation behind great songwriters. Although the song is a tribute from Veloso to Roberto Carlos, it is most readily associated with the voice of Gal Costa, and because of their close professional and personal relationship, the subject of the tribute is often seen as Veloso himself: "Eu vi muitos cabelos brancos/ Na frente do artista/ O tempo não pára e no entanto ele nunca envelhece" (I saw many grey hairs/ On the artist's brow/ Time doesn't stop but somehow he doesn't grow old).

While "Força estranha" draws attention to what Veloso considers as the transcendental possibilities of singing, "Como dois e dois" focuses on the act of singing and the question of emotional sincerity – whether we are privy to the singer's "true" emotions. Veloso refers to this explicitly, assuring, "Mas eu não minto, não minto ..." (But I don't lie, I don't lie). This theme is taken up in "Drama", which deals precisely with the theatre of emotions of the love song. The imagery of the lyrics centres on the physicality of performing *música romântica*, and equates voice directly with identity, stressing the existence of the performing persona. The lyrics of the song are as follows, beginning with a direct echo of the line quoted above from "Como dois e dois":

Eu minto, mas minha voz não mente
Minha voz soa exatamente
De onde no corpo da alma de uma pessoa
Se produz a palavra eu
Dessa garganta tudo se canta
Quem me ama, quem me ama

Adeus, meu olho todo teu
Meu gesto é no momento exato
Em que te mato
Minha pessoa existe
Estou sempre alegre ou triste
Somente as emoções
Drama!
E ao fim de cada ato
Limpo num pano de prato
As mãos sujas do sangue das canções ...

(I lie, but my voice doesn't lie/ My voice sounds exactly/ Like the place in the body of the soul of a person/ Where the word "I" is produced/ From this throat everything is sung/ Farewell to the one who loves me, who loves me/ My gaze is all yours/ My gesture is the exact moment/ In which I kill you/ My persona exists/ I'm always happy or sad/ Only emotions/ Drama!/ And at the end of every act/ I wipe clean on a cloth/ The hands which songs have bloodied ...)

The question of sincerity is acknowledged as a crucial one for the popular love song. The song opens by suggesting that in terms of emotional honesty, song lyrics can be problematic, (for example because of the influence of romantic ideology on the personal rhetoric, or because they are dreamed up entirely from the imagination). However, "minha voz não mente" – the desiring body as expressed in the voice – is a more reliable indicator of sincerity. The third line then locates the voice as the meeting place of the two central articulations of desire in the tradition of *música romântica*: body and soul, the sexual and the sublime. The voice transacts between the two and so helps us to understand the nature of our desires and the nature of our selves. In the body, or as the fifth line of the song specifies, in the throat, the word or notion of "I" is made material. Whether the words are imagined or ideologically laden, performing them allows listeners to enter into and participate in scenarios which may recall or illuminate lived experience, as well as fuel the fantasies through which we can give form to our desire. Vocal gesture, then, is a form of communication which conveys the presence of the performer, a presence which seduces the listener and puts our emotions at his mercy: "Meu gesto é no momento exato/ Em que te mato". The performer himself emerges bloodied from the scenes of love's battles, because whether these are real or imagined circumstances which he narrates, he is living them for the audience, living with us our vulnerabilities and disappointments.[3]

The song "Drama" appears on the album of the same name by Veloso's sister, Maria Bethânia, well known for her taste for melodramatic love songs. The first four lines that open with the declaration of honesty are delivered almost in a speaking voice, which suggests that the performer is "talking straight". The extremely restrained musical arrangement supports this impression, bereft as it is of the musical conventions of the love song and the romantic discourses suggested by them. In the line which refers to the throat, however, strings are introduced to evoke a wistful and nostalgic sentimentality and gradually an underlying staccato beat builds up to the powerful exclamation "Drama!", appropriately accompanied by what sounds like tango music. The restrained introduction serves as an important commentary on the flourish of the rest of the song: while love songs are about dramas and narratives, roles and characters, the sincerity comes from the way in which they are performed, the way in which the emotions and desire are articulated by the voice.

The question of the nature of desire is enlarged to take in issues of race and gender in Veloso's important and complex song "Eu Sou Neguinha?" (Am I Your Black Beauty?). The word "Neguinha" is a colloquialism for "darling", or "sweetheart" and is derived from "nega", which has the same usage, but can also refer to a black woman. It is worth quoting the lyrics of the song in full:

> Eu tava encostad'ali minha guitarra
> No quadrado branco vídeo papelão
> Eu era o enigma, uma interrogação
> Olha que coisa à toa, boa, boa, boa, boa, bo-a
> Eu tava com graça
> Tava por acaso ali, não era nada
> Bunda de mulata, muque de peão
> Tava em Madureira, tava na Bahia
> No Beaubourg, no Bronx, no Brás
> E eu e eu e eu e eu
> A me perguntar:
> Eu sou neguinha?
> Era uma mensagem lia uma mensagem
> Parece bobagem, mas não era não
> Eu não decifrava, eu não conseguia
> Mas aquilo ia e eu ia e eu ia e eu ia e eu ia
> Eu me perguntava: era um gesto hippie, um desenho estranho
> Homens trabalhando, pare, contramão
> Era uma alegria, era uma esperança
> E era a dança e dança ou não ou não ou não ou não ou não
> tava perguntado: Eu sou neguinha? Eu sou neguinha? Eu sou neguinha?
> Eu tava rezando ali completamente
> Um crente, uma lente, era uma visão
> Totalmente terceiro sexo totalmente terceiro mundo terceiro milênio
> carne nua nua nua nua nua nua nua
> Era tão gozado, era um trio elétrico, era fantasia
> Escola de samba na televisão
> Cruz no fim do túnel, becos sem saída
> E eu era a saída, melodia, meio-dia dia dia
> Era o que dizia: Eu sou neguinha?
> Mas via outras coisas: via o moço forte
> E a mulher macia den'da escuridão
> Vi o que é visível, via o que não via
> O que a poesia e a profecia não vêem mas vêem vêem vêem vêem
> É o que parecia
> Que as coisas conversam coisas surpreendentes

130   BRAZILIAN POPULAR MUSIC

Fatalmente erram acham solução
E que o mesmo signo que eu tento ler e ser
É apenas um possível ou impossível em mim em mim em mil em mil em mil
E a pergunta vinha: Eu sou neguinha? Eu sou neguinha?

(I leaned my guitar down there/ Against the square white video box/ I was the enigma, a question/ See what a random thing, but it's good, good, good, good, go-od/ I was full of charm/ I was there by chance, I was nothing/ *Mulata's* behind, servant's brawn/ I was in Madureira, I was in Bahia/ In Beaubourg, the Bronx, Brás/ And I and I and I and I/ Asked myself/ Am I your black beauty? .../ It was a message I was reading a message/ It looked like nonsense, but it wasn't/ I didn't decipher it, I couldn't/ But it was slipping away and I was slipping away, away, away/ I asked myself: was it a hippy sign, a strange design/ Men at Work, Stop, One Way/ It was joy, a hope/ It was a dance the dance or not or not or not or not/ I was asked: Am I your black beauty? Black beauty? Black beauty?/ I was deep in prayer there/ A believer, a lens, I was a vision/ Totally third sex, totally third world, third millennium/ Naked naked naked naked naked naked naked flesh/ It was so much fun, music in the street, a costumed fantasy/ Samba school on TV/ Cross at the end of the tunnel, dead-end streets/ And I was the way out, the melody, mid-day day day/ I was my own question: Am I your black beauty?/ But I saw other things: I saw the strong young man/ And the woman's soft skin in the darkness/ I saw what is visible, I was seeing what was not/ What poetry and prophecy see and don't see see see see see/ It is what it seemed/ Things tell surprising stories/ They make fatal errors they find solutions/ And the same sign that I try to read and be/ Is only one possibility or impossibility in me in me in millions millions millions/ And the question came: Am I your black beauty? Black beauty?)

Beginning with the title, the song poses a contentious and rather surprising question, given that the singer is obviously neither black, nor female. The question represents a bold challenge to perceptions about collective, unified identity, asserting right from the first the mutability of signs of identity based around race and gender. In Stuart Hall's discussion of "sliding identities", identities are seen as ways of understanding the constant transformations of who we are, in forms we are required to take on. In other words one has to take up a position in order to say anything and "such positional identities are narratives, ... they are stories we tell ourselves about ourselves. They are necessarily fictional."[4] It is the fictional nature of identities that leads us to see them as arbitrary in a linguistic sense, but identities cannot slide infinitely or they will deny meaning. Veloso refers to the consequent elusiveness of meaning repeatedly in the song, ("Era uma mensagem lia uma mensagem/ Parece bobagem mas não era não ... Eu me perguntava: era um gesto hippie, um desenho estranho/ Homens trabalhando pare contramão ... E que o mesmo signo que eu tento ler e ser/ É apenas um possível ou impossível ..."). However, although they undermine the idea of a politics constructed around fixed identities, these signs are not arbitrary, but to follow Hall's argument, they advocate an identity politics which is located between reality and desire.

The initial question of the song's title immediately suggests a confusion of the subject with the object of desire, a confusion that Veloso uses throughout the song to question the relationship between the two. In the first line of the song Veloso is yet another artist about to make use of a fantasy-object – the dark-skinned or *mulata* woman – who is fundamental to so many forms of popular expression in Brazil and to music in particular. However, the positions are suddenly thrown into disorder, as he becomes the enigma, the object of another's gaze, framed within the video screen. The song begins to function as an attempt to close the gap between the self and the distant muse. It seeks to do this by complicating the positioning process to the point where the singer is simultaneously the gazing subject, the medium of the gaze and the vision: "Um crente, uma lente, ... uma visão". This struggle against the polarised opposition of self and other constitutes the lyrical and musical movement of the song, its reiterated questions and repetitive phrasings.

Veloso also considers the politics of making music that bears the influence of Brazil's African heritage. As Susan McClary observes in her consideration of what makes music political, "the musical power of the disenfranchised – whether youth, the underclass, ethnic minorities, women or gay people – more often resides in their ability to articulate different ways of construing the body, ways that bring in their wake the potential for different experiential worlds."[5] The song challenges the racist stereotyping that reduces black identity to the "*mulata's* behind ", by situating blacks historically in terms of the diasporic experience. It therefore moves beyond simplistic equations such as black bodies = sensuality, to acknowledge how Brazil's black population's use of their bodies, in music, dance, religious practices, carnival, has opened "different experiential worlds". Because these forms of cultural expression have spread widely in Brazil, these ways of experiencing the world have also been made open to non-black Brazilians – Veloso, too, can be a believer and a dancer. Frequently, however, this can lead to appropriation of forms of black cultural expression – the reduction of carnival to a commercialised television spectacle, for example. The song ends by reiterating the call to close the gap between the self and the enigma and to this end, continuing the process of questioning which is not afraid of confusing signs, messages and identities: "E que é o mesmo signo que eu tento ler e ser/ É apenas um possível ou impossível em mim em mim em mil em mil ...".

The song comes from the 1987 album *Caetano*, which acknowledges the composer's debt to the black music of Bahia ("José"; "Depois que o ilê passar" [After Ilê Pass By]; "Ia omim bum" [a homage to *candomblé* priestess Mãe Meninha]). The visuals also evoke this heritage: conceived by the plastic artist Luiz Zerbini and photographed by Flávio Colker, the image shows the composer in the foreground being handed a cassette tape by a black hand, with young black men in carnival costume on Rio's Grumari beach in the background. Musically,

"Eu sou neguinha?" is a stylised form of dub, a self-conscious translation of the genre. Veloso draws attention to the act of translating by the vocal gestures which accompany lines 5, 11,17, 23, and so on, repeating and drawing out sounds in an imitation of the dub echo which is created by studio engineers' prolonging of the recorded voice.[6] Other idioms of black music also converge within the space of the song: there are elements of funk; the soulful women's backing vocals; Carlinhos Brown's Bahian drums. By the end of the song, which stages a "dialogue" with the female chorus, the question has become an affirmation, heightened by Veloso's high-pitched approximation to the women's voices.[7]

The question of mutability is also crucial in the song "O quereres" (Your Wanting), from the 1984 album *Velô*:[8]

> Onde queres revólver sou coqueiro
> E onde queres dinheiro sou paixão
> Onde queres descanso sou desejo
> E onde sou desejo queres não
> E onde não queres nada, nada falta
> E onde voas bem alto, eu sou o chão
> E onde pisas o chão minha alma salta
> E ganha liberdade na amplidão
> Onde queres família, sou maluco
> E onde queres romântico, burguês
> Onde queres Leblon, sou Pernambuco
> E onde queres eunuco, garanhão
> Ah! Bruta flor do querer
> Ah! Bruta flor, bruta flor
>
> Onde queres o ato, eu sou o espírito
> E onde queres ternura, eu sou tesão
> Onde queres o livre, decassílabo
> E onde buscas o anjo sou mulher
> Onde queres prazer, sou eu que dói
> Onde queres tortura, mansidão
> Onde queres um lar, revolução
> E onde queres bandido sou herói ...

(Where you want a revolver I'm a palm tree/ And where you want money I'm passion/ Where you want rest I'm desire/ And where I want desire you don't/ And where you want nothing, nothing is missing/ And where you fly high, I am the ground/ And where you are grounded my soul soars/ And gains freedom in deep space/ Where you want family, I'm crazy/ And where you want a romantic, I'm bourgeois/ Where you want Leblon, I'm Pernambuco/ And where you want a eunuch, I'm a playboy/ Oh! Brute flower of desire/ Oh! Brute flower, brute flower/ Where you want the act, I am the spirit/ And where you want tenderness, I'm a turn-on/ Where you want free verse, I'm decasyllables/ And where you seek an angel, I'm a woman/ Where you want pleasure, I feel pain/ Where you want torture, I'm kindness/ Where you want a home, I'm revolution/ And where you want a bandit I'm a hero ...)

The lyrics are structured as an interchange between two lovers, in which the tortuousness of the desiring imagination makes it very difficult to arrive at a consensus about sexual, social and political identities. The relationship is not portrayed in terms of a clash between two clearly defined oppositional stances, as the lovers' positions keep changing, in order to avoid being fixed as the object of the other's desire: "Onde queres descanso sou desejo/ ... Onde queres o ato, eu sou espírito". Both parties are asserting the right to express their conflicting narratives of desire, narratives that articulate their own understanding of social experience and its imagined alternatives. The song enacts how ideologies about love and social roles are subject to transformation and distortion by the individual – for whom "real life" is not so neat and tidy – unsettling the categories which order official realities

> [Eu queria querer-te e amar o amor
> Construir-nos dulcíssima prisão
> Encontrar a mais justa adequação
> Tudo métrica e rima e nunca dor
> Mais a vida é real e de viés
> E vê só que cilada o amor me armou
> Eu te quero e não queres como sou
> Não te quero e no queres como és

(I wanted to love you and to love love/ Construct for us the sweetest prison/ Find the most perfect proportions/ All metre and rhyme and without pain/ But real life is all awry/ And see what a trap love set for me/ I want you and you don't want me as I am/ I don't want you and you don't want you as you are)].

In this individual space, subjectivity may be in a different relation to the prevailing order – disrupting or challenging it, but it is never outside of it. Veloso appears to be defiantly re-stating the importance of the private undermining of public norms with which his work was consistently concerned during the years of dictatorship, which would finally come to an end the following year. The use of the form of the love song is significant, given *engagé* songwriters' rejection of the idiom of romance as a valid form of social commentary in the early part of Veloso's career. "O quereres" is a reply to his critics over the years who have accused him of political alienation ("Onde queres o ato eu sou espírito ... Onde queres comício, flipper-vídeo" [Where you want the act I am the spirit ... Where you want political rallies, I want video games]). Additionally, as Charles Perrone has observed, it is a reflection on his often difficult relationship with his public.[9] Importantly, "O quereres" is also a rock song ("E onde queres romance, [sou] rock n' roll" [And where you want romance [I'm] rock n'roll]) a form derided by the cultural left. However, in the tenderly intoned refrain, "Ah bruta flor do querer" (the sighing "Ah!" having been a prominent feature of the *samba-canção*), Veloso injects romantic sensibility into the rock song. The interjection suggests that the different musical forms can coexist, just as different cultural-political viewpoints should, in order to stimulate discussion and dialogue. Indeed by the song's end, the seemingly irreconcilable desires: "Onde queres revólver sou coqueiro" (Where you want a revolver I'm a palm tree), have ceased to conflict so starkly: "onde queres coqueiro sou obus" (where you want a palm tree I'm a howitzer).[10]

This song can be situated in the context of the debate on "patrulhas ideológicas" (ideology patrols) that was raging in the artistic and intellectual communities during the late 1970s and early 80s. The term arose out of an interview with film-maker Carlos (Cacá) Diegues, first published in the newspaper *Estado de São Paulo* in August 1978 and republished by the *Jornal do Brasil* the following month. In the interview, originally titled, "Cacá Diegues: por um cinema popular sem ideologias" (Cacá Diegues: for an ideology-free popular cinema), Diegues defended the right to artistic freedom from the imposition of any ideological pressures. Diegues was referring specifically to the conditions of film production in Brazil. The state body EMBRAFILME monopolised the production, exhibition and distribution of films and many directors, Diegues included, occupied positions of responsibility within the organisation. However, the right-wing press turned Diegues's comments into an attack on left-wing ideology, coining the provocative term "patrulhas ideológicas", despite Diegues's insistence that he was referring not to a political, social or cultural category, but to systems of pressure which sought to patrol any form of Brazilian cultural expression which could not be easily codified. Occurring during the period of *abertura*, when military rule was being relaxed to some degree, the polemic over "patrulhamento" (patrolling) disrupted the unified front to the military regime that oppositional groups had managed to maintain. Veloso became embroiled in the debate by denouncing the left's "patrolling" of his work since the Tropicália period. He was severely criticised by cultural figures such as film-maker Glauber Rocha, for becoming drawn into what Rocha saw as a purely cynical anti-communist attack by the conservative press.[11] Add to this debate the initiation of the campaign for direct elections (Diretas-Já) on 25 January 1984, and "O quereres" can be seen as an affirmation of the right to creative freedom and political choice.

Another, earlier love song which deals with the question of the expectations of the public and the mixing of song forms is "Não identificado" (Unidentified Object) from the 1969 album *Caetano Veloso*. This song could easily be subtitled "Or How to Write a Love Song". The lyrics explicitly treat the issue of intention and reception of popular romantic music, identifying the addressee: "uma canção pra ela"(a song for her), genre: "um iê-iê-iê romântico" (a romantic iê-iê-iê), the locality: "uma canção brasileira" (a Brazilian song) and its status as a product aimed at a market: "pra lançar depois do carnaval" (to release after carnival). The song, therefore, recognises that within the love song there are certain norms being expressed, and they are not just those of the singer, but also of the listening public and the recording industry.

The song's musical and vocal styles oscillate between pop romance and rock, referring implicitly to the polemic surrounding the opposition between the two forms in the Western music industry. From 1956 and the emergence of Elvis Presley as a superstar until punk music in the late seventies, rock was the dominant language of most global popular music and made various ideological claims for itself, in contrast to pop music. Where rock saw itself as the expression of a community of Western youth, pop was thought to pander to the masses; where rock was sincere and authentic, pop was commercial and cynical; while rock was initially the result of small-scale industrial production and artistic, "organic" technology, pop emerged from mass industrial production and was technological, artificial and cold.[12] Using the trope of love and romance Veloso juxtaposes both forms of musical expression in the space of this song. While rock may have held the ideological centre ground, as a Tropicalist, Veloso uses pop anthropophagically in an ironic self-consciousness of its sentimentality and its place within a commercial system. Additionally, the rock rebellion was based around a new, more open approach to sexuality and considered the romance of pop a dubious form of sexual politics. In the song, the aggressively masculine, Hendrix-inspired psychedelic rock guitar contrasts markedly with the mostly intimate, whispered sweet nothings of the vocals and while the electric guitar takes the solo, virtuoso work, the muted sound of Gilberto Gil's acoustic guitar maintains the rhythm. Rogério Duprat's studio effects evoke the space-age futurism of the title and give a nod to the supposed technological and artificial nature of pop, which in fact has the last word, or more accurately, the last sound, the whining feedback that conjures up a moving spaceship in the imagination.

In mixing rock with romance Veloso was of course following the precedent set by Roberto and Erasmo Carlos, with their *iê-iê-iê romântico*. In subjecting rock to a process of romanticisation, Roberto and Erasmo deprived it of much of its rebellious charge. Genre is how we understand what music is attempting to do and whether it is fulfilling its intentions; it recognises the collective, industrial production of music and also allows for a social understanding of music.[13] It is easier to manage value judgements that are based on the understood conventions of a particular genre, and this applies to both the music industry and the authorities. As Andrew Ross points out, for the former, genre fusion is difficult to market, while for the latter it is difficult to police as a social phenomenon.[14] In terms of the industry, Veloso's commitment to resisting homogeneity in taste cultures has meant that he did not have a gold record in Brazil until 1981 and his avant-garde 1972 album *Araçá Azul* broke the record for the highest number of returns to record stores when it was released. Yet he has been allowed creative freedom by his recording label, Philips, later taken over by the major corporation Polygram, in apparent recognition that this resistance plays a major part in fuelling his musical production. Tied into this is his deliberate use of genre mixture to disturb political and social conventions, most notable during the Tropicália period, but evident throughout his career. Criticism in a daily newspaper of his 1979 album

Cinema Transcendental by the critic José Ramos Tinhorão, known for his cultural left, nationalist agenda, makes clear what was at stake in terms of "purity" vs. borrowing:

> In fact, on the very first track of the *Cinema Transcendental* album, why add those pseudo-modern sounds on the bass and keyboards to the basic accompaniment, which is a lovely background rhythm beaten out on a real Northeastern triangle? And on the second track, "Oração ao Tempo" (Prayer to Time), if Caetano's obvious intention was to create an overall sound of *samba de roda* refrains, why not just do so courageously, instead of diluting the rhythm and allowing an unimaginative chorus to produce pale imitations of North American soul? In the same way, on "Beleza Pura" (Pure Beauty), why that internationally-oriented chorus spoiling the wonderful Caetano-esque/Bahian quality of the song? ...
>
> This is all very discouraging because whenever Caetano Veloso *submits his uniquely Brazilian poetry to the appropriate form of music*, he produces beautiful work ...
>
> What a great poet, but with such little understanding of his *ideological responsibility* to his contemporaries![15]

Tinhorão, undoubtedly, would not have approved of the love song "Baby" from the *Tropicália* album, which mixes the genres of pop with bossa nova and recognises the extent to which foreign influences form an integral part of contemporary Brazilian life and culture. The song considers the development of a pop culture in urban Brazil and presents a society and culture defined by commodities. The song also reflects on the extent to which choices about individual as well as social identity have become commodity choices:

> Você precisa saber da piscina
> Da margarina, da Carolina, da gasolina
> Você precisa saber de mim
> Baby, baby eu sei que é assim
> Baby, baby eu sei que é assim
> Você precisa tomar um sorvete
> Na lanchonete
> Andar com a gente, me ver de perto
> Ouvir aquela canção de Roberto

(You need to know about swimming pools/ About margarine, Carolina, gasoline/ You need to know about me/ Baby, baby, I know it's so/ You need to have an ice cream/ At the snack-bar/ Hang out with us, see me up close/ Check out that song by Roberto.)

The use of the commercial pop song genre is appropriate to the character portrayed in the song, who defines herself[16] in terms of commodities: "Você precisa saber da piscina/ Da margarina .../ Da gasolina/ Você precisa saber de mim". The use of these commodities is articulated in the musical form and some of the lexicon of romance, with its association with pleasure and self-discovery, to highlight how elements of mass consumerism are used in private ways. In this context, popular music, which was beginning to take on some of the characteristics of a mass form in Brazil in 1968 when "Baby" was written, forms a link between mass culture and the realm of the private, because of the ways in which individuals apply popular song imaginatively to their personal lives. In "Baby", therefore, popular song forms a bridge between the social world and private life. The subject voice invites her potential lover to understand both how she relates to society and to access her private world through popular music. The two songs referred to in the lyrics, "Carolina", by Chico Buarque and "that song by Roberto" (Carlos) are at opposite ends of the musical spectrum. They reflect the range of possibilities available to the listener for identification with and expression of cultural, social and political agendas within popular song. Buarque, a singer-composer in the samba mould, as mentioned previously, was one of the most censored artists under the dictatorship, and Carolina represents a martyr-like figure oppressed by the brutality of the military regime. This contrasts sharply with Roberto Carlos's Brazilian rock and hedonistic values, which proclaim "to hell with everything" in the face of contemporary socio-political realities.

The second half of the song suggests the ideological confusion that occurs in the zone in which consumption becomes culture, particularly when it is a consumption of foreign commodities:

> Você precisa aprender inglês,
> Precisa aprender o que eu sei
> E o que não sei mais
> Não sei, comigo vai tudo azul
> Contigo vai tudo em paz
> Vivemos na melhor cidade da América do Sul
> Da América do Sul
> Você precisa, você precisa, você precisa ...
> Não sei, leia na minha camisa
> Baby, baby, I love you ...

(You need to learn English/ You need to learn what I know/ And what I don't know anymore/ Don't know, everything's cool with me/ Everything's OK with you/ We live in the best city in South America/ In South America/ You need to, you need, you need .../ Don't know, read it on my T-shirt/ Baby, baby, I love you ...)

The polemical issue of the internationalisation of Brazilian culture and society is also raised in the references to English, which are deeply ironic and ambivalent. The question of cultural borrowing is reiterated in the use of the pop song genre, but is complicated by combining pop with bossa nova. Bossa nova, of course, represents one of Brazil's most famous musical exports, but is itself a form which combines samba with North American jazz. The question of consumption and appropriation of mass culture is further problematised in the song by suggesting that it is available only to a select group, those who live "in the best city in South America" and who belong to certain sectors of society (You need to ... hang out with us).

Gal Costa's vocals and Rogério Duprat's arrangement for "Baby" on the *Tropicália* album remain for many the definitive recording, with the subject voice of the song more often identified with Costa than with Veloso. Although many of Veloso's songs have been recorded by women, he rarely writes lyrics in a female subject voice, a strategy for which Chico Buarque is famous. However, throughout his career, Veloso has attracted attention because of his expressions of desire for men, in song lyrics, interviews and performances, and as a star his sexuality has long been the subject of public speculation. One certainly gets the impression that he courts this attention and interest in his sexuality and that in public spaces, on the stage, or at social events, he is performing, or representing, various sexual postures. Given the artist's high profile, this posturing appears aimed at making pointed statements, provoking comment and shocking. His right to diversity in the presentation of his sexual self is closely linked to the right to cultural and artistic diversity that he advocates so strongly.

The shock value of expressions of non-heterosexual desire was evident in the furore that greeted "Menino do Rio" (Boy from Rio), released on the album *Cinema Transcendental*. The subject of the song is a *carioca* beach bum, but has also been associated with a street-kid, in part because of a parallel and contemporary song by Chico Buarque, "Pivete" (Kid), which is an expression of solidarity with street-children and a tribute to their will to survive. "Menino do Rio", however, does not constitute a straightforward denunciation of deprivation or social inequity. It is written as a love song, in which the body of the young boy is the focus of unabashed erotic contemplation: "Menino do Rio/ Calor que provoca arrepio/ Dragão tatuado no braço/ Calção corpo aberto no espaço/ Coração de eterno flerte/ Adoro ver-te ..." (Boy from Rio/ So hot you send shivers down my spine/ Dragon tattoo on your arm/ In shorts with your body open to the breeze/ Heart of an eternal flirt/ I love to look at you). The undisguised pleasure he describes on viewing the boy's body, recalls the relationship between subject and object that he seeks to question in "Eu sou neguinha", with the boy cast as the marginal and victimised other. On one level the performer's desire for the boy conveys the predatory nature of the relationship between the haves and the have-nots in Brazilian society. However, criticism and denunciation of the boy's marginalised position in society are also channelled through an articulation of desire. The artist's desire for the boy also works as a metaphor for the desire for social justice, for the opportunity to realise dreams and pursue happiness. Additionally, the boy himself is presented as a desiring subject who will not simply allow himself to be stereotyped and mythologised, but instead shapes the performer's desire and makes the relationship between the two one of exchange and interaction: "O Havaí seja aqui/ Tudo que sonhares/ Todos os lugares/ As ondas dos mares/ Pois quando eu te vejo eu desejo o teu desejo ..."

(May you find paradise here/ All that you dream of/ All the places that you want to be/ All the waves of all the seas/ Because whenever I look at you I desire what you desire).[17]

"Cajuína" (Cashew Wine), also from the *Cinema Transcendental* album and dedicated to a friend from the North-eastern city of Teresina, is another composition which unites desire for another man with a statement on human suffering. The song appears to suggest that love and respect for fellow human beings is the first step in the struggle against social injustice. At the time that the song was released, however, it was taken by some to be a gay anthem:

> Existir-mos: a que será que se destina?
> Pois quando tu me deste a rosa pequenina
> Vi que és um homem lindo e que se acaso a sina
> Do menino infeliz não se nos ilumina
> tampouco turva-se a lágrima nordestina
> Apenas a matéria vida era tão fina
> E éramos olharmo-nos intacta retina
> A cajuína cristalina em Teresina.

(We exist – what is our destiny, who knows?/ Then when you gave to me that tender little rose/ I saw beauty in a man who might escape the fate/ Of the unhappy boy life failed to illuminate/ Nor did our North-eastern tears grow dimmer by the year/ Only that the stuff of life was just so rare/ And I looked deep into your eyes, intact retina/ Crystal clear cashew wine in Teresina.)

"Vampiro" (Vampire) completes the trilogy of songs from this 1979 album devoted to sexual diversity. Written by Jorge Mautner as early as 1958, the song is a particularly dark and unconventional portrayal of desire and the erotic. Set to tango music, the atmosphere of the song is one of high drama and heightened emotions, an atmosphere appropriate for the tumultuous and conflicting feelings associated with complete freedom of choice with respect to sexual identity, as advocated in the song's lyrics. Mautner himself has stated that the song is rooted in the experiences and emotions of a bisexual lifestyle and the tortuousness of pleasure and desire, and seeks to destroy the cosy certainties of conventional romantic discourse:[18] "E eu sinto aquela coisa no meu peito/ Eu sinto aquela grande confusão/ Eu sei que eu sou um vampiro/ Que nunca vai ter paz no coração" (I feel that something deep inside me/ I feel that great confusion/ I know that I'm a vampire/ Whose heart will never find peace). The song uses vampirism to explore the ambiguities of desire, drawing on images of sado-masochism, blood and wounding, to suggest deep and disturbing passions, which can lead to a loss of control: "E vou sugando o sangue dos meninos/ E das meninas que eu encontro/ Por isso é bom não se aproximar/ Muito perto dos meus olhos/ Senão eu te dou uma mordida/ Que deixa na sua carne aquela ferida ..." (And I go along sucking the blood of the boys/ And girls who cross my path/ That's why it's best to avoid my gaze/ Or I'll sink my teeth into you/ And leave that wound upon your flesh ...).

Despite suggesting the dangers of these passions, the song seeks to view sexual culture in terms of diversity rather than perversity.

The question of Veloso's sexuality on public display is an important one and continued to be so, even after the radicalism of *Tropicália*. His status in Brazil means that his appearances in public are given extensive coverage on television and in the press. He has always played, or had thrust upon him, a role as commentator on Brazilian life that far surpasses the brief of an entertainer, a leftover perhaps of the role played by artists under the dictatorship. Frequently solicited for, or freely giving his views on political, economic or social events, he even initiated a self-imposed ban on comments to the media in 1979, claiming a fear of over-exposure. At the time his very silence was the subject of public attention and speculation. In a sense, therefore, Veloso has always "performed" his views, comments and personal politics. Nearly 20 years after *Tropicália*, one such "performance" of his ambiguous sexuality provoked an outcry and furious debate on the significance of his behaviour for gender relations in Brazilian society, and the implications of showcasing non-heterosexual behaviour on television.

The occasion was the programme *Chico & Caetano*, a series of twelve weekly shows on TV Globo hosted with Chico Buarque, to which different guest performers were invited. The show was aired in 1986, the year after the return to democracy in Brazil, and became something of a platform from which Veloso sounded attitudes to social democracy and individual freedom in the wake of political change. During the fifth programme in the series, Veloso performed a duet with Paulo Ricardo, lead singer of the rock group RPM, which had had a hit with a remake of Veloso's "London, London". Contrasting markedly with Chico Buarque's conservative dress sense, Veloso sported *dhoti*-style trousers, sandals and an earring. At various points during the show, before the appearance of Paulo Ricardo, his behaviour is coquettishly feminine: he places his hands on his hips, his vocal style is extremely soft and intimate and he cultivates the most self-consciously shy and vulnerable expressions when the camera zooms in for the close-ups. His performance with Ricardo was executed in the manner of a male/female duet and punctuated with lingering, sensuous looks and prolonged, repeated and intimate embraces.[19]

The effects of this incident and the debate it provoked are clearly summarised in a contemporary newspaper article, which reports:

> Interpreters of Caetano's career and personality say that his behaviour in the video is intentional: he definitely wants to shock hard-line machos all over Brazil. Others have already stated that this is the final straw with regard to displays of homosexuality on television ... and have called on Mr. Roberto Marinho [the owner and chief executive of TV Globo] to take the necessary steps.

The article goes on to ask: "But, from what is evident in the video, what could Caetano's sensual affront mean for our national culture?"[20] It concludes that Veloso, for all his sexual ambiguity, is adored by women because he realises their own repressed sexuality, and constitutes a threat to machos precisely because women consider him an ally, as well as because of his undermining of orthodox masculine role models. The writer also makes an interesting point with regard to the gendered reception of Veloso's songs. He proposes that in terms of address, Veloso chooses to privilege his female public and suggests that his alliance with a feminine and even feminist viewpoint reflects a desire that his voice and his music should arise out of the most marginal and marginalised areas of cultural life.

In this chapter I have sought to address the question of Veloso's use of the tradition of *música romântica*. In addition to raising issues of gender and sexuality, many of the love songs, including those with a less complicated romantic discourse, use desire and love to refer to the actual process of musical creation. In "Ela e Eu" (She and I), for example, the perfect relationship is described as "Como a própria perfeição da rima para amor" (Like the very perfection of a rhyme in a love song). In "Remelexo" (Swaying), the dancing body of the girl he desires generates and sustains the sounds and rhythms of the samba. "Eu Te Amo" (I Love You) contains a reference to the activity of singing which equates it with the expression of love, while "Minha Voz Minha Vida" (My Voice My Life) goes further to suggest that singing is not just an expression of emotions, but that the performer sings in order to live those emotions. Here singing and the voice actually open up the possibilities of life and love: "Meu amor acredite/ Que se pode crescer assim pra nós/ Uma flor sem limite/ É somente porque eu trago a vida aqui na voz" (My love believe/ That for us can grow thus/ A flower without limits/ And all because I carry life here in my voice). "Eclipse Oculto" (Mysterious Eclipse), on the other hand, talks about love from the point of view of a consumer rather than a producer of music, charting the ups and downs of a relationship framed within references to the music of Djavan and the late Tim Maia, two prominent performers of romantic music in Brazil. These references suggest the way in which we use songs as markers of memory, identifying or associating a particular song or singer with an experience or relationship. The relationship described in the song is difficult, not conforming to romance as portrayed in such songs: "Tipo de amor que não pode dar certo na luz da manhã/ E desperdiçamos os blues do Djavan" (The kind of love that doesn't work out in the cold light of day/ And we just frittered Djavan's blues away). The lovers theorise the relationship to the point where they lose sight of the question of fundamental sexual desire: "Demasiadas palavras/ Fraco impulso da vida/ Travada a mente na ideologia/ E o corpo não agia" (Too many words/ Weak impulse for living/ Minds blocked by ideology/ And our bodies not stirring). However, the relationship to which they aspire is expressed in terms of popular song, a recognition of its role in providing ways of thinking about and the language for talking about desire and love: "Quero ser seu amor/ Quero ser seu amigo/ Quero que tudo saia/ Como o som do Tim Maia/ Sem grilos de mim/ Sem desespero sem tédio sem fim" (I want to be your lover/ I want to be your friend/ I want our love to belong/ In a Tim Maia song/ No broken hearts to mend/ No despair no tedium no end).

It is clear that Veloso's love songs also comment on the part played by music in socialising the individual and in disseminating dominant ideologies of gender identity. The song "Tem que ser você" (It Has to Be You) refers directly to the heterosexual conventions of the love song: "Tem que ser você/ Tem que ser mulher/ Tudo no lugar certo/ Tem que ser você/ Tem que ser assim …" (It has to be you/ It has to be a woman/ Everything in its rightful place/ It has to be you/ It has to be this way …). This song was understood by some of his public to be a definitive statement by Veloso on his sexuality, but the song actually works precisely against such fixity. As Veloso himself said of the song: "After I recorded 'It Has to Be You', Tomás Improta [a Brazilian musician] said to me that with that song, I had finally defined my sexuality … I don't agree. These things are always of the moment, I never have firm definitions."[21] The song ostensibly sets out a hegemonic model of gender organisation,[22] but simultaneously resists it in the performance style and with asides and interstitial comments. Veloso delivers almost the entire song in a deep and exaggeratedly manly voice, which is a highly unusual vocal style for him, and which suggests at once that he is projecting "someone else's" voice and ideas. The melody is overly repetitive and this is reinforced by the lyrics, with almost every phrase beginning with "it has to" or "everything has". The overall effect is dogmatic and insistent. Yet this authoritative discourse of unequivocality is interrupted on occasion by a comment suggesting the need for openness to the mysteries of desire: "Tudo tem seu momento/ … Tudo tem seu segredo …" (Everything has its moment/ … Everything has its secret). An aside addressed to other men is inserted into the rhetoric as if it were an inadvertent slip: "E homens, o amor-mentira/ Pode ser tão bonito" (And men, love's illusions/ Can be so beautiful), but he then reminds himself of social expectations concerning sexuality: "Mas o céu do meu sexo/ Tem que ser você … Tem que ser a flor …" (But celestial joy for my sex/ Has to be you … Has to be the flower). About halfway through the song the heavy jazz funk rhythms are interrupted by a high pitched whoop and followed by a passage of disco music, highly significant given disco's body politics, and making the return to the more plodding rhythm all the more marked. The song ends with the jazz-funk fusion sound, but now with some strings added which lighten the mood and suggest that the sound and the discourse with which it is associated in the song has been affected by another, alternative discourse.

Veloso repeatedly challenges conservative morality in his legitimisation of diverse representations of gender and sexuality. What he also makes clear is that these representations are always liable to change, and although they are individual expressions, they cannot be severed from their social context. I would like to return to the newspaper article that suggests that Veloso allies himself with a female perspective in order to position his voice from the margins of cultural life. For Veloso, this is one position among many. He has oscillated between the margins and the mainstream throughout his career, and has been censured for locating himself in both, because the politics of the former is generally thought to be incompatible with what can be seen as co-option into the latter. In the cultural politics of the 1960s his attempts to expose the dialectical relationship between the two were misunderstood as an attempt to reconcile two mutually excluding opposites, and the latter view still proved tenacious in subsequent periods. Veloso's inhabiting of both spaces seems to me to be a running commentary on what Stuart Hall sees as the changing field of cultural struggle, based around a constant tension between popular culture and dominant culture. Hall describes the relations between the two thus:

> I think there is a continuous and necessarily uneven and unequal struggle, by the dominant culture, constantly to disorganise and reorganise popular culture; to enclose and confine its definitions and forms within a more inclusive range of dominant forms. There are points of resistance; there are also moments of suppression. This is the dialectic of cultural struggle. In our times it goes on continuously, in the complex lines of resistance and acceptance, refusal and capitulation, which make the field of culture a sort of constant battlefield. A battlefield where no once-for-all victories are obtained but where there are always strategic positions to be won and lost.[23]

This statement recognises that "almost all cultural forms will be contradictory ... composed of antagonistic and unstable elements. The meaning of a cultural form and its place or position in the cultural field is *not* inscribed inside its form."[24] Veloso's mediation of the tensions between margins and mainstream and his resistance to fixity of form reflect a sensitivity to this view of cultural dynamics. It is no accident that a large part of his repertoire is constituted of songs of love. The relational context contained in them serves as a space from which to explore his concern with the balance of cultural relations. The intensity and charge of the performances of Veloso's love songs also acknowledge that although our most private emotions may be culturally shaped, they are no less valid and vividly experienced for that. He makes use of and challenges the conventions of the tradition to draw out the ambivalence of the articulation of desire and identity, using the relationship with the listener, which is so fundamental to the genre, to explore and question social and gender relationships. Ultimately, his most important contribution to the tradition of *música romântica* in Brazil is an intellectualised approach which acknowledges love and relationships as valid subjects for discussion and as useful for talking about a society and its politics, but which does not then deny its listeners the pleasures of the body.

Notes

1. "Lobo Bobo" (Silly Wolf) (1959), one of the first compositions of the songwriting partnership of Carlos Lyra and Ronaldo Bôscoli, provoked a great deal of criticism for the frivolity of its lyrics, using the idea of Red Riding Hood and the Wolf to describe Boscoli's assiduous courtship of Nara Leão.

2. Os elogios de Caetano foram ainda mais enfáticos para Roberto Carlos, ao cantar as músicas que fez para o ex-lider da jovem guarda, que 'formam uma trilogia'. "Dois e Dois", "Muito Romântico" e "Força Estranha" são, de acordo com o compositor baiano, 'como fotografias de Roberto Carlos tiradas por mim ou feitas por ele através de mim.

   Dulci: "*Muito* – Um 'show' muito 'odara'", *Jornal do Brasil*: no date: Museu da Imagem e do Som, Rio de Janeiro. Emphasis mine.
3. See Simon Frith's illuminating discussion of the question of sincerity in popular music, in Chapter 8 of *Performing Rites*, 158–82.
4. Hall, "Fantasy, Identity, Politics", 63–9.
5. McClary, "Same as it Ever Was", 34.
6. I am grateful to Sean Stroud for this observation.
7. In an interesting twist, "Eu sou neguinha?" was also a hit for the late Cássia Eller, an openly gay, white, female performer, sung in what sounds remarkably like a rumbling baritone.
8. On the album cover the word "Velô", the first four letters of the artist's surname, is written so that at a glance it can be read either as "velô" or as "love".
9. Perrone, *Masters of Contemporary Brazilian Song*, 87.
10. Veloso's vocals are executed in such a way as to suggest cycles of dialogue; his style contrasts that of Gal Costa in her rendition of "O quereres" (*Mina D'Agua Do Meu Canto*. Warner Chappell. 7432126323-2. 1995), which conveys a more aggressive, confrontational and distinctly female affirmation of sexual subjectivity.
11. Pereira and Buarque de Hollanda, *Patrulhas ideológicas*, 7–9, 18 and 24. Veloso went so far as to create a "Patrulha Odara" to counter attacks on his album *Muito* for what was seen as its lack of political commitment. Even friends and sympathisers such as Hélio Oiticica criticised his response, which was meant to turn the tables on the relationship between the "patrulheiro" (patroller) and the "patrulhado" (patrolled), but which Oiticica believed merely perpetuated intolerance.
12. These oppositions are taken from Hesmondhalgh, 'Rethinking Popular Music after Rock and Soul', 195–212.
13. See Hesmondhalgh, 'Rethinking Popular Music after Rock and Soul', 195–212.
14. Ross and Rose (eds), *Microphone Fiends*, 149.
15. De fato, logo na primeira faixa do disco *Cinema Transcendental*, por que acrescentar pseudos sons modernos do baixo e dos teclados ao acompanhamento básico, que soa ao fundo marcando ritmo bonito de um triângulo bem nordestino? E na segunda faixa, *Oração ao Tempo*, se a intenção evidente de Caetano foi usar o tom geral dos estribilhos de samba de roda, por que não evidenciar corajosamente isso, em vez de diluir seu ritmo para permitir a um coro sem imaginação produzir sovados efeitos do canto *soul* dos norteamericanos? Da mesma forma, em *Beleza Pura*, por que o coro de gosto internacional estragando o clima tão gostosamente caetanobaianista da música? ...

    Isso tudo é muito desalentador porque, quando Caetano Veloso, afinal, submete sua poesia tão brasileira à forma musical adequada, resultam obras lindas ...

    Que grande poeta, para tão pequena compreensão de sua responsabilidade ideológica perante os contemporâneos!

    Tinhorão, "Como seria bom se a música de Caetano e Chico Buarque correspondesse à sua poesia", *Jornal do Brasil*, 12/12/1979. My emphases.
16. The subject voice of this song is frequently identified with Gal Costa, who recorded it on the *Tropicália* album.

17. The 1983 song "Salva-Vida" is another frank erotic appreciation of the male body, in which the artist lets go of fear to experience this variant of desire. The sea is invoked as a potent sexual metaphor, reinforcing the idea that this unconventional desire is a form of both spiritual and material renewal, which saves the artist from a feeling of world-weariness: "Místico pôr-do-sol no mar da Bahia/ E eu já não tenho medo de me afogar/ Conheço um moço lindo que é salva-vida/ … Que é fera na doçura, na força, e na graça/ Ai, ai, quem dera/ Que eu também pertenecera a essa raça/ Salva-vida onda nova nova vida vem do novo mar …" (Mystical sunset in Bahia/ I no longer fear drowning/ I meet a beautiful boy who's a life-guard/ … With a wild tenderness, strength and grace/ Oh, oh, who would think/ That we two belong to the same race/ Safeguarder-of-lives new wave new life emerging from the new sea …)
18. Interview with the author, 7/08/98.
19. Moraes Neto, "Caetano calou", *Jornal do Brasil*, 08/10/87; Souza, "Fala, Caetano: a voz do anjo torto", *Jornal do Brasil*, 27/10/87; Aragão, "Novo disco de Caetano chega às lojas amanhã cercado de expectativa diante de seu 'silêncio'", *O Globo*, 27/10/87; Silva, "O sempre supreendente Caetano", *Última Hora*, 28/10/87; Cerqueira, "Sem fala, Caetano é só voz e instrumento", *A Tarde*, 16/01/88; Machado, "E Caetano falou", *A Tarde*, 16/01/88.
20. Hermeneutas e intérpretes da carreira e da personalidade de Caetano Veloso dizem que o seu comportamento no vídeo é propositual: – ele quer certamente chocar os machistas de cintura dura, espalhados por esse Brasil afora. Outros já afirmam que chegara o momento limite de manifestação homossexual diante das câmeras de tevê … e que o Senhor Roberto Marinho deveria tomar as suas providências.

    Mas o que poderia significar para a cultura nacional o afrontamento sensual de Caetano, nas formas em que se manifesta no vídeo?

    Porto, "O sexo dos mitos", *Correio Brasiliense*, 26/08/86.
21. (Depois que eu gravei *Tem que ser você*, Tomás Improta me disse que, com essa música, eu afinal tinha definido minha sexualidade … Eu não acho. Essas coisas são sempre de momento, nunca tenho definições definitivas.) Cited in Fonseca, *Esse Cara*, 45.
22. The idea of hegemonic and resistant models of gender organisation in music, based on Gramscian concepts, is taken from McClary's *Feminine Endings*, 8.
23. Hall, "Notes on Deconstructing the Popular", 234.
24. Hall, "Notes on Deconstructing the Popular", 235.

Conclusion

This book has sought to contribute to an approach to studying Brazilian popular music informed by the diverse codes of performance that produce meaning in popular song. It has attempted to shed light on how these codes function to produce the effects to which we as listeners respond. It is intended that this work may play a small part in the development of a line of study of popular music in Brazil underpinned by two key considerations. The first is an awareness of and sensitivity to the multidimensional nature of popular song; the second is a concern to elaborate methods for studying popular music that are mindful of the crucial questions of the enjoyment and pleasure of the listener.

That Caetano Veloso has maintained an awareness of the mass appeal and of the entertainment function of popular music, while cultivating an intellectual approach to music-making, has brought him criticism. This was well-illustrated in 1997 with the release of his album, *Livro* (Book) and the publication of his memoirs *Verdade Tropical* (Tropical Truth). Both the album and the book examine how artistic and cultural practices of the past and present, both erudite and popular, intertwine in popular music expression. The launch of a book about music and an album called "book" highlights the multidiscursive nature of popular music for Veloso, and the book offers a number of insights into cultural identity and the national question. Some critics, however, saw the publication of the dense, over-long memoirs as a pretentious attempt to intellectualise Tropicália in book form and consecrate Veloso's place within Brazilian cultural history. It may well be true, as one of his detractors comments, that Veloso appears to identify Brazil with his own image, seeing himself as "the embodiment and the spectacle of all Brazilian racial, sexual and cultural contradictions".[1]

The music video of the song "Livros", which appeared on that 1997 album, demonstrates this conflation of the subjective with the national in Veloso's work and iconography. It emphasises Veloso's role as mediator between different cultural traditions in Brazil – between popular song and literature – and represents his life and career as analogous to the country's cultural history. The video clip's opening scene is filmed in black and white, with Veloso singing the opening lines to "Chão de Estrelas" (Carpet of Stars, 1937). Many commentators share the opinion that the song's lyrics, written by the journalist and poet Orestes Barbosa (1893–1966), are among the most beautiful in Brazilian popular music. In a 1956 chronicle on Barbosa written by no less a literary luminary than the poet Manuel Bandeira, the latter declared: "If there were a competition … to determine the most beautiful verse ever written in Portuguese, I think it would be that one by

Orestes that goes, 'you trampled on the stars distractedly ...'".[2] This is the line that Veloso borrows for the first line of the song "Livros", invoking this standard of the meeting of popular song and literary traditions, but also distorting it by altering the adjective "distraída" (distractedly) to "desastrada" (clumsily), which suggests the songwriter's freedom to both draw on and transform the words of the poet. The video presents us with an ambivalent take on literary culture. The first image we see in colour is of a boy dressed as a man, dragging a pile of books behind him, in what appears to be a reference to the cumbersome weight of erudite cultural heritage. The boy-as-man figure punctuates the whole video and is equated with the figure of Veloso himself, in whom artistic traditions of the past and present meet. This encounter is not a straightforward one, and is signified in the video through the play on time, which is not presented as linear, but whimsical and difficult to control. In keeping with the song lyrics, the relationship between the artist and the book is represented in very physical terms. Veloso dances on books, lies on them and rolls his body over them, as the literary text is demystified and turned into an object of the performer's desire. As he did in the live shows based on the album, the act of reading is conspicuously performed in the video (with reading glasses as a prop). How do we, in turn, read his gesture? Is it parody, a disruption of the aura of literature through popular song performance? At one point in the video clip Veloso reads from a book in French, lip-synching the words out of time to isolate and emphasise the action. On the one hand, this moment seems to suggest the disjuncture between popular culture and the first-world ideal of Brazil's intellectual elites. On the other hand, it apparently reconciles this disjuncture through the performer's own ostentatiously demonstrated ability to read in French.

Various commentators have observed Veloso's passage from Tropicalist iconoclast to part of the canon of Brazil's cultural heritage, as exemplified in his publication of a book that presumes to offer a kind of official "truth" on the movement in which he participated.[3] The fact that Veloso is very much a consecrated cultural figure today, however, does not on its own account for the pretensions of the book's title and the over-ambitiousness of its scope. In fact, Veloso's years in the public eye have always been characterised by pronouncements on the big issues surrounding Brazilian culture that present his personal views as certainties. To return to the criticism cited previously, if Veloso does see himself as the embodiment of all of the contradictions of Brazil, it is, however, undeniable that this critical self-absorption has yielded many significant and thought-provoking perspectives on Brazilian identity. Despite the ponderous conviction and finality of its title, the *Tropical Truth* memoirs attempt to wrestle with some of the paradoxes and open-ended ambiguities of Brazilian society and culture. Its most important contribution to cultural criticism, like Veloso's career, is a consideration and questioning of the function and practice of songwriting in negotiating the vexed question of what it means to be Brazilian.

Notes

1. Braga-Pinto, 2000, 105.
2. (Se se fizesse aqui um concurso (…) para apurar qual o verso mais bonito de nossa língua, talvez eu votasse naquele de Orestes: "tu pisavas os astros distraída …".) Cited in Severiano and Homem de Mello *A canção no tempo: Vol. 1*, 155.
3. See Sovik, 2000, on this and for a summary of reviews and criticism of the book.

Appendix
Interview with Caetano Veloso[1]

Lorraine Leu: I'd like to begin with a question about the performer and the voice. In the intitial phase of your career, up to *Araçá Azul*, you seemed to be developing a new cult of the voice. But at the same time that interest in the qualities of the voice in itself, that experimentation with the voice, was a challenge, a provocation, for many listeners. You seemed to want to attract and repel the public at the same time. Was there a conscious intention to do this?

Caetano Veloso: Overall I had a conscious desire to establish a dialogue between what I was doing and the public that was consuming what I was doing. I didn't think of it in terms of conflict, I wanted it to be a dialogue, which ended up almost like a debate. So, in fact, I did want to both attract and repel people. If this was evident in the area of the voice I can't say if it was done consciously, or at least in such a controlled way. However, I don't think I can answer "no" to your question. My intention to comment on different styles, particularly in the Tropicalist period, to attract and repel, is also present in the emission of the voice, even if it's unconscious.

LL: Apart from the iconography of the superstar that represents a fundamental code of popular music in general, at times the lyrics of your songs have a strong visual dimension. You've been a film director, you compose soundtracks for films and have just released a CD in homage to Fellini. Does the image enter into the actual creative process of your songs?

CV: Without a doubt, because when I was a boy I didn't plan on being a musician. I played the piano, I knew all of the songs played on the radio, but I also drew and painted and what I really wanted was to be a film director. The older I got the more I wanted to be a director. By the time I was 18 I got to be a film critic, I wrote reviews for a paper in Santo Amaro for a year, and I wrote a few articles on film for some newspapers in Salvador. So, that visual aspect, it's from my imagination, without a doubt it's present in everything I do, even when it's a song without words.

LL: Is it that you see the images when you compose?

CV: It's not quite like that, you know how people sometimes see without actually seeing? You imagine a visual reality without needing to transform it into an actual visual image. It has a visual quality, but it's experienced mentally.

LL: The albums that you released in 1975, *Jóia* and *Qualquer Coisa*, are very significant albums in your career, in which you explored language to its limits. Do you think they had something in common with the poetry of João Cabral, I mean, that sense of the fragility of communication and language. You said at that time that you were afraid of language failing, "falling into a vacuum", do you still have that fear?

CV: Communication really is precarious, but I don't know that you're always that aware of the threat, sometimes you're more aware, sometimes less. But João Cabral was a writer who didn't believe or didn't want to believe in the passivity of the writer in relation to the states of mind in which he found himself. He liked to attribute poetic creation to a lucid and deliberate will to do something. And personally, although I do something totally different, on the whole I have that sensation that I write songs most of the time not because I'm swept away by a creative impulse, but because they are songs I planned to write, issues I planned to address, and that's more or less how I end up approaching it.

LL: Do you think that popular song has become the most fertile space for poetic creation in Brazil today?

CV: Perhaps it always has been. In Brazil it has really been a very fertile space, since the thirties, in the songs of Noel Rosa. Also in songs by Dorival Caymmi and many of Wilson Batista's songs and other Brazilian sambistas, like Cartola, at times. You really do often find such an intense poetic power in simple popular songs.

LL: What is curious in Brazil as well, is how within the space of the popular song "high" and "low", erudite and popular culture, often meet.

CV: Perhaps because although there are extraordinary individual expressions of high culture in Brazil, we don't have the means of expressing ourselves in the area of high culture that might make it a solid, strong area of expression.

LL: So it has to enter into dialogue with popular culture ...

CV: It enters into dialogue in such an intimate way that one of the greatest poets of João Cabral's generation, Vinícius de Moraes, who was also a diplomat like Cabral, became the most prolific lyric writer of bossa nova and never returned to his books.

LL: Highly significant, that relationship between poetry and popular music ...

CV: It is, popular music is dominated by song, there's instrumental music, there was such a sophisticated development of this through jazz, you know? But what has dominated popular music through the years is song, the sung word. That's the raw material of popular music and the sung word is precisely a kind of popular poetry that developed ... that comes from a tradition of popular music, but that also drew on erudite poetry and that came to occupy a place that didn't exist before the 20th century. If you listen to a song by Gershwin, sometimes you can't make any direct comparison with Schubert or Verdi, and sometimes it's better than Schubert or Verdi. It has a sense of form, of economy, a creative capacity, it's a very compact piece, with very balanced proportions – melodic sequences, harmonic structure, in combination with the ideas and the rhythm of the words. They're really unique pieces, of a specific type of creation, which is popular song for the mass public, to be sung on stage at popular venues and then recorded and played on radio for millions of people to hear. They're often works with a perfection that any creator, in any area, in any period would envy. In the sixties, rock 'n' roll, the most "lowly" and commercial form of popular music, was taken up by groups of English teenagers, rescued really, it was like a real redemption of the mass appeal, the element of mass entertainment that popular music represents. Abandoning all pretence at sophistication, harmonic or melodic complexity, or the delicacy that had developed in the lyrics of some of the great American songs, the Beatles and the Rolling Stones took the garbage of popular culture and presented it as the highest artistic expression of something that they perceptively captured at the time.

LL: A kind of re-reading of popular culture ...

CV: Without a doubt, it turned the idea of high and low culture on its head, within the space of low culture. But not just there, because the Beatles wrote – and in this regard, we Tropicalists shared their approach – they were attracted to 20th century experimental music, to erudite experimental music.

LL: The music was often experimental and the lyrics at times so banal ...

CV: A mixture of banal, colloquial with experimental; of the commercial with the ultra-demanding. There was a confusion between high and low culture created by this reversal in the history of rock 'n' roll which changed the judgement criteria of things forever.

LL: You mentioned the sung word a while ago, let's talk about the sung/spoken word. In the soundtrack to *Orpheus*, you mix a *samba-enredo* with rap ...

CV: Yes, this was dictated by the character in the film and it's what's happening in Brazil now; in the *favelas* of the big cities rap is what they're consuming and producing more than anything else. And furthermore, today, rap is like an attitude that is almost intolerant and exclusive. Many of them reject samba, fans of samba and the rest of Brazilian popular music. Rap has become a vehicle of affirmation and confrontation, you know?

LL: Outside of tradition?

CV: Outside of tradition and like an aggressive form of expression of the most deprived sectors of society, which are mainly black, which also makes the question of race explicit in a way that is not traditional in Brazil either.

LL: But do you think that rap is an "imported" and "foreign" phenomenon, or does it have anything in common with existing traditions in Brazil?

CV: It does! It's not that it's foreign, it's a question of assimilation by Brazilian popular music of what's going on in the international music scene, and that is a Brazilian tradition. And on the other hand it's an expression of the diaspora. And in Brazil it's growing at an incredible rate, what is curious is how it's growing directly in the *favelas* and through people from the *favelas*. This is the most interesting and important event in Brazilian music at the moment, this growth of rap music, which is not taking place through the conventional channels. And has a public made up exclusively of people from the *favelas* ...

LL: It's winning over another kind of audience now though, isn't it?

CV: There's rap made for the middle classes like Gabriel o Pensador, who's very good and sells very well with everyone, but these radical rappers from the *favela* groups, they're hardly known by the middle classes in the cities, and they're loved by people from *favelas* in cities all over Brazil, in particular the group Racionais MCs, they're a phenomenon, and they've already sold almost a million records without appearing on TV Globo, without giving interviews to the conventional magazines, without accepting contact with the mainstream press.

LL: It's a challenge to the organisation of the music industry ...

CV: It's a challenge and a very important sociological issue, which also becomes aesthetically important.

LL: You must be the Brazilian composer who has reflected most consciously on the continuities in the tradition of popular music. However, you are also responsible for radical ruptures to that tradition. How do you see the relationship between tradition and rupture in your work?

CV: That's the story of my life! I always find myself trying to examine that relationship and interpret it as best I can. We were talking about the high level of poetry in music lyrics and I'm precisely from that generation to which Chico Buarque belongs, he does everything with lyrics that we talked about, taking them to an unimaginably high level. So he's the highest expression of popular music and also represents the continuity side of Brazilian popular music. While I, on the other hand, observed the relationship between continuity and rupture and decided to emphasise the element of rupture. That's really what Tropicalism was, it was a decision at which I arrived, stimulated by conversations with Gilberto Gil and by the things that I was listening to, discussing, and by other conversations too, with my sister, Bethânia and with friends who were not necessarily associated with popular music. So Chico took precisely this element of continuity in bossa nova and explored it to its limits. And what I wanted from bossa nova was to take the element of rupture. Bossa nova was also a scandal when it emerged – a huge rupture, but it was a huge rupture that would have precisely the effect of maintaining continuity. Or in other words, regenerating the creative material of Brazilian popular music. And this was what Tropicalism sought to do as well, what I did and in a way, what has characterised my performances over the years, has been an interest in always reviving the value of rupture, whenever rupture is actually necessary and appropriate, because of its capacity to regenerate what is vital within a tradition.

LL: You mentioned rupture in performance. For a long time you presented yourself in public as a very ambiguous figure, constantly changing. Why did you feel obliged to recreate your image so much in the sixties and seventies?

CV: I don't know that I felt obliged to do this. I always acted on the presupposition that we were presenting those songs on TV. At the time that we started our careers television was the main means by which popular music was developing, which makes that question of high and low culture even more interesting, because it was television that was precisely the privileged vehicle for those new songs which were in competition with each other and which were being discussed by university students. I mean, they were discussed in order to determine whether they represented the right ideological position and the best solution to the aesthetic problems of popular music creation in Brazil. And all of this through television with an audience present, it's curious ...

LL: And how did your performances respond to this?

CV: Well I wanted to emphasise the fact that we were involved in the mass media. And I wanted to make explicit the idea of an image specially designed for television. So it was both a kind of re-affirmation of what I was doing, it was mass media entertainment and a critique of the mass media and its attitudes. So we were parodying those images at the same time that we created them – I mean, we had no illusions that simply by singing a few songs we could influence the political position of the listener, or make the best aesthetic choices to save the purity of Brazilian national identity. At the end of the day, that just seemed ingenuous to us. First of all we wanted to say that we were there as television personalities singing for millions of people and that in this world of mass entertainment interesting things were happening, including experimentation with form and political daring ... And this daring was evident for example, when I sang "É Proibido Proibir" with green and black plastic clothes, with beads around my neck and necklaces of electric wires and plugs and my hair the way it was, and Os Mutantes with science fiction-style clothes. And at another time I wore African garments, or suddenly I appeared in a suit, or Bahian robes over jeans ...

LL: So dressing like that was for television?

CV: Well, it began with television and then we took it to the stage, to shows, to emphasise the point that a show is, after all, a show. It's not that I wanted to formalise the show as a theatrical spectacle, with specially designed clothes; it wasn't that, but that uniform, everyone singing in black tie, that's how everyone dressed at that time on TV and for shows, everyone singing in their smoking jackets ... So we went on stage with our African clothes, Indian beads, plastic clothes ... Throughout my career, my appearance has taken the most varied forms, because from the beginning we wanted to make clear our awareness of ourselves as stage and screen personalities ...

LL: The awareness of belonging to the culture industry ...?

CV: Well, what we had to do was to be aware of that and involve ourselves in that and not passively accept formal wear for television and live performances, but effect a critique of clothing as well. A critique of appearance so we could feel free in that world of mass entertainment. It's a world that is often very conformist because of the concern to maintain an audience or sell a product, so the tendency would be to do everything not to displease the public, to increase sales. Sometimes the individual ends up as this conformist figure in order to be accepted by the majority, a kind of Hollywoodian repression of the personalities of the artists. Our generation wanted to do away with all that.

LL: And do you think that it took so long to get your first gold record because you refused to conform in this way?

CV: I do, I never sell many records. At the moment I'm selling for the first time but it's something out of the ... it's not what's expected of me! [laughter] Not even I expected it! But in any case it's not something that's seen as laudable by the Brazilian press, because it seems to look a bit suspect, it doesn't go down well with them. I also appeared in the magazine *Caras* which is a celebrity magazine, and they think that it shouldn't be done, it just shouldn't ... [laughter]. I'm supposed to play the role of the artist who is against show business and who's not a celebrity, but an artist ...

LL: Which is a bit difficult for you, as you're heavily involved in the world of show business ...

CV: I am a celebrity, I belong to show business, yes, I love it. I love that environment, of artists, singers, musicians, actresses, I like it, I always have. And I belong to that world and I don't want to pretend that it's otherwise.

LL: Many of your songs allow the listener to enter into the creative process of the song, enter and participate in the development of the song. Where does this willingness to dialogue with the listener come from? Is there a poetic or musical influence, for example, that influenced you in this regard?

CV: You know, I had a natural tendency towards that. Maybe because of my temperament and maybe because of what was going on at the time. I studied philosophy, which reveals a vocation for reflection and also a desire to share with people who are dialoguing with me the process by which I arrive at certain conclusions. I grew up in the fifties and sixties, and was becoming an adult in my own right and beginning to work in popular music at that time. The decade of the sixties saw a return in the mass media to some of the avant-garde concepts of the beginning of the century. And these vanguards frequently contained a meta-linguistic dimension, this was clear, for example, in the work of Godard whom I loved more than anyone else – he's my favourite director because of this. It was that tendency for a work to seem as though it were commenting on itself, we see it in Brecht, and it comes from the experimental art at the beginning of the century, Dadaism, Cubism. This interest in meta-language – in the literature of James Joyce, the poetry of e.e. cummings – this was all taken up again by avant-garde musicians in the fifties, by poets, and particularly by Brazilian poets in the fifties, the Concretists, Augusto de Campos, Haroldo de Campos, Décio Pignatari and others, but these three in particular, who sought us out eventually because they found a certain affinity with what we were doing, and it interested them, even though we weren't aware of what they were doing. But it was a tendency that, in a way, was heading in the same direction as their poetry. And at that time they introduced us to Oswald de Andrade, the most interesting Modernist of all and we were amazed to see how what Oswald had written and done confirmed our tendencies and inspirations. It's also the time when the work of North American pop artists became known, which also has that dimension like Godard's films and is not dissimilar to the attitude of the Beatles and the Rolling Stones with regard to rock, which I spoke about at the beginning of our conversation. So all of this contributed to making my work, as opposed to the work of other colleagues who are just extraordinary – I mention Chico because I believe him better than myself, than any of us – so as opposed to him, but also to the work of Edu Lobo, or Ivan Lins and other Brazilian composers as a whole, instead of making a product which was as finished as possible, as beautiful as possible and you present it ready and independent of yourself, I ended up, or was always inclined to produce a ... a destruction of the final object in favour of a demonstration of what the making of the object involved ...

LL: The process itself ...

CV: Yes, so the process becomes more interesting that the final product. This is quite typical of the sixties and it involves all the questions of meta-language and self-reference and self-parody, parody of other things, implicit and explicit commentary. On the whole, an invitation to the listener, the consumer, to dialogue – an open dialogue. And they're also very dirty pieces, broken compositions, more unfinished in a sense. Because their purpose is to pose the question, "What is this song?". "Why am I producing popular music now, here?" This becomes the thing which both obstructs and resolves the composition.

LL: And finally, Caetano, what are your projects for the future, and how do you see the immediate future of Brazilian popular music?

CV: Well, Brazilian popular music has always been very strong, so I am necessarily optimistic about popular music in Brazil. With regard to my personal projects, I tend to think in the short term, at most in the medium term. So I know that I'd like to put on more of the *Livro* shows, based on the *Prenda Minha* album, particularly in Europe, where I haven't taken it yet. And afterwards I'd like to concentrate on creating new things, maybe write another book. I wrote a book on the experiences of Tropicalism, called *Verdade Tropical* and I really enjoyed writing, I'd like to stop for a while to write, because I never stopped while I was writing the last book ...

LL: You were recording the whole time, weren't you?

CV: Recording, performing at shows, travelling, and writing at the same time. I need a bit of a break, to sit quietly in a corner, somewhat away from it all, to write, go somewhere every day, not stay at home. But I'd also like to do some other things, a record like the one I made of Latin American songs, *Fina Estampa*, but this time with North American songs. I'd really like to do it and it's a big challenge.[2] And on the other hand I'd like to make a new record with new things, more capricious than *Livro* which was a record I thought turned out well, but I was writing that book *Verdade Tropical* and recording at the same time ...

LL: *Livro* turned out as a very hybrid product ...

CV: It is, it's very hybrid and I like the fact that it is, but I want to take that hybridity further and arrive at something else that I can only glimpse now, but which I need to be able to see more clearly. And in the medium term I'd like to make another film.

LL: Thank you very much, Caetano.

(08/11/99)

Notes

1. This is an edited and translated version of an interview originally conducted in Portuguese.
2. This has since been released as *A Foreign Sound* (Universal Music. 6 02498 08621. 2004).

Bibliography

Books and Articles

As a guide for those who may be new to the study of Brazilian popular music, I have grouped separately from the rest of the bibliography some key works on Brazilian popular music – MPB in particular – written in Portuguese, followed by some useful publications currently available in English. In the discography key albums are marked out in bold.

Portuguese

Calado, Carlos. *Tropicália: A história de uma revolução musical* (São Paulo: Editora 34: 1997).
Campos, Augusto de. *Balanço da bossa e outras bossas* (São Paulo: Editora Perspectiva: 1993).
Castro, Ruy. *Chega de Saudade: A História e as histórias da bossa nova* (São Paulo: Companhia das Letras: 1995).
Favaretto, Celso. *Tropicália: Alegoria, Alegria* (São Paulo: Kairós: 1979).
Galvão, Walnice. "MMPB: uma análise ideológica", *Aparte*, n. 2, maio/jun. 1968, republished in *Saco de gatos: Ensaios críticos* (São Paulo: Duas Cidades: 1976), pp. 93–119.
Napolitano, Marcos. "A música popular brasileira nos anos 60: Apontamentos para um balanço historiográfico", *História: Questões e Debates*, Ano 15, N° 28, 1998, pp. 123–49.
Severiano, Jairo, and Mello, Zuza Homem de. *A canção no tempo: 85 anos de músicas brasileiras, Vol. 1: 1901–1957* (São Paulo: Editora 34: 1997).
Severiano, Jairo, and Mello, Zuza Homem de. *A canção no tempo: 85 anos de músicas brasileiras, Vol. 2: 1958–1985* (São Paulo: Editora 34: 1998).
Tatit, Luiz. *O Cancionista; A Composição de canções no Brasil* (São Paulo: Edusp: 1996).
Tinhorão, José Ramos. *História social da música popular brasileira* (Lisboa: Editorial Caminho: 1990).
Tinhorão, José Ramos. *Pequena história da música popular: da modinha ao Tropicalismo* (São Paulo: Art Editora: 1986).
Veloso, Caetano. *Verdade Tropical* (São Paulo: Companhia das Letras: 1997).
Wisnik, José Miguel. "The Gay Science: Literature and Popular Music in Brazil", *Journal of Latin American Cultural Studies*, 5.2, Nov. 1996, pp. 191–202

(Originally published as "Gaia ciência: literatura e música popular no Brasil", in *Revista de occidente*, 174 (1995), pp. 53–72).

English

Castro, Ruy. *Bossa Nova: The Story of the Brazilian Music that Seduced the World* (Chicago: A Capella: 2000).
Dunn, Christopher. *Brutality Garden: Tropicália and the Emergence of a Brazilian Counterculture* (Chapel Hill and London: University of North Carolina Press: 2001).
McGowan, Chris and Pessanha, Ricardo. *The Brazilian Sound: Samba, Bossa Nova and the Popular Music of Brazil* (Philadelphia: Temple University Press: 1998).
Perrone, Charles A. *Masters of Contemporary Brazilian Song: MPB 1965–1985*, (Austin: University of Texas Press: 1993).
Perrone, Charles A. and Dunn, Christopher. *Brazilian Popular Music and Globalization* (Gainesville: University Press of Florida: 2001).
Stroud, Sean. "'Música é para o povo cantar': Culture, Politics and the Brazilian Song Festivals, 1965–1972", *Latin American Music Review*, Volume 21: Number 2: Fall/Winter 2000, pp. 87–117.
Treece, David. "Guns and Roses: bossa nova and Brazil's music of popular protest, 1958–1968", *Popular Music* (1997) Volume 16/1, pp. 1–29.
Treece, David. "Rhythm and Poetry: Politics, Aesthetics and Popular Music in Brazil since 1960", in Anny Brooksbank Jones and Ronaldo Munck (eds), *Cultural Politics in Latin America* (Basingstoke: Macmillan: 2000).
Veloso, Caetano. *Tropical Truth: A Story of Music and Revolution in Brazil* (New York: Alfred A. Knopf: 2002).

"A Imagem do Som de Caetano Veloso", exhibition catalogue (Rio de Janeiro: Francisco Alves: 1998).
Almirante. *No Tempo de Noel Rosa* (Rio de Janeiro: Francisco Alves: 1977).
Anderson, Benedict. *Imagined Communities: Reflection on the Origin and Spread of Nationalism* (London: Verso: 1991).
Anderson, Perry. 'Marshall Berman: Modernity and Revolution', in *A Zone of Engagement* (London: Verso: 1992), pp. 24–45.
Andrade, Mário de. *Aspectos da Música Brasileira* (São Paulo: Livraria Martins: 1965).
Andrade, Mário de. *Dicionário Musical Brasileiro* (Belo Horizonte: Editor Itatiaia Limitada: 1989).
Andrade, Oswald de *Obras Completas: do Pau-Brasil à Antropofagia e às Utopias* (Rio de Janeiro: Civilização Brasileira: 1970).
Aufderheide, Pat. "Music videos: The Look of the Sound", *Journal of Communication*, Winter 1986, p. 77.

Ávila, Affonso. "Barroco, Estilo de vida, Estilo das Minas Gerais", in *Brasil Barroco: entre céu e terra* (Exhibition catalogue, Petit Palais, Paris, 04/11/99–06/02/00), pp. 95–104.
Bahiana, Ana Maria. *Nada será como antes – MPB nos anos 70* (Rio de Janeiro: Civilização Brasileira: 1980).
Bakhtin, Mikhail. *Rabelais and His World* (Bloomington: Indiana University Press: 1984).
Bar, Décio. *Acontece que ele é baiano*, in *Realidade*, Vol. 3:33, Dec. 1968.
Baroni, Mario. "The Concept of Musical Grammar", *Music Analysis*, 2:2, 1983, pp. 175–208.
Barthes, Roland. *Image, Music, Text* (London: Fontana: 1977).
Barthes, Roland. "The Grain of the Voice", in Simon Frith and Andrew Goodwin (eds), *On Record: Rock, Pop and the Written Word* (London: Routledge: 1990), pp. 293–300.
Bauman, Richard. "Verbal Art as Performance", *American Anthropologist*, 77, 1975, pp. 290–311.
Béhague, Gerard. "Bossa and Bossas: Recent Changes in Brazilian Urban Popular Music", *Ethnomusicology*, 17:2, May 1973.
Béhague, Gerard. "Brazilian Musical Values of the 1960s and 1970s: Popular Urban Music from Bossa Nova to Tropicália", *Journal of Popular Culture*, 14:1, Winter 1980.
Blacking, John. "Towards an Anthropology of the Body", in *The Anthropology of the Body* (London, New York, San Francisco: Academic Press: 1977).
Booth, Mark W. *The Experience of Songs* (New Haven and London: Yale University: 1981).
Boretz, Benjamin. "Meta-variations: Studies in the Foundations of Musical Thought (I)", *Perspectives of New Music*, 8, 1969, pp. 1–74.
Bradford Burns, E. *A History of Brazil* (New York: Columbia University Press: 1980).
Braga-Pinto, César, "How to Organize a Movement: Caetano Veloso's Tropical Path", *Studies in Latin American Popular Culture*, Vol. 19, 2000, pp. 103–12.
Buarque de Hollanda, Heloísa. *Impressões de Viagem: CPC, Vanguarda e Desbunde: 1960/1970* (São Paulo: Brasiliense: 1981).
Buarque de Hollanda, Heloísa, and Gonçalves, Marcos A. *Cultura e participação nos anos 60* (São Paulo: Brasiliense: 1984).
Cammack, Paul. "Brazil: The Long March to the New Republic", *New Left Review*, No 190, Nov/Dec 1991, pp. 21–58.
Campos, Augusto de, Pignatari, Décio and Campos, Haroldo de. *Teoria da Poesia Concreta* (São Paulo: Livraria Duas Cidades: 1975).
Campos, Haroldo de. "Poesia do Barroco", in *Brasil Barroco: entre céu e terra* (Exhibition catalogue, Petit Palais, Paris, 04/11/99–06/02/00), pp. 145–8.
Campos, Haroldo de. *Ruptura dos Gêneros na Literatura Latino-Americana* (São Paulo: Perspectiva: 1977).

Canclini, Néstor García. *Culturas híbridas: Estrategias para entrar y salir de la modernidad* (Mexico City: Grijalbo: 1989).
Candido, Antônio. "The Brazilian Family", in T. Lynn Smith and Alexander Marchant (eds), *Brazil: Portrait of a Half Continent* (New York: Dryden Press: 1951), pp. 291–312.
Cardoso, Fernando Henrique. "On the Characterization of Authoritarian Regimes in Latin America", in David Collier (ed.), *The New Authoritarianism in Latin America* (Princeton: Princeton University Press: 1979), pp. 33–57.
Chambers, Iain. *Urban Rhythms* (London: Macmillan: 1985).
Chaves, Celso Loureiro. "Memórias do passado no presente: a fenomenologia de *Transa*", Studies in Latin American Popular Culture (2000), Volume 19, pp. 73–82.
Chediak, Almir (ed.). *Caetano Veloso Songbook 1* (Rio de Janeiro: Lumiar: 1994).
Chediak, Almir (ed.). *Caetano Veloso Songbook 2* (Rio de Janeiro: Lumiar: 1994).
Clarke, Gary. "Defending Ski Jumpers: A Critique of Theories of Youth Subcultures", in Simon Frith and Andrew Goodwin (eds), *On Record: Rock, Pop and the Written Word* (London: Routledge: 1990), pp. 81–96.
Cone, Edward. *The Composer's Voice* (Berkeley: University of California Press: 1974).
Coutinho, Afrânio. *An Introduction to Literature in Brazil* (New York: Columbia University Press: 1969).
Cubitt, Sean. *Timeshift: On Video Culture* (London: Routledge: 1991).
Da Matta, Roberto. *Universo do Carnaval: Imagens e Reflexões* (Rio de Janeiro: Pinakotheke: 1981).
Da Matta, Roberto. *Carnivals, Rogues and Heroes: An Interpretation of the Brazilian Dilemma* (Notre Dame: University of Notre Dame Press: 1991).
Durant, Alan. *The Condition of Music* (London: Macmillan: 1984).
During, Simon, (ed.). *The Cultural Studies Reader* (London: Routledge: 1999).
Durst, Rogério. *Madame Satã: Com o diabo no corpo* (São Paulo: Brasiliense: 1985).
Dyer, Richard. "Don't Look Now: The Male Pin-Up", *Screen* 23: 3–4 (October 1982), pp. 61–72.
Dyer, Richard. "In Defense of Disco", in Simon Frith and Andrew Goodwin (eds), *On Record: Rock, Pop and the Written Word* (London: Routledge: 1990), pp. 410–18.
Eco, Umberto. "The Frames of Comic Freedom", in Thomas Sebeok (ed.), *Carnival* (Berlin: Mouton: 1984), pp. 1–9.
Enciclopédia da Música Brasileira (São Paulo: Art Editora/Publifolha: 1998).
Favaretto, Celso. "A canção tropicalista e a Tropicália de Hélio Oiticica", paper presented at BRASA III, King's College, Cambridge, 7–10 Sep., 1996.
Fausto, Boris. *A Concise History of Brazil* (Cambridge: Cambridge University Press: 1999).
Fonseca, Heber. *Esse Cara* (Rio de Janeiro: Editora Revan: 1993).
Foucault, Michel. *The History of Sexuality* (London: Penguin: 1981).

Franchetti, Paulo and Pécora, Alcyr. *Caetano Veloso: Literatura Comentada* (São Paulo: Abril: 1981).
Frank, Arthur W. "For a Sociology of the Body", in M. Featherstone et al. (eds), *The Body: Social Process and Cultural Theory* (London: Sage: 1991), pp. 36–102.
Freire, Paul. *Cultural Action for Freedom* (Harmondsworth: Penguin: 1972).
Freire, Paul. *Pedagogy of the Oppressed* (Harmondsworth: Penguin: 1972).
Freitas Filho, Armando, Hollanda, Heloísa Buarque de and Gonçalves, Marcos Augusto (eds). *Anos 70: Vol. 2: Literatura* (Rio de Janeiro: Europa Empresa: 1979–80).
Freyre, Gilberto. *The Masters and the Slaves: A Study in the Development of Brazilian Civilisation* (New York: Alfred A. Knopf: 1963).
Freyre, Gilberto. *The Mansions and the Shanties: The Making of Modern Brazil* (New York: Alfred. A. Knopf: 1963).
Frith, Simon. *Sound Effects: Youth, Leisure, and the Politics of Rock'n'Roll* (New York: Pantheon Books: 1981).
Frith, Simon. *Facing the Music: Essays on Pop, Rock and Culture* (London: Mandarin: 1990).
Frith, Simon. *Music For Pleasure: Essays in the Sociology of Pop* (Polity Press/ Basil Blackwell: Cambridge/Oxford: 1989).
Frith, Simon, and Goodwin, Andrew (eds). *On Record: Rock, Pop and the Written Word* (London: Routledge: 1990).
Frith, Simon, Goodwin, Andrew and Grossberg, Lawrence (eds). *Sound and Vision: The Music Video Reader* (London: Routledge: 1993).
Frith, Simon. *Performing Rites: On the Value of Popular Music* (Oxford: OUP: 1996).
Garcia, Walter. *Bim Bom: A Contradição sem conflitios de João Gilberto* (São Paulo: Paz e Terra: 1999).
Gil, Martha. *Carmen Miranda: A Pequena Notável* (São Paulo: Círculo do Livro: 1989).
Gonzalez, Mike and Treece, David. *The Gathering of Voices: The Twentieth Century Poetry of Latin America*, with Mike González (London: Verso: 1992).
Goodwin, Andrew. *Dancing in the Distraction Factory: Music Television and Popular Culture* (London: Routledge: 1993).
Green, Lucy. *Music on Deaf Ears: Musical Meaning, Ideology and Education* (Manchester: Manchester University Press: 1988).
Guerra, Guido. *Vicente Celestino: O Hóspede das Tempestades* (Rio de Janeiro: Editora Record: 1994).
Hall, Stuart. "Notes on Deconstructing the Popular", in Raphael Samuel (ed.), *People's History and Socialist Theory* (London: Routledge & Kegan Paul: 1981), pp. 227–40.
Hall, Stuart and Jefferson, Tony (eds). *Resistance Through Rituals: Youth Subcultures in Post-War Britain* (London: Unwin Hyman: 1989).

Hall, Stuart. 'Fantasy, Identity, Politics', in Erica Carter, James Donald and Judith Squires (eds). *Cultural Remix: Theories of Politics and the Popular* (London: Lawrence & Wishart Ltd: 1995), pp. 63–69.

Harwood, Dane L. "Universals in Music: A Perspective From Cognitive Psychology", *Ethnomusicology*, 20:3, 1976, pp. 521–33.

Hebdige, Dick. *Subculture: The Meaning of Style* (London: Routledge: 1997).

Hennion, Antoine. "The Production of Success: An Antimusicology of the Pop Song", in Simon Frith and Andrew Goodwin (eds), *On Record: Rock, Pop and the Written Word* (London: Routledge: 1990), pp. 185–206.

Hesmondhalgh, David. "Rethinking Popular Music after Rock and Soul", in James Curran, David Morley and V. Walkerdine (eds), *Cultural Studies and Communications* (London: Arnold: 1996), pp. 195–212.

Hughes, Walter. 'In the Empire of the Beat: Discipline and Disco', in Andrew Ross and Tricia Rose (eds), *Microphone Fiends: Youth Music, Youth Culture* (London/New York: Routledge: 1994), pp. 147–57.

Johnson, Randal. "Tupy or not Tupy: Cannibalism and Nationalism in Contemporary Brazilian Literature and Culture", in John King (ed.), *Modern Latin American Fiction: A Survey* (London: Faber & Faber: 1987), pp. 41–59.

Kiefer, Bruno. *A modinha e o lundu* (Porto Alegre: Editora Movimento: 1977).

King, John. *Magical Reels: A History of Cinema in Latin America* (London: Verso: 1990).

Koestenbaum, Wayne. *The Queen's Throat: Opera, Homosexuality and the Mystery of Desire* (London: Penguin: 1994).

Kramer, Lawrence. *Music as Cultural Practice: 1800–1900* (Berkeley: University of California Press: 1990).

Krausche, Valter. *Música Popular Brasileira* (São Paulo: Brasiliense (1983).

Laing, Dave. "Music Video: Industrial Product, Cultural Form", *Screen*, Vol. 26, No.1, 1985.

Lomax, Alan. *Folk Song Style and Culture* (Washington D.C.: American Association for the Advancement of Science, Publication no. 88: 1968).

Lucchesi, Ivo and Korff Dieguez, Gilda. *Caetano. Por que não?: Uma viagem entre a aurora e a sombra* (Rio de Janeiro: Leviatã: 1993).

Lynch, Joan D. "Music Videos: From Performance to Dada-Surrealism", *Journal of Popular Culture*, Vol.18, No.1, 1984.

Maciel, Luiz Carlos. *Geração em Transe: Memórias do Tempo do Tropicalismo* (Rio de Janeiro: Nova Fronteira: 1996).

Magaldi, Cristina. "Adopting imports: new images and alliances in Brazilian popular music of the 1990s", *Popular Music*, Volume 18/3, 1999.

Mariz, Vasco. *A Canção Brasileira* (Rio de Janeiro: Civilização Brasileira: 1977).

Matos, Gregório de. *Gregório de Matos: Poesias selecionadas* (São Paulo: FTD: 1993).

Matos, Claudia. *Acertei no Milhar: Samba e Malandragem no Tempo de Getúlio* (Rio de Janeiro: Paz e Terra: 1982).

Matos, Maria Izilda Santos de. *Dolores Duran: Experiências Boêmias em Copacabana nos Anos 50* (Rio de Janeiro: Bertrand Brasil: 1997).
McCann, Bryan. *Hello, Hello Brazil: Popular Music in the Making of Modern Brazil* (Durham and London: Duke University Press: 2004).
McClary, Susan and Walser, Robert. "Start Making Sense!: Musicology Wrestles with Rock", in Simon Frith and Andrew Goodwin (eds), *On Record: Rock, Popular and the Written Word* (London: Routledge: 1990), pp. 277–92.
McClary, Susan. *Feminine Endings: Music, Gender, and Sexuality* (Minnesota: University of Minnesota Press: 1991).
McClary, Susan. "Same as it Ever Was: Youth Culture and Music", in *Microphone Fiends: Youth Music and Youth Culture* (New York/London: Routledge: 1994), pp. 29–40.
McGowan, Chris, and Pessanha, Ricardo. *The Billboard Book of Brazilian Music : Samba, Bossa Nova and the Popular Sounds of Brazil* (New York: Billboard Books: 1991).
McRobbie, Angela. "Settling Accounts With Subcultures: A Feminist Critique", in Simon Frith and Andrew Goodwin (eds), *On Record: Rock, Pop and the Written Word* (London: Routledge: 1990), pp. 66–80.
Mello, Maria Amélia (ed.). *20 Anos de resistência: Alternativas da cultura no regime militar* (Rio de Janeiro: Espaço e Tempo: 1986).
Melly, George. *Revolt into Style: The Pop Arts in Britain* (London: Allen Lane/The Penguin Press: 1970).
Melo Neto, João Cabral de. *João Cabral de Melo Neto: Antologia Poética* (Rio de Janeiro: José Olympio: 1986).
Meneses, Adélia Bezerra de. *Desenho Mágico: Poesia e Política em Chico Buarque* (São Paulo: Hucitec: 1982).
Menezes, José Luiz Mota. "O Barroco no país do açúcar", in *Brasil Barroco: entre céu e terra* (Exhibition catalogue, Petit Palais, Paris, 04/11/99–06/02/00), pp. 85–94.
Merquior, José Guilherme. *De Anchieta a Euclides: Breve história da literatura brasileira* (Rio de Janeiro: José Olympio: 1979).
Michaelis Dicionário Ilustrado, Vol. II (São Paulo: Melhoramentos: 1961).
Middleton, Richard. *Studying Popular Music* (Milton Keynes: Open University Press: 1990).
Morelli, Rita. *Indústria Fonográfica: Um Estudo Antropológico* (Campinas: UNICAMP: 1991).
Nattiez, Jean-Jacques. "Reflections on the Development of Semiology in Music", *Music Analysis*, 8:1–2, pp. 21–75.
Neto, Torquato. "Texto de *Os Últimas Dias de Paupéria*", reproduced in *O Estado de São Paulo, Cultura*, 7/08/93.
Novo Dicionário Aurélio, 1ª edição, 11ª impressão (Rio de Janeiro: Nova Fronteira: 1975).
O som do Pasquim (Rio de Janeiro: Codecri: 1975).

Ortiz, Renato. *A Moderna Tradição Brasileira: Cultura Brasileira e Indústria Cultural* (São Paulo: Brasiliense: 1994).
Parker, Richard. *Bodies, Pleasures and Passions: Sexual Culture in Contemporary Brazil* (Boston: Beacon Press: 1991).
Pereira, Carlos Alberto M. and Hollanda, Heloísa Buarque de. *Patrulhas ideológicas, marca reg.: Arte e engajamento em debate* (São Paulo: Brasiliense: 1980).
Pereira, Maria Isaura de Queiroz. *Carnaval Brasileiro* (São Paulo: Brasiliense: 1992).
Perrone, Charles A. *Seven Faces: Brazilian Poetry Since Modernism* (Durham, London: Duke University Press: 1996).
Phelan, Peggy. *Unmarked: The Politics of Performance* (London: Routledge: 1993).
Ramos, Fernão. "Uma forma histórica de cinema alternativa e seus dilemas na atualidade", in Maria Amélia Mello (ed.), *20 Anos de resistência: Alternativas da cultura no regime militar* (Rio de Janeiro: Espaço e Tempo: 1986), pp. 81–94.
Resende, Beatriz. "Brazilian Modernism: The Canonised Revolution", in Vivian Schelling (ed.), *Through the Kaleidoscope: The Experience of Modernity in Latin America* (London: Verso: 2001).
Ridenti, Marcelo. *Em Busca do Povo Brasileiro: artistas da revolução, do CPC à era da tv* (Rio de Janeiro/São Paulo: Record: 2000).
Rodrigues Filho, Lupicínio (ed.). *Foi Assim* (Porto Alegre : L &PM Editores: 1995).
Ross, Andrew, and Rose, Tricia (eds). *Microphone Fiends: Youth Music, Youth Culture* (London/New York: Routledge: 1994).
Rowe, William, and Schelling, Vivian. *Memory and Modernity: Popular Culture in Latin America* (London: Verso: 1991).
Saia, Luiz Henrique. *Carmen Miranda* (São Paulo: Brasiliense: 1984).
Salomão, Waly. *Hélio Oiticica: Qual é o parangolé?* (Relume Dumará/Prefeitura do Rio de Janeiro: Rio de Janeiro: 1996).
Sant'Anna, Affonso Romano de. *Música popular e moderna poesia brasileira* (Petrópolis: Vozes: 1978).
Santiago, Silviano. *Uma Literatura nos Trópicos* (Rio de Janeiro: Editora Perspectiva: 1978).
Savage, Jon. "The Gender Bender", *The Face*, 7 (November 1970).
Savage, Jon. "Androgyny", *The Face*, 38 (June 1983).
Savage, Jon. 'Tainted Love: the influence of male homosexuality and sexual divergence on pop music and culture since the war', in Alan Tomlinson (ed.), *Consumption, Identity and Style: Marketing, Meanings and the Packaging of Pleasure* (London: Comedia/Routledge: 1990).
Schelling, Vivian (ed.). *Through the Kaleidoscope: The Experience of Modernity in Latin America* (London: Verso: 2000).

Schreiner, Claus. *Música Brasileira: A History of Popular Music and the People of Brazil* (London: Marion Boyars: 1993).

Schwarz, Roberto. "Culture and Politics in Brazil, 1964–1969", in *Misplaced Ideas: Essays in Brazilian Culture* (London: Verso: 1992), pp. 19–32.

Sevcenko, Nicolau. "Entre a ordem e o caos: colonialismo, escravidão e barroco no Brasil", in *Brasil Barroco: entre céu e terra* (Exhibition catalogue, Petit Palais, Paris, 04/11/99–06/02/00), pp. 61–7.

Shaw, Lisa. *The Social History of the Brazilian Samba* (Aldershot: Ashgate: 1999).

Sherman, Barry L. and Dominick, Joseph R. "Violence and Sex in Music Videos: TV and Rock n' Roll", *Journal of Communication*, Winter, 1986.

Shore, Michael. *The Rolling Stone Book of Rock Video* (London: Sidgwick & Jackson: 1985).

Shuker, Roy. *Understanding Popular Music* (London, New York: Routledge: 1994).

Siqueira, Baptista. *Modinhas do Passado* (Rio de Janeiro: Folha Carioca Editora Ltda: 1979).

Skidmore, Thomas. *The Politics of Military Rule in Brazil, 1964–1985* (New York: Oxford University Press: 1988).

Sloboda, John A. *The Musical Mind: The Cognitive Psychology of Music* (Oxford: Clarendon Press: 1985).

Solie, Ruth A. *Musicology and Difference: Gender and Sexuality in Music Scholarship* (Berkeley: University of California Press: 1995).

Solt, Mary Ellen (ed.). *Concrete Poetry – A World View* (Bloomington: Indiana University Press: 1970).

Sontag, Susan. *Against Interpretation* (London: André Deutsch: 1987).

Sovik, Liv. "Tropicália, Canonical Pop", *Studies in Latin American Popular Culture*, 19, 2000, pp. 113–28.

Steiner, Wendy (ed.). *The Sign in Music and Literature* (Austin: University of Texas Press: 1981).

Storr, Anthony. *Music and the Mind* (London: Harper Collins: 1993).

Tagg, Philip. "Fernando the Flute", seminar at the Centre for the Study of Brazilian Culture and Society, King's College London, 13th March, 1997.

Thompson, Grahame F. "Approaches to Performance", *Screen*, 26 (5), 1985: 81, pp. 78–90.

Tinhorão, José Ramos. *Música Popular: Os Sons Que Vêm da Rua* (São Paulo: Edições Tinhorão: 1976).

Tinhorão, José Ramos. *O Samba Agora Vai – A Farsa da Música Popular no Exterior* (Rio de Janeiro: JCM: no date).

Tinhorão, José Ramos. *Música Popular: do Gramofone ao Rádio e TV* (São Paulo: Ática: 1981).

Tolman, Jon M. "The Context of a Vanguard: Toward a Definition of Concrete Poetry", *Poetics Today*, 3:3 (Summer 1982), pp. 149–66.

Treece, David. "Melody, Text and Luis Tatit's *O Cancionista*: New Directions in Brazilian Popular Music Studies", *Journal of Latin American Cultural Studies*, 1996, 5.2, pp. 203–16.

Treece, David. "Tropicália: A Canção Popular e a Cultura de Massas", *Studies in Latin American Popular Culture*, Volume 19 (2000), pp. 51–5.

Treece, David. "Between Bossa Nova and the Mambo Kings: the Internationalization of Latin American Popular Music", in *Travesia*, Volume 1: 2, pp. 65–66.

Tupinambá, Martha de Ulhôa. "Música romântica in Montes Claros: inter-gender relations in Brazilian popular song", *British Journal of Ethnomusicology*, Vol. 9/I, 2000, pp. 11–40.

Turner, Bryan S. "Recent Developments in the Theory of the Body", in Mike Featherstone et al. (eds), *The Body: Social Process and Cultural Theory* (London: Sage: 1991), pp. 1–35.

Vasconcellos, Gilberto. *Música Popular: De olho na fresta* (Rio de Janeiro: Graal: 1977).

Veloso, Caetano. *Alegria, Alegria*, Waly Salomão (ed.) (Rio de Janeiro: Pedra Q Ronca: 1977).

Ventura, Zuenir. *1968: O Ano que não terminou* (Rio de Janeiro: Nova Fronteira: 1988).

Vieira, Else Ribeiro Pires. "Liberating Calibans: Readings of *Antropofagia* and Haroldo de Campos's Poetics of Transcreation" in Susan Bassnett (ed.), *Postcolonial Translation: Theory and Practice* (London/New York: Routledge: 1999), pp. 95–113.

Walker, John A. *Cross-Overs: Art Into Pop/Pop Into Art* (London: Comedia/ Methuen: 1987).

Walser, Robert. *Running with the Devil: Power, Gender and Madness in Heavy Metal Music* (Hanover: University Press of New England: 1993).

Yudice, George. "A Funkificação do Rio" in Micael Herschmann (ed.), *Abalando os Anos 90: Funk e Hip-Hop – Globalização, Violência e Estilo Cultural* (Rio de Janeiro: Rocco: 1997), pp. 24–49.

Zolov, Eric. "*Rebeldismo* in the Revolutionary Family: Rock 'n' Roll's Early Challenges to State and Society in Mexico" in *Journal of Latin American Cultural Studies*, Vol. 6, No. 2, Nov. 1997, pp. 201–16.

Zolov, Eric. *Refried Elvis: The Rise of the Mexican Counterculture* (Berkeley: University of California Press: 1999).

Newspapers and Magazines

A.C.M., et al. "Depois de 26 anos, um manifesto sem revolução", *O Globo*, 11/08/93.

Abreu, Caio Fernando. "Comprei calças de cetim verde-amazônia", in *O Estado de São Paulo, Cultura*, 7/08/93.

Alves Leite, Marcos. "Caetano Veloso: alegria infinita para a música", *Enfoque*, 06/06/85.
Anon. "Caetano Veloso", *O Globo*, 19/08/78.
Anon. "Caetano Veloso", *O Estado de São Paulo*, 17/08/78.
Anon. "Caetano emociona em tributo a Fellini", *O Globo*, 26/11/97.
Anon. "Caetano não obteve êxito", *O Estado de São Paulo*, 03/03/70.
Anon. "Caetano no templo do caetanismo", *Veja*, 19/01/72.
Anon. "Caetano Veloso reafirma suas convicções", *Jornal do Brasil*, 27/09/68.
Anon. "Caetano Veloso, novo disco com Gil e Bethânia", *O Globo*, 04/03/81.
Anon. "Caetano Veloso: na velocidade do tempo, assumindo novas posturas e se renovando", *Correio Brasiliense*, 24/12/84.
Anon. "Caetano volta ao palco com bigode", *A Folha de São Paulo*, 13/08/86.
Anon. "Caetano, *Velô* e Cia", *A Tarde*, 12/12/84.
Anon. "Casamento de Caetano deu em versos de cordel", *Ultima Hora*, 23/01/68.
Anon. "CD homenageará o movimento", *O Globo*, 26/10/97.
Anon. "Deixando sangrar", *Diário de Notícias*, 12/08/71.
Anon. "O Tropicalismo é nosso, viu?", *Revista Realidade*, December, 1968.
Anon. "Orgulho pelo recorde de devoluções", *Jornal do Brasil*, 02/06/87.
Anon. "Os críticos musicais segundo Caetano Veloso: Racistas e preconceituosos, que não gostam de dançar", *O Globo*, 31/01/79.
Anon. "Polícia Federal quer saber quem fez a capa do LP com Caetano nu", *O Dia*, 07/08/75.
Anon. "A Arte de Velô em Eu Sou o Show", *Correio Brasiliense*, 19/08/85.
Anon. "A situação atual/O novo disco", *Jornal da Tarde*, ?/07/71 (Museu da Imagem e do Som, Rio de Janeiro)*.
Anon. "Caetano vaiado pára *show* e xinga a platéia", *Jornal do Brasil*, 26/11/73.
Anon. "Caetano vaiado xinga o público e acaba detido", *Jornal do Brasil*, 26/11/73.
Anon. "Caetano Veloso apresenta: *O Cinema Falado*", *Folha de São Paulo*, 06/09/86.
Anon. "Caetano Veloso: Nem herói nem mártir: impresível como sempre", *O Globo*, 19/08/78.
Anon. "Especial Rádio JB – Caetano Veloso", *Jornal do Brasil*, 20/08/75.
Anon. "Os encontros de um duo afinado", *Revista Programa*, 24/09/93.
Anon. "*Tropicália 2*, faixa por faixa", *Revista Programa*, 24/09/93.
Anon. "Uma colcha de retalhos coloridos", *Revista Programa*, 24/09/93.
Aragão, Diana. "A volta de *Araçá Azul*", *Jornal do Brasil*, 02/06/87.
Aragão, Diana. "Novo disco de Caetano chega às lojas amanhã cercado de expectativa diante de seu 'silêncio'", *O Globo*, 27/10/87.
Aragão, Diana. "Caetano, beleza quase pura": *O Globo*: no date (Museu da Imagem e do Som: Rio de Janeiro)*.
Azevedo, Eliane. "Quem são as canalhas?", *Veja*, 20/11/91.
Bahiana, Ana Maria. "Caetano e seu novo LP, *Bicho*: Dançar ajuda a pensar melhor", *O Globo*, 10/04/77.

Bahiana, Ana Maria. "Caetano Veloso: Os muitos nomes e as cores várias de quem não tem nada a ocultar", *O Globo*, 28/03/82.
Bahiana, Ana Maria. "Caetano, com seu *Velô*. A Tropicália continua viva", *O Globo*, 23/06/84.
Bahiana, Ana Maria. "Velô no Canecão", *O Globo*, 21/06/84.
BASF. "Rock in Brasil: O Balanço das gerações", leaflet, Projeto Cultural das Empresas do Grupo BASF no Brasil, São Paulo, 1986.
Benavides, Roberto. "Caetano: Quarentão e adolescente", *Jornal do Brasil*, 10/08/85.
Brito, Hagamenon. "Caetano Veloso radiografa o caos do Brasil", *A Tarde*, ?/12/91 (Museu da Imagem e do Som, Rio de Janeiro)*.
Brito, Hagamenon. "*Circuladô* é o ápice estético de Caetano", *A Tarde*, 08/12/92.
Camacho, Marcelo. "Bate-Papo Baiano", *O Dia*, 21/08/93.
Campos, Augusto de. "Festival de viola e violência", *Correio da Manhã*, 26/10/67.
Capinan, José Carlos, et al. "O senhor da canção", *A Tarde*, 09/03/96.
Carlos, Antônio. "Caetano, sem lenço, sem documento", *Jornal do Brasil*, 11/01/68.
Castello, José. "Caetano entre o Ben e o Mautner", *Jornal do Brasil*, 03/03/88.
Castro, Acyr. "Um novo interlúdio em busca das reinvenções", *O Globo*, 05/06/73.
Cerqueira, José. "Sem fala, Caetano é só voz e instrumento", *A Tarde*, 16/01/88.
Chaves, Celso Loureiro. "Giro Completo, Caetano, Caetano", *A Tarde*, 11/12/93.
Cury, João Wady. "Morte da Tropicália será exibida na Globo", *O Estado de São Paulo, Cultura*, 7/08/93.
Dayrell Porto, Sergio. "O sexo dos mitos: Quem tem medo do Caetano?", *Correio Brasiliense*, 26/08/86.
Dias, Mauro. "A volta da língua áspera e feroz do poeta", *O Globo*, 15/11/84.
Dulci, Estevam. "*Muito* – um 'show' muito 'odara' com Caetano e a platéia de 'short' e camiseta", *Jornal do Brasil*, no date (Museu da Imagem e do Som, Rio de Janeiro)*.
Dumar, Deborah. "Neguinha, para os íntimos", *O Globo*, 07/11/87.
Espírito Santo, Solange. "Acima da ansiedade subdesenvolvida", *Diário do Grande ABC*, 04/10/83.
Esquivel, Edvaldo, F. "*Araçá Azul*: A volta do fruto proibido", *A Tarde*, 10/06/87.
Essinger, Silvio. "Soul Brasil", 02/06/00, Clique Music Internet site.
Fernandes, Paula, et al. "Haiti nas retinas do Brasil", *O Globo*, 06/08/93.
Ferreira, Mauro. "Um CD cheio de experiências", *O Dia*, ?/12/97 (Museu da Imagem e do Som, Rio de Janeiro)*.
Ferreira, Mauro. "Um novo olhar tropical", *O Dia*, 22/11/97.
Fonseca, Albenísio. "Flagrantes de 'Cae' no camarim", *A Tarde*, 26/10/89.
Freitas, Jorge. "De verde e rosa, Caetano canta 'Odara' e todos dançam", *Última Hora*, 14/12/79.
Garrido, Luís Cláudio. "Latinocaetano", *A Tarde*, 28/07/94.

Garrido, Luís Cláudio. "Resistente ao tempo", *A Tarde*, 19/11/97.
Gonçalves, Marcos Augusto. "A Virada de Caetano", *Folha de São Paulo*, 26/05/84.
Gonçalves, Marcos Augusto. "*Velô*: A língua veloz de um novo Caetano", *Folha de São Paulo*, 15/11/85.
Grünewald, José Lino. "Caetano, cambalacho", *Correio da Manhã*, 13/03/70.
Guimarães, Ângela. "Caetano, em DVD", *A Tarde*, 17/04/2000.
Halfoun, Eli. "Caetano: já é alegria demais", *Última Hora*, 2/12/67.
HB. "O Outro retrato de um estrangeiro", *A Tarde*, 26/10/89.
Lobato, Eliane. "O Haiti não é mais aqui", *Isto É*, 12/10/94.
Lobato, Eliane. "Os ecos de Caetano", *O Globo*, 08/06/87.
Louchard, Aimée. "A noite encantada de Caetano Veloso na Praça da Apoteose", *O Globo*, 06/10/86.
Machado, Béu. "E Caetano falou", *A Tarde*, 09/03/88.
Machado, Paulo Sérgio M. Text from the booklet accompanying the album *Dolores Duran & Tito Madi*, part of the series *Nova História da Música Popular Brasileira*, Abril Cultural, 1978, p. 11.
Maciel, Luiz Carlos. "O pensamento voltado para a doçura de existir", *O Globo*, 26/10/97.
Maria, Cleusa. "*Cores Nomes*: Caetano Veloso num momento de generosidade", *Jornal do Brasil*, 24/03/82.
Maria, Cleusa. "Caetano, simplesmente velô", *Jornal do Brasil*, 21/06/84.
Mello, Luiz Antonio. "Caetano, de volta ao Canecão", *Jornal do Brasil*, 02/05/81.
Miguel, Antônio Carlos et al. "A petulância de viver a verdade tropical", *O Globo*, 22/11/97.
Miguel, Antônio Carlos. "O futuro do Tropicalismo no Haiti", *O Globo*, ?/?/93 (Museu da Imagem e do Som, Rio de Janeiro)*.
Moraes Neto, Geneton. "Caetano calou", *Jornal do Brasil*, 08/10/87.
Moreira, Célia. "Caetano: o longe ficou mais próximo", *Jornal do Brasil*, 12/08/71.
Moretz-Sohn, Cláudia. 'Visual assumido na capa do disco', *O Globo*, 7/11/1987.
Motta, Nelson. "Aparição, martírio e glória de Caetano Veloso", *O Globo*, no date (Museu da Imagem e do Som, Rio de Janeiro)*.
Motta, Nelson. "Caetano interditado", *O Globo*, 07/08/75.
Motta, Nelson. "De surpresa em surpresa, a trajetória de Caetano", *O Globo*, 18/12/77.
Motta, Nelson. "Nos, nus, e a música: coeur-razon nas palavras de Caetano", *O Globo*, 12/04/81.
Nery, Sebastião. "O Grande Rio", *Tribuna da Imprensa*, 19/12/70.
Olivieri, Rita. "Fino Caballero", *A Tarde*, 01/04/95.
Philips Catalogue, 09/1975.
Queiroz, Rachel de. "Êsse Caetano Veloso", *Jornal do Brasil*, 10/03/68.
Rangel, Maria Lucia. "Caetano Veloso: Extraordinariamente gostável mesmo sem fazer o modelito nacional", *Jornal do Brasil*, 12/12/79.

Rocha Lima, Irlam. "Eu faço algo de 2ª categoria", *Correio Brasiliense*, 15/06/85.
Rodrigues, Apoenan. "Outras palavras", *Isto É*, 15/05/96.
Rosa, Gideon. "Caetano erudito", *A Tarde*, 04/12/93.
Santos, Joaquim dos. "A Apoteose de Caetano", *Jornal do Brasil*, 19/09/86.
Santos, Joaquim dos. "O 'sóbrio' Caetano", *Jornal do Brasil*, 07/11/87.
Silva, Beatriz Coelho. "O sempre surpreendente Caetano", *Última Hora*, 28/10/87.
Silveira, Emilia. "Caetano: Só a vontade de cantar", *Jornal do Brasil*, 17/08/75.
Souza, Okky de. "A poesia das ruinas", *Veja*, 04/12/91.
Souza, Tárik de and Luiz Carlos Mansur. "Duas noites para a história", *Jornal do Brasil*, 06/10/86.
Souza, Tárik de. "Caetano e Gil, 15 anos depois", *Jornal do Brasil*, 07/04/81.
Souza, Tárik de. "Caetano: É preciso dar um tempo", *Jornal do Brasil*, 12/05/74.
Souza, Tárik de. "Crítica música; *Fina Estampa*", *Jornal do Brasil*, 23/09/95.
Souza, Tárik de. "Dois violões e duas vozes em ritual mágico", *Jornal do Brasil*, 01/10/94.
Souza, Tárik de. "Fala, Caetano: a voz do anjo torto", *Jornal do Brasil*, 27/10/87.
Souza, Tárik de. "O gênio multiplicado de *Velô*", *Jornal do Brasil*, 15/11/84.
Sukman, Hugo. "Cada vez mais 'loco por ti' ", *Jornal do Brasil*, 13/05/94.
Sukman, Hugo. "Caetano reencontra o cinema", *O Globo*, 20/07/96.
Suzuki Junior, Matinas. "A outra banda de Caetano Veloso", *Folha de São Paulo*, 24/09/86.
Tinhorão, José Ramos. 'Como seria bom se a música de Caetano e Chico Buarque correspondesse à sua poesia', *Jornal do Brasil*, 12/12/1979.
Ventura, Mary. "Temporada de outono", *Jornal do Brasil*, 02/05/74.
Zappa, Regina and Ernesto Soto. "Caetano, o místico racional", *Jornal do Brasil*, 22/11/97.
* (Dates missing at source)

Discography

Caetano Veloso

Domingo, Polygram. 6328 392. 1967.
Caetano Veloso, Philips. R765.026L. 1968.
***Tropicália ou panis et circensis*, Philips. 6436303. 1968.**
Caetano Veloso, Philips. R765.086 London. 1969.
Caetano Veloso, Philips. 6349 007. 1971.
Transa, Philips. 6349 026. 1972.
Araçá Azul, Philips. 824 691-1. 1972.
Gal Costa, *Índia*, Philips. 6349.077. 1973.
Qualquer Coisa, Philips/Polygram. CD 838 558-2. 1975.

Jóia, Philips/Polygram. CD 838 559-2. 1975.
A Arte de Caetano Veloso, Fontana. 6470 541/2. 1975.
Bicho, Philips/Polygram. 6349 327. 1977.
Muito (dentro da estrela azulada), Philips. 6349.382. 1978.
Cinema Transcendental, **Philips/Polygram. CD 838 289-2. 1979.**
Outras Palavras, Philips/Polygram. 6328 303. 1981.
Cores, Nomes, Philips/Polygram. 6328 381. 1982.
Caetano, História da Música Popular Brasileira, Abril Cultural. HMPB - 10. 1982.
Uns, Philips/Polygram. CD 812 747-2. 1983.
Velô, **Philips/Polygram. 824 0241. 1984.**
Caetano Veloso, Nonesuch. CD 846 9196-2. 1986.
Totalmente Demais, Philips/Polygram. 830145-1. 1986.
Caetano, Philips/Polygram. 832938-1. 1987.
Música Popular Brasileira: Entrevistado: Caetano Veloso, Museu da Imagem e do Som, São Paulo. Cassette. 13/02/87.
Estrangeiro, Philips/Polygram. CD 838 297-2. 1989.
Circuladô, **Philips/Polygram. 501 639-1. 1991.**
Circuladô Vivo, Philips/Polygram. 518 070-2. 1993.
Tropicália 2, **Philips/Polygram. CD 518 178-2. 1993.**
Fina Estampa, Philips/Polygram. CD 522745.2. 1994.
Livro, **Philips/Polygram. CD 536 584-2. 1997.**
Prenda Minha, Philips/Polygram. CD 538 332-2. 1998.
Orfeu (soundtrack), Natasha Records. CD 292.105. 1999.
Caetano Veloso Singles, Philips/Polygram. CD PHCA-1090. 1999.
Noites do Norte, Universal Music. 044001 65272. 2001.

Other Artists

Antônio Adolfo, *Feito em Casa*, Artezanal. LP-A-001. 1977.
Antônio Adolfo, *Viralata*, Artezanal. LP-A-003. 1979.
Wilson Batista, *História da Música Popular Brasileira*, Abril Cultural. MPB 35. 1971.
Chico Buarque, *Chico 50 anos: O Malandro*, Philips/Polygram. CD 522800-2. No date.
Roberto Carlos, *Roberto Carlos*, CBS. S 64757. 1972.
Roberto Carlos, *Roberto Carlos*, Columbia. CD 850.285/2 – 464245. 1985.
Vicente Celestino, *História da Música Popular Brasileira*, Abril Cultural. MPB 25. 1970.
Gal Costa, *Mina D'Agua Do Meu Canto*, Warner Chappell. 7432126323-2. 1995.
Cândido das Neves and Catulo Paixão Cearense, *História da Música Popular Brasileira*, Abril Cultural. HMPB - 42 - B. 1978.
Dolores Duran and Tito Madi, *História da Música Popular Brasileira*, Abril Cultural. HMPB - 46 - B. 1978.

João Gilberto, *O Talento de João Gilberto*, EMI. 152 422183/4. 1986.
João and Astrud Gilberto, *The Girl from Ipanema*, Sarabandas. CD 306. 1993.
Tom Jobim, *História da Música Popular Brasileira*, Abril Cultural. MPB 16. 1970.
Tom Jobim, *Inédito*, BMG/Jobim Music. 7432132920-2. 1998.
Carmen Miranda, *The Lady in the Tutti Frutti Hat*, Harlequin. CD 133.
Sérgio Ricardo, *História da Música Popular Brasileira*, Abril Cultural. MPB 37. 1971.
Lupicínio Rodrigues, *História da Música Popular Brasileira*, Abril Cultural. MPB 10. 1970.
Geraldo Vandré, *História da Música Popular Brasileira*, Abril Cultural. MPB 34. 1971.
Geraldo Vandré, *Geraldo Vandré: Prá não dizer que não falei das flores*, Som Maior. 303.2001-B. 1979.
Various, *10 anos da bossa nova, n° 3*, Fontana. 6488 028. 1974.
Various, *Festivais – Volume 1*, GloboDisk. CD 0028-2. 1997.
Various, *II Festival Internacional da Canção Popular, Rio*, CODIL. CDL - 13.003. 1967.
Various, *III Festival Internacional da Canção Popular, Rio*, CODIL. CDL - 13.017. 1968.
Various, *3° festival da música popular brasileira, Volume 1 (TV Record)*, Philips. R765. 014L. 1967.
Various, *3° festival da música popular brasileira, Volume 2 (TV Record)*, Philips. R765. 015L. 1967.
Various, *3° festival da música popular brasileira, Volume 3 (TV Record)*, Philips. R765. 016L. 1967.

Videography

"Caetano – Circuladô Vivo", Polygram Video, 086 195 - 3, 1992.
"Caetano Veloso – Un Caballero de Fina Estampa", Polygram Video, 011 228 - 3, 1995.
"Festivais MPB – Anos 60, TV Record", Arquivo Projeto Alta Fidelidade, Universidade de Paraná, Curitiba.
Tropicália 20 anos, Julio Lerner and Christiane Ballerini, Centro de Produção de Vídeo, Museu da Imagem e do Som, São Paulo: 0-36/88.
"Yes, Nós Temos Memória", Museu da Imagem e do Som, São Paulo: 0-36/88.
"Programa Livre: Caetano Veloso", SBT, 03/12/97, 15:30-16:30.

Various music videos (including "Livros") supplied by Alex Perreira at Polygram do Brasil.

Extracts of television interviews and programmes kindly made available by Roberto Luiz, Caetano Superbacana Veloso Fã Clube, "Disco Voador Records", Loja N° 77-B, Shopping Orixás Center, Politeama, Salvador, Bahia.

Centro de Documentação Rede Globo

"TV Ano 25 – Festivais da Record 66, 67, e 68; FIC 68, 69 e 70", N° Documento: 51-0101635; N° Cassete: 0101635/0101635: 01/01/66.
"Musical com Caetano Veloso – 'Felicidade'", N° Documento: 51-0041245; N° Cassete: 0041235/0041245: 07/07/74.
"Caetano Veloso – Show no Seis e Meia do Carlos Gomes", N° Documento: 50-0000059; N° Cassete: 0000048/0000119: 07/07/77.
"Serie Grandes Nomes: Caetano Emanuel Viana Teles Veloso", N° Documento: 51-0015417; N° Cassete: 0015417: 05/06/81: 05/06/81.
"Show de Caetano Veloso 'Cores, Nomes' – Canecão", N° Documento: 50-0041545; N° Cassete: 0041541/0041569: 19/05/82.
"Entrevista Caetano Veloso sobre os seus 40 anos, seu sucesso e sobre o momento atual da história política brasileira", N° Documento: 50-0044112; N° Cassete: 0044093/0044120; 06/08/82.
"Show de Caetano Veloso no Canecão – 'Uns'", N° Documento: 50-0055273; N° Cassete: 0055273/0055279: 09/06/83.
"Tropicalismo", N° Documento: 51-0030695 ; N° Cassete: 0030695/0030696: 15/12/83.
"Entrevista de Caetano Veloso sobre seu show 'Velô', que estreia em São Paulo", N° Documento: 50-0068901; N° Cassete: 0068900/0068906: 26/05/84.
"Show 'Velô' de Caetano Veloso no Canecão", N° Documento: 50-0069403; N° Cassete: 0069403/0069404: 22/06/84.
"Show 'Totalmente Demais' de Caetano Veloso, no Teatro João Caetano, no Rio de Janeiro", N° Documento: 50-0101154; N° Cassete: 0101148/0101156: 13/08/86–15/08/86.
"Chico & Caetano: 5° programa da serie", N° Documento: 51-0050146; N° Cassete: 0050146/0050146: 15/08/86.
"Show de Caetano Veloso no Scala Dois, Rio de Janeiro", N° Documento: 50-0117234; N° Cassete: 0117234/0117239: 05/11/87.
"Show 'Estrangeiro' de Caetano Veloso no Canecão", N° Documento: 50-0137164; N° Cassete: 0137161/0137164: 29/06/89.
"Entrevistas com Caetano Veloso e Gilberto Gil feitas por Regina Casé (material bruto)", N° Documento: 50-0174308; N° Cassete: 0174308/0174308: 10/02/91.
"Entrevistas com Caetano Veloso e Gilberto Gil feitas por Regina Casé", N° Documento: 50-0174309; N° Cassete: 0174309/0174309: 10/02/91.
"Clip de Caetano Veloso e Gilberto Gil cantando 'Haiti'; Imagens da época da Tropicália", N° Documento: 51-0086776; N° Cassete: 0086769/0086776: 08/08/93.

"Retrato Falado; Caetano Veloso fala de si, de suas posições políticas", Nº Documento: 51-0096324; Nº Cassete: 0096317/0096327: 09/10/94.

"Show de Caetano Veloso 'Fina Estampa' no Metropolitan, no Rio", Nº Documento: 50-0210710; Nº Cassete: 0210708/0210712: 21/09/95.

"Caetano Veloso fala de seu show; Trecho do clip 'Tieta'", Nº Documento: 50-0226470; Nº Cassete: 0226463/0226474: 18/02/97.

Index

(References to illustrations are in **bold**)

Ávila, Affonso 14
Abreu, Caio Fernando 41–2
absurdism 38
AI-5 *see* Fifth Institutional Act
Alves, Lúcio 61, 62
Amado, Jorge, *O Pais do carnaval* 16
Anderson, Benedict 86
Anderson, Perry 88
Andrade, Joaquim Pedro de, *Macunaíma* 5
Andrade, Mário de 105
Andrade, Oswald de 155
   antropofagia theory 4, 86
   works
      Manifesto Antropofágico 86–7
      O Rei da Vela 5, 87
antropofagia theory 4, 86
Araújo, Guilherme 30, 31, 35
Araújo, Mozart de 103
Arcadianism 13
authoritarianism 19

baião 63, 67
Bakhtin, Mikhail 16
bananas, Tropicalist symbol 40
Banda Black Rio 12
Bandeira, Manuel 146–7
Barbosa, Orestes, 'Chão de Estrelas' 146
baroque literature 13
baroque tradition 13–14
   language experiments 14
   religious manifestations 14
   and Tropicália 42
Barroso, Ari 33
Beatles 155
   'Help' 97–8
   Veloso on 151
   Veloso's cover versions 97–8
   White Album 87

beguin 63
bel canto style 61, 104
Ben, Jorge 60
body, the
   deregulation 43
   and patriarchy 42–3
   and social meaning 42
   Veloso's use of 45
bolero 33, 63, 67
bossa nova 1, 2, 33, 40, 63, 108, 111, 112–13, 137
   discrediting of 9
   influence on Veloso 124–5
   lyrical simplicity 113–14
   situational music 113
   Veloso on 9–10, 152
   verbal/musical blurring 84
   vs protest song 62
Brasilia, construction 1, 39
Brazil, African heritage 131
Bressane, Julio, *Matou o familia e foi ao cinema* 5
bricolage, subversive power of 38
Buarque, Chico 1, 10, 28, 36, 42, 70, 80, 140, 152, 155
   Roda Viva 6, 27
   'Samba e Amor' 96–7
Burns, Bradford 109

Cabral, João 8, 150
Calado, Carlos 35
Caldas Barbosa, Domingos 103, 104
   'Lundum em Louvor de uma Brasileira Adotiva' 106
camp culture 33
Campos, Augusto de 28, 79, 110, 117, 155
   Balanço da bossa e outras bossas 10

Campos, Haroldo de 13–14, 87, 155
  'Branco' 92
canção de rádio 60, 61
Canclini, Néstor García 87–8
Candido, Antônio, *Formação da literatura brasileira* 13
cannibalism, cultural 4, 86–7, 93–4, 96
Cardoso, Fernando Henrique 19
Carlos, Erasmo 114–15, 116, 118, 119, 135
Carlos, Roberto 60, 65, 135
  songs 116–18
  style 118–19
  Veloso, influence on 126–7
carnival
  gender roles 16–17
  transgressivism 15–16, 44
  transvestism 17
Castro, Ruy 114
Celestino, Vicente 60, 107–8, 114
Celso, Zé 5, 6, 27
Chambers, Iain 116, 117, 119
Chaves, Celso Loureiro 75, 77
Cinema Novo 4–5
Concretists 87, 92–3, 99, 155
coronelismo 18
Costa, Gal 38, 63, 67, 68, 90, 127, 138
counter-culture, and festivals 26–7
Coutinho, Afrânio 14
CPCs (Centros Populares de Cultura) 2
crooners 61–2
cultural memory 86
cummings, e.e. 155

Da Matta, Roberto 15, 16, 17
deboche 67, 68
desbunde 38
Discoteca do Chacrinha 45–6
Diegues, Carlos (Cacá) 134
Divino, Maravilhoso programme 46
  photos **52–3**
Djavan 141
Drummond, Carlos 8
Duprat, Rogério 38, 44, 67, 135, 138
Duran, Dolores, 'A Noite do Meu Bem', lyrics 111–12
Dyer, Richard 33

Eco, Umberto 16
EMBRAFILME agency 5, 134
eroticism, ideology 18
Estado Novo 18, 32

fado 70
fan clubs, influence 62
Farney, Dick 61
Faro, Fernando 46
Favaretto, Celso 4, 7
  Tropicália: Alegoria, Alegria 10
favelas 7, 151, 152
festivals, and counter-culture 26–7
  see also song festivals
Fifth Institutional Act (AI-5) 2, 3, 36, 69, 86
folklore, traditions, and national identity 2
Foucault, Michel 43
Frank, Arthur 43
Freire, Paulo 2
Freyre, Gilberto 16
Frith, Simon 67

gender roles
  carnival 16–17
  modinha 105
  patriarchy 17–18
Gershman, Rubem 6–7
Gil, Gilberto 24, 27, 29, 36, 38, 65, 67, 70, 135, 152
  imprisonment 25, 47
  photo **48**
Gilberto, João 9, 62, 84, 111, 114, 117
  vocalisation 125
Gismonti, Egberto 12
Goulart, João 2

Halfoun, Eli, on Veloso 30
Hall, Stuart 143
happenings 6–7, 8, 46
Hebdige, Dick 37, 38
  Subculture: The Meaning of Style 25, 26
history, and memory 86
hunger, aesthetic of 5

'ideology patrols' 134
iê-iê-iê 40, 63, 65, 127

audience for 114–15
romanticisation 135
see also rock music
ISEB (Instituto Superior de Estudos Brasileiros) 2

Jabor, Arnaldo 5
jazz fusion, Brasilianised 12
Jobim, Tom 28, 36
Jovem Guarda 114, 115

Kiefer, Bruno 103
Koestenbaum, Wayne, *The Queen's Throat* 67
Kubitschek, Juscelino 1–2, 40, 113

landowners, power 18
language
  and memory 86, 98
  Veloso's use of 89–92, 97–8, 149–50, 155
language experiments, baroque tradition 14
Leão, Nara 8
Lima, Lezama 14
literature
  baroque 13
  and song 93
Lomax, Alan 59
love songs
  tradition 103–19
  Veloso's 124–43
lundu 105, 106–7
Lyra, Carlos 8

McClary, Susan 61, 131
machismo 19, 43
Madi, Tito 111
Maia, Tim 12, 141
malandro 84
  clothes 32–3
MAM (Museu de Arte Moderna) 7
Manchete magazine, publicity 40, **50**
Marcuse, Herbert, *Eros and Civilisation* 19
Martinez, José Celso 37, 42, 87
mass media, and Tropicália 44–5
Matos, Gregório de 14
Melly, George, *Revolt into Style* 25

Melo Neto, João Cabral de
  influence on Veloso 88–9
  works
    Morte e Vida Severina 87, 88
    'Psicologia da composição' 88
Melodia, Luiz 12
memory
  continuity 94–5
  cultural 94, 95, 100
  fragility 86
  and history 86
  and language 86, 98
Messias, José, 'Madrugada e Amor' 97
Middleton, Richard 37
militarism 43
military regime 3, 19
Miranda, Carmen 5, 60
  as Tropicalist icon 32, 33
moda 103
modinha
  development 104
  gender roles 105
  performance aspects 105
  and social identity 103
  styles 106
  vocal style 104
Motta, Nelson 46
MPB (Música Popular Brasileira), emergence 1, 2, 10, 13
mulher boêmia 108–9
música romântica 124, 141, 143
musical excerpts 64, 66, 68, 79

Napolitano, Marcos 8–9
national identity, and folkloric traditions 2
Neoclassicism 13
Nero, Torquato 41

Oiticica, Hélio 4, 7, 41
Ortiz, Renato 2
Os Mutantes 34, 35, 38, 45, 67, 68, 153
  photos **48**, **49**, **50**, **52**

Panama hat 33
parangolés 7
Parker, Richard 15, 17–18
Pascoal, Hermeto 12

patriarchy
   and the body 42–3
   gender roles 17–18
Pessoa, Fernando 78
Pignatari, Décio 155
plastic arts 4, 7
poema processo 8
poetry
   performance 8
   and popular music 150–51
polysemy, cultural style 25–6, 37
'popular', meaning 3, 11
popular music
   analysis 61
   criticism 8, 10
   foreign influences 12
   Golden Age 61
   and poetry 150–51
   role 9
   and style 25–6, 32–3
   Veloso on 9
   see also protest song
populism 3–4
preguiça 25, 29, 38, 119n4
private, public spheres 18
protest song 8, 27, 44, 60, 84
   vs bossa nova 62

radio, Golden Age 60, 76
rap
   samba, fusion 99
   Veloso on 151–2
Regina, Elis 117
Reis, Mário 61
religious manifestations, baroque tradition 14
Ricardo, Paulo 140
Ricardo, Sérgio 28
Rocha, Glauber 134
   Terra em Transe 3–4
rock music 114, 115, 151
   function 115–16
   values 116
   see also iê-iê-iê
Rodrigues, Lupicinio 108
   songs 109–11
Rolling Stones 151, 155

Ross, Andrew 135
rumba 67

samba 33, 40, 70, 151
   rap, fusion 99
samba-canção 24, 33, 63, 70, 111, 112, 113, 118
   emergence 107
Santiago, Silviano 45
   on Veloso's style 37–8
Santos, Nelson Pereira dos, *Como era gostoso o meu francês* 5
Satã, Madame 33
Seixas, Raul 115
Sevcenko, Nicolau 13, 14
Silva, Orlando 60, 61, 62
song
   and literature 93
   see also love song
song festivals 11, 12, 28, 34, 125
   aggression at 27–8
songwriting
   facets 86
   polarisation 85
   'prefixing' 90
soul music 12
style
   and popular music 25–6, 32–3
   subcultural 25–6, 37
   Veloso's 31–2, 37–8, 43–4, 47

tango 33, 70
tango-canção 108
Tatit, Luis 84, 117
   O Cancionista 59–60, 61
Teatro Arena, *Opinião* 3
Tel Quel 26
television use
   Tropicália 46
   Veloso 45–7, 153
theatre, of violence 5–6
Tinhorão, José Ramos 9, 62, 103, 136
Tiso, Wagner 12
toada 40, 65, 73
Tornado, Toni 12
transcreation concept 87, 96
transgressivism, carnival 15–16, 44

transvestism
  carnival 17
  Veloso 17
Treece, David 11–12, 37, 84–5, 113
Tropicália 27
  and the baroque tradition 42
  clothes 41–2
  iconography 38
  installation 4, 7
  lyricism 42
  and mass media 44–5
  music 10–11
  politics 37
  television use 46
  Veloso on 152–3
Tropicalists 4, 5, 6, 8, 11, 12, 15, 27
  banana symbolism 40
  Carmen Miranda as icon 32
  musical style 33
  vs traditionalists 35
Turner, Bryan 42
TV Globo Festival 35

Udigrudi 5

Valente, Assis 47
Vandré, Geraldo 28–9, 36
  'Caminhando' 35, 85
Vargas, Getúlio 18, 19, 109
Veloso, Caetano
  albums
    Araçá Azul 59, 62, 78, 79–80, 85, 135, 149
    Caetano Veloso 4, 63, 72, 126, 134
    illustration **51**
    Cinema Transcendental 136, 138, 139
    Domingo 62–3
    Fina Estampa 156
    Jóia 85, 87, 93, 149
      bird concept 89
    Livro 146
    Muito 125–6
    Noites do Norte 98
    Prenda Minha 156
    Qualquer Coisa 85, 87, 93, 95, 149
      Beatles songs 97–8
  cover versions 96–7
  cultural borrowing 96
  fusion elements 97
  Transa 59, 74–5, 77
  Tropicália 4, 38, 44, 67, 138, 140
    illustration **49**
    vocalisations 67
  Velô 98, 132
androgyny 46
  on the Beatles 151
  body use 45, 46
  on bossa nova 9–10, 152
  bossa nova, influence of 124–5
  as cultural mediator 146–7
  discography 170–71
  exile 59, 72
  game show popularity 24
  image changes 45, 153
  images, use of 149, 153
  imprisonment 25, 47
  interview with 149–56
  language, use of 89–92, 97–8, 149–50, 155
  love songs 124–43
  memoirs, *Verdade Tropical* 146, 147, 156
  musical influences 63, 124
  photos, **frontispiece 48–53**
  on popular music 9
  public rant 36
  on rap 151–2
  record sales 154
  sexuality, ambiguous 43, 138, 140–41, 142
  songs
    'A Little More Blue' 72
    'A terceira margem do rio' 93
    'Acrilírico', lyrics 71
    'Alegria, Alegria' 26, 29–30, 65–6
      lyrics 40–41
      musical excerpt 66
      structure 66, 74
      vocalisation 66
    'Alfômega', vocalisation 71
    'Anoiteceu' 47
    'Asa, asa' 89–90
    'Asa Branca' 73–4, 80

'Atrás do trio eléctrico' 70
'Avarandado' 63
'Baby', lyrics 136–8
'Cajuína', lyrics 139
'Canto do povo de um lugar' 94
'Carolina' 70, 137
'Chão de Estrelas' 146
'Come dois e dois', lyrics 127–8
'De conversa', vocalisation 78–9
'De palavra em palavra', vocalisation 79
'Dindi' 126
'É Proibido Proibir'
  lyrics 34
  performance 34–6, 38, 45, 78, 85, 153
  structure 78
  vocalisation 78
'Eclipse Oculto' 141
'Ela e Eu' 141
'Enquanto seu lobo não vem' 68–9
  musical excerpt 68
'Eu sei que vou te amar' 125–6
'Eu Sou Neguinha'
  as dub 132
  lyrics 129–31
'Eu te Amo' 141
'Força estranha' 127
'Gilberto Misterioso'
  musical excerpt 79
  vocalisation 79
'Gravidade' 90
'Hino ao Senhor do Bonfim' 69
'In the Hot Sun of a Christmas Day' 73
'Irene' 70
'It's A Long Way' 76
'Jóia', lyrics 93–4
'Lingua'
  lyrics 98–9, 100
  rap basis 99
'Livros' 147
'London, London' 73, 140
'Lost in the paradise' 70
'Lua, Lua, Lua, Lua' 91, 92, 93
'Maria Bethânia' 73

'Marinheiro só' 70
'Menino do Rio', lyrics 138–9
'Minha Senhora' 63
'Minha Voz Minha Vida' 141
'Muito romântico', lyrics 126–7
'Não identificado' 134–5
'Nine Out of Ten' 75
'Nostalgia' 75
'O quereres', lyrics 132–4
'Os argonautas' 70
'Parque Industrial' 67–8
'Pipoca Moderna' 91
'Qualquer Coisa', lyrics 95–6
'Relance' 90
'Remelexo' 141
'Saudosismo', lyrics 124–5
'Superbacana' 40
'Tem que ser você' 142
'Triste Bahia' 75, 76–7
'Tropicália' 38, 63–4
  lyrics 39–40
  musical excerpt 64
  origins 64
  quotations 65
  structure 64
  vocalisation 64–5, 70–71
'Tudo, tudo, tudo' 90, 91
'Vampiro', lyrics 139
'You Don't Know Me' 59, 76
  structure 75
  vocalisation 75–6
style 31–2, 37–8, 43–4, 47
television use 45–7, 153
transvestism 17
on Tropicália 152–3
videography 172
vocal style 60, 62–80
wedding 31
vocal style 59
  modinha 104
  Veloso's 60, 62–80

Walser, Robert 61
Wisnik, José Miguel 93

Zé, Tom 38, 67, 68